MW01615333

THE
FOR HALEY

An Insider's Account of the Largest Search Mission in Arkansas History

Tim Ernst

The photograph on the front cover is of Hawksbill Crag, in the Upper Buffalo Wilderness Area of the Ozark National Forest, Arkansas. This is one of the main features that Haley and her hiking group went to see on their short hike in April of 2001. She disappeared a few minutes later. The search and rescue efforts were centered around this famous landmark. Photo by Tim Ernst.

Library of Congress Control Number: 2001118931
ISBN 1–882906–45–4

Wilderness books by Tim Ernst

Arkansas Hiking Trails guidebook
Buffalo River Hiking Trails guidebook
Ozark Highlands Trail guidebook
Ouachita Trail guidebook
Arkansas Dayhikes guidebook (mid-2002)
Arkansas Waterfalls guidebook (mid-2002)

Arkansas Portfolio picture book
Wilderness Reflections picture book
Buffalo River Wilderness picture book
Arkansas Spring picture book

All books may be ordered direct from the author:
Tim Ernst
CLOUDLAND.NET
HC 33, Box 50–A
Pettigrew, AR 72752
Toll-free order line: 800–838–HIKE
Web Page: www.Cloudland.net
E-mail: TErnst@ArkansasUSA.com

Thank you
for all your
love and
prayers.
♡ Haley

TABLE OF CONTENTS

Art By Haley Z.

INTRODUCTION

It would be best if you grabbed a box of tissues before reading this book. This is the story of the search for Haley Zega, a six-year-old girl who got lost while hiking in one of the most remote and rugged wilderness areas in the central United States. She wandered for three days and two nights, scrambled down steep slopes, waded the Buffalo River, bushwhacked through a thick jungle of twisted vines and sharp briars, made friends with a caterpillar, and may have been kept company by the spirit of a little girl who had been murdered long ago.

Haley's saga captivated the region, as the world watched and held their collective breaths that she would be found alive. A massive search and rescue mission was mounted that included 80 organizations, hundreds of searchers in the woods, and thousands of others in communities providing support. Helicopters flew grid patterns day and night, teams of tracking dogs scoured the slopes, rope teams worked the faces of tall bluffs in the darkness, ground teams turned over every leaf in a five-square mile area, the Governor prayed. What began as a short hike to show a grandchild the wonders of nature turned into the largest search and rescue mission in Arkansas history.

This is a story of courage, of hope, and of despair. It is the story of exhausted volunteers who would not give up. It is the story of a community of strangers who dropped everything and came together for a little girl they did not know. And it is the story of the greatest moment in many of these people's lives.

Since I live in a log cabin right in the middle of the search area, I was called in to help search right away, and was one of the first on the scene. Haley's parents, Steve and Kelly Zega, headquartered at the cabin during the ordeal. It was here where they experienced their darkest hours, and their greatest moment of triumph.

I was never interested in writing a book about all of this—I take nature pictures and write hiking trail guidebooks for a living. Yet as the weeks passed after Haley was found, the details of her ordeal kept running through my mind, and I became obsessed with this story. There were still so many unanswered questions—how did Haley elude the searchers for so long, what route did she take to get down off of the dangerous bluff and descend more than 700 feet to the river below, where did she spend each night, and how in the world did she survive it all? I decided that the only way I could get any peace was to go looking for the answers and write it all down.

With the enthusiastic support of the Zega family, I began to put together the first several chapters of this book, expanding on notes that I had already written during the ordeal that were published in my online *Cloudland Journal*. I watched hours of video tapes from the many television reports of the mission, poured over hundreds of pages of newspaper articles and official mission documents, and spoke with many who participated.

Then I sat down with the two men who ran the search, and learned what a monumental and complicated mission it really was. There were criticisms from searchers and government officials about how the mission was run, complaints from the mission managers about the huge number of untrained volunteers whose numbers overwhelmed them, and lots of rumors. I wanted to address all of those issues, find the truth, and publish the facts.

I wanted to hear what the volunteers had to say too. Many wrote to me with their own personal accounts of long hours in the woods, dealing with the bureaucracy, their deep depression when no clues were found, and the elation when Haley emerged alive and unhurt.

One of the most moving chapters was written by Haley's parents. I wanted them to tell us what it was like going through this terrible ordeal, what they were thinking, how they coped with it all. There were a few light moments too. You will laugh. You will certainly cry.

Because the last few minutes of the hike that Sunday morning when Haley disappeared were so important, I asked the last person to see her, her grandmother Joyce Hale, to detail it all for us. She also gives us some insight into her own feelings as the clock ticked away and there was no sign of her only granddaughter.

The person most associated with efforts to find lost children in Arkansas is Colleen Nick. Her own daughter, Morgan, was taken from her in 1995. Colleen was with the Zegas throughout Haley's ordeal, and an entire chapter here is devoted to her thoughts and emotions of that time. It is important to note that a portion of the proceeds from sales of this book will go to the Morgan Nick Foundation, and Colleen's continued fight to bring young people home safely.

You will find one short section near the end of the book that every parent should read—and have their children understand—about what a child should do if lost in the woods (Lost in the Woods Program, page 230). If you are a parent and do nothing else with this book, *please read this section!*

There is a chapter about the trip to Arkansas by the *Dateline NBC* crew who spent several days in the sweltering summer heat to film Haley's story. It rained a lot during their visit, they got to see a giant rattlesnake, and for some reason the crew members were all wearing dog collars.

Towards the back of the book there is a listing of the agencies and organizations that were on-site during the search. Also a collection of poems and songs that were written about Haley.

And finally, I spent time with Haley herself, and many long hours and days out in the wilderness trying to figure out her route. I describe that trip in great detail, the rugged terrain that she traveled, some of the obstacles she encountered and conquered, and what it must have been like for her. There is a map of her hike, and also a map that shows the route followed by the two men on mules who found her.

Out of respect for the family I did not take any photographs during the search and rescue mission. There are, however, several historical photographs included in the book that were taken of Haley at the time of her rescue. And there are several other photographs of main characters or places that I took since the rescue—these are all original images taken with a small digital camera.

The illustrations that you will find at the beginning of each chapter were drawn by Haley. Most of them represent things that she saw during her ordeal. And while they may not be great works of art, my wife tells me that they are actually very good for a six-year-old child! Haley loves to draw.

The map on the opposite page shows the general lay of the land and principal locations that are talked about in the book. Haley was lost in the Upper Buffalo Wilderness Area, a remote and rugged section of Newton County in northwest Arkansas. Cell phone coverage in this area is rare, and vehicles are allowed only on a couple of rough, gravel county roads.

Please note that much of this book was written by those who lived this drama, and I have retained their original language—the text has not been highly processed (although the editors had to work overtime on my narrative!). I believe that you will find the passages easy to read, humorous at times, but will tug at the very depth of your heart.

What I offer here is certainly not the complete account of this event—there are hundreds more stories that are worth telling. But I hope it will go a long way to explain what actually happened, and gives you some sense of what the searchers and family members were going through.

Now, its time to reach for that box of tissues. Enjoy.

Tim Ernst

If you find typos in this book, they are here for a reason—
some people enjoy looking for them, and I strive to please as many readers as possible!

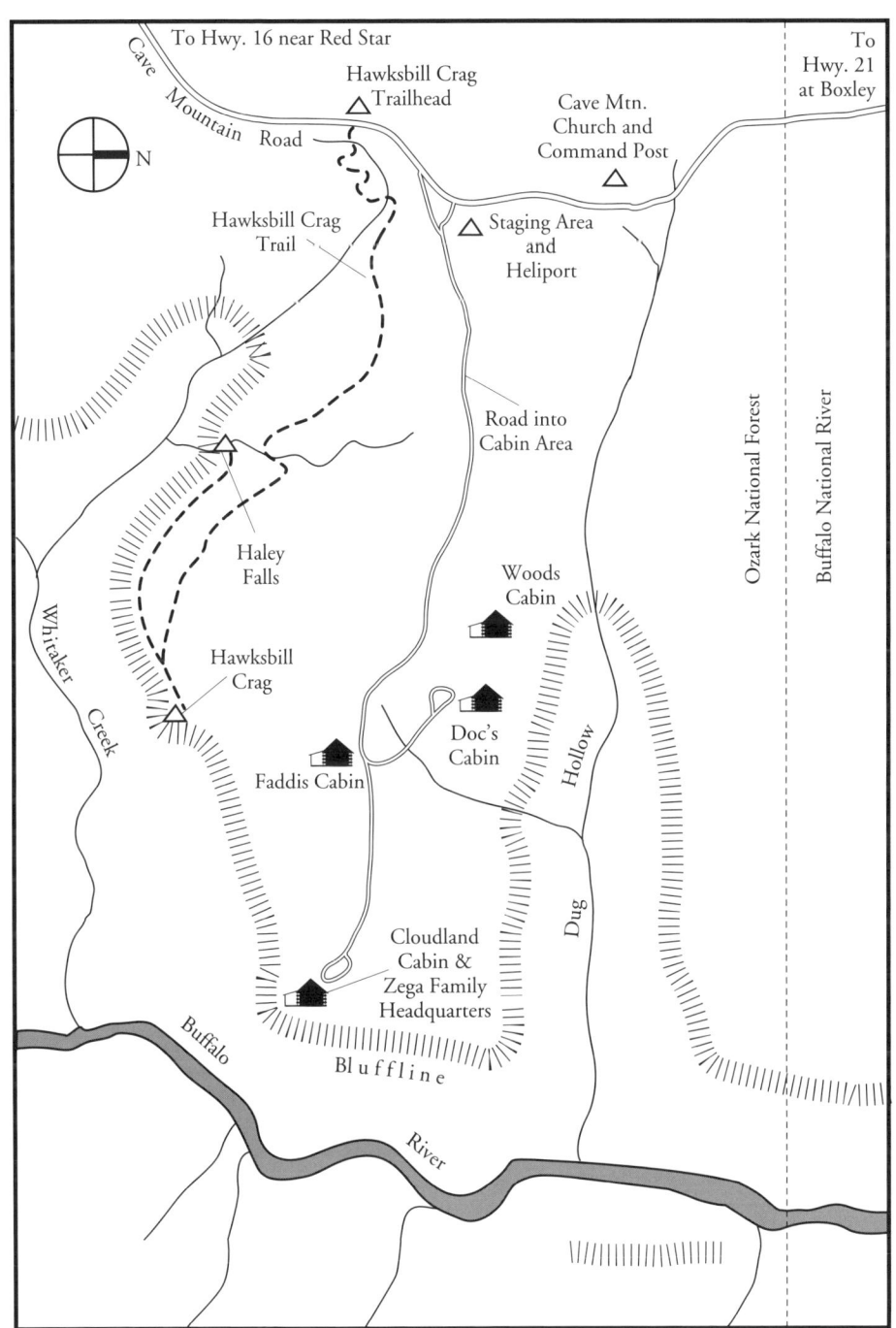

Overall Map of the Area

Chapter 1
DAY ONE

S unday, April 29, 2001. What began as a beautiful spring day in the Ozarks would turn out to be one of the most difficult times ever at Cloudland, my log cabin home that sits at the edge of the 13,000 acre Upper Buffalo Wilderness Area in Newton County, Arkansas. I had just completed a grueling schedule, consisting of many weeks of giving photography workshops and chasing waterfalls for a new waterfall guidebook, and hadn't gotten home until the wee hours of this particular morning. I was exhausted and ready for a break.

My dear wife Pam and I were on a short hike around Cloudland. We were newlyweds. So new, in fact, that Pam still lived in Republic, Missouri—she would be moving down to the cabin as soon as her eight-year-old daughter Amber got out of school for the year. We saw our neighbor Robert "Doc" Chester working on a dead tree he had just cut down. He told us that a group of hikers had just left the Faddis cabin, planning to hike down to the famous Hawksbill Crag (a point of rock that juts out over the forest and is shown on the cover of this book), a group that included a bouncing little girl. Doc's eyes always sparkle when he speaks of a child. He has a lot of friends that use his Faddis cabin as a beginning location for a hike into the adjacent wilderness area.

Ours was just a short hike; and soon we were back at the cabin, starting on our own chores for the day. I sat down at the computer and began to write up the events of the past couple of days to post on my online *Cloudland Journal* web page. The phone rang a few minutes later—it was Doc Chester. He said that someone from the hiking group had just returned and had told him that the little girl had gotten lost. He asked if I could please go over to the Crag and help search for her?

A chill ran down my spine as visions of the tall bluffline in that area flashed through my head—I was not ready to find a child at the bottom of it. I quickly loaded up a fanny pack with some supplies, handed Pam a two-way radio, and hit the door running.

Just below our cabin, there is a primitive trail that runs near the top of that bluffline, all the way to the Crag. I was on that trail within three minutes of getting the phone call and began my search as I moved towards the Crag. Pam took up a position on the lower back deck of our cabin to keep an eye on the trail in case the little girl came along after I had gone. Little did we know that Haley had already hiked down this trail, passed the cabin, and was at that very moment heading in the opposite direction, probably within a couple of hundred yards of us. That is the closest she would be to another human being for three days.

When I arrived at the Crag just past noon I found a lady standing there with a couple of other hikers. She had borrowed the hiker's cell phone and was trying to talk to someone about the little girl, but she was not having much luck due to poor reception (those coverage maps that you see at cell phone stores are not too accurate—there is very little cell phone coverage out in the wilderness areas of Arkansas, especially with those little hand-held units). This lady was Haley's grandmother, Joyce Hale, who I had first met a couple of weeks before, at one of my slide programs in Fayetteville. She was calm but very serious as she gave me a bit of information about Haley, including her name, description, what she was wearing, and where they had last seen her. Haley was wearing a grey t-shirt, black shorts and black and white tennis shoes. "Wow!" I thought. With these colors, Haley would be a difficult object to spot. Joyce said that other hikers in the area had already begun to search up above the bluffline. I told her that I intended to go down through a crack in the bluffline nearby and search the base of the bluff. I radioed all of this information back to Pam, then rushed to the bluffline.

Joyce also told me a bit of info about the last few moments before Haley had disappeared. Haley had wanted to go look at a waterfall along the trail, but they did not have the time to do so because they needed to turn back and go eat lunch. Haley was not happy about this and had sat down on a rock for a moment. She then reluctantly followed the group, but back at a distance, often out of sight. The group had turned around and headed back towards the Crag. Some of them stopped to wait for Haley to catch up, while others went on (there were a total of five adults on the hike with Haley—her parents were not with them). Within a few minutes, Haley had disappeared, and the search began. Her grandmother told me that Haley was a bit upset at not being able to see the waterfall, and was also upset because they would not carry her when they decided to turn around and go back. (The grandfather did go down to see the waterfall—it is a *big* leap to get down to the lower bench to view this double-decked waterfall.) So Haley was not pleased with the grown-ups.

My very first thought when Doc had said Haley was lost between the Crag and the waterfall was that she had fallen over the bluff. The bluffline in this area is very tall—80-100 foot dropoffs—and I knew she probably would not survive such a fall. I also knew that it is not always a straight path to the ground from way up there, and she might have landed in a treetop or on a ledge.

I hurried to the spot where the break in the bluffline was located and made it to the bottom of the bluff. I began to carefully search the drip line (the point on the ground where water falling off the bluff hits the ground). I had a pair of unofficial "bloodhounds" with me, our dogs Aspen and Lucy. Even though neither of these dogs were trained to find people, I figured they would let me know if they found Haley out there in the brush somewhere.

Within minutes I came across two large rocks that had fallen off the bluff. They had made an impact in the ground and scattered fresh dirt around the area. Rocks do fall off blufflines from time to time, but this dirt looked very fresh. My heart pounded, and my mind raced. I broke out into a cold sweat. I carefully searched the area, then widened my search down the hillside. Nothing. I looked up at every single branch of each tree in the vicinity (in case she had become lodged in a branch after falling). Nothing. I stood back and scoured the tall bluff for any signs. Nothing. I moved on along the bluffline.

One thing that kept racing through my head was that while I was very focused on what I was doing, the *last* thing that I wanted to find on my search was Haley. The reason was, if I had found her down there, I would be finding a body and not a smiling little girl. Having just become a dad for the first time a month ago, all of this really hit home. I hoped to God that I did not find her. *Please* let someone *else* find her, someone up on *top* of the bluff!

By the time I reached the end of my immediate search area—the waterfalls near where she had disappeared—I could hear a number of folks in the woods calling out her name and looking for her. The foliage was so thick, that while some of these folks were only a couple of hundred yards away, I did not ever see them. Lucy was barking at them, and someone from one of the groups yelled out and asked if I had tracking dogs with me. "Negative," I replied. These folks were apparently just hikers who had been out on the trail when Haley disappeared, and joined in on the search. I had no idea who they were.

It appeared that this end of the search area was being covered, so I turned around and headed back along the base of the bluffline, doubling my efforts to scour every single inch of ground, trees and bluff that I could possibly see. I continued along the base of the bluff under Hawksbill Crag, and then all the way to the far end of the bluffline right below my cabin. At one point I looked up and saw one of the other members of Haley's hiking party, Dennis Boles. He had climbed down to a ledge high above, and was searching. There was a grim expression on his face.

During all of this I was in radio contact with Pam, who was still at the cabin. She was manning the phone and acting as a clearing house for the search, plus was staying out on the back deck with the binoculars, looking and calling out Haley's name. Milancy McNamara, a neighbor, called the house. A couple had knocked on her door with the news of Haley's disappearance, and Milancy had called us to find out who to contact about it. Pam relayed the message to me, and I told her to tell them to call the Newton County Sheriff's Office, and to do so right away. By this time, Joyce had already made her way back out to the Faddis cabin and had contacted the Sheriff's Office on the phone there.

Once I arrived at the end of the bluffline, I climbed back up to our cabin. I gathered up a few more supplies, called Milancy to see what the Sheriff's Office had said, then headed out again to search the trail above the bluff between the cabin and the Crag a second time. Just as I was walking out the door, I thought about a radio announcement that I had heard some time ago about how police departments were now issuing Teddy bears to their officers to give comfort to children. I stepped into my own little girl's bedroom and grabbed a small stuffed animal and placed it into the top of my pack.

I raced down the trail, both wanting to cover a lot of ground, yet knowing that I needed to search *everything* I passed as well as I could. I have trained my eyes over the years to spot certain colors or patterns while hiking fast—I do this when taking pictures. For instance, when I am looking for some great firepink wildflower shots, I plug the color *red* into my brain and scan the forest floor for anything red. It was going to be tough to look for the "grey and black" of Haley's t-shirt though, but that is what I plugged into my brain.

I followed the trail to the Crag and found no one there, then went up to the next bench and searched a while, then up to the next one, then another. This went on for the next hour or two. Much of the Ozarks is what we call "bench" land. A bench is simply a linear step in the hillside that runs along fairly level, then drops off steeply below and may level out again on another bench. Benches can be anywhere from a few feet wide to several hundred feet or more. Often these level benches will follow contours for a long way. They make great locations for hiking trails. If you hike along the outer edge of one bench, you can generally look down and get a good view of the bench below. The Upper Buffalo area is prime bench land, and sometimes you can get on a bench and hike all day, remaining at the same general altitude.

Pam was still at her post with the phone and binoculars when I returned to our cabin dejected. Both of us milled around on the back deck for a little while, not really knowing what to do next. Pam had to return to her home and child in Missouri, something she absolutely *hated* to do, especially at this point in the search. I had to continue looking, so I kissed my wife goodbye and headed back out into the woods once again.

I had wanted Pam to keep my springer spaniel Aspen at the cabin, so she held onto him and her dog Lucy until I disappeared into the forest. A short time later, while Pam and the dogs were down on the lower deck, Pam said that Aspen just jumped up and shot off. Somehow this dog knew that my little hike was something really important, something that perhaps he could help out with, and there would be no keeping him back at the cabin. A few minutes later Aspen came racing up next to me. He sort of looked up at me with this "*I am going to help with this whether you like it or not*" attitude, then charged out ahead in search of Haley. That very same attitude would arrive with hundreds of volunteers who would later join the search.

I returned to the Crag area—still no one else around—and made my way up to and along a short bluffline that is a bench or two above the big bluff. There are many little nooks and crannies along this bluff—perfect hiding places for a little girl if she was trying to get away. Aspen and I crawled into and sniffed around every single one of them (he did most of the sniffing!).

A little while later I came out to the road near the Faddis cabin where I talked to several people who had been involved in the search, including Dennis Boles, who I had seen earlier on the bluffline, and Doc Chester. They both told me of the growing group of officials out at the main trailhead, which included the Forest Service, Park Service, and Sheriff's Department. I turned around and headed back into the woods.

I continued to search in my own little area east of a line between the Crag and the Faddis cabin. I never saw another soul in this area. Pam had long since headed for home, and had called from the cell phone in her car (when she found a spot where the phone would work) to report that there was a large group gathering up along the road.

An hour later I was still out searching when a helicopter came flying by, very low, overhead. And then another one appeared going in the opposite direction. A chill came over me—it wasn't until that very moment that I realized the gravity of the situation. There was a little girl out here, lost in the forest. It was a potential life-threatening situation, and a genuine and major search had begun for her. I don't know, but something about those helicopters just hit me right square between the eyes. I sat down on a rock and cried. The tears were for Haley, and for my own daughter Amber, who I was really just beginning to get to know.

I had always looked at the wilderness as a beautiful and exciting place to be, a place that brought me great joy, gave me a career, and even brought my lifemate and bride Pam to me. But now the fact that these very same wild woods might have taken the life of one so innocent was tearing my heart out. I found myself down on my knees, begging for the life of someone I had never laid eyes on. How in the world could this magical place turn so ugly?

The incredibly *loud* sound of a helicopter passing directly overhead brought me back to reality, and I got up and moved on.

I knew these woods where I searched like the back of my hand. So well, in fact, that it was not uncommon for me to wander around through them in the dark, without a flashlight, not the least bit concerned where I was going at all. I could move through this forest without a care in the world, soaking up the beauty and conversing in my own way with the plants and animals. Each step today though, took on a new meaning. Quite literally the very next move—indeed any step—could bring shouts of elation, or a sight of horror beyond comprehension. I was prepared physically for the rigors of this search, but not mentally, not for the uncertainty of each moment. I tried not to think about all of that, as I wiped the sweat from my brow and moved on.

One of the times that I returned to our cabin, I spent some time down on the lower deck watching the helicopters working. The view from this deck is a vast scene of wilderness, all the way from Hawksbill Crag to the right, most of the Whitaker Creek Drainage out in front, five miles of the Buffalo River drainage, and back to the left the hilltops of the community of Mossville. The bluffline where Hawksbill Crag sits wraps throughout the wilderness for many miles, and much of it can be seen from the deck.

A helicopter was doing something rather incredible out there. At first it was flying very close to the bluffline over at the Crag. The pilot was flying nose-in, looking straight into the bluff. Then he inched his way along the bluffline towards my direction. I could not believe how *close* he was getting to the bluff! I ran upstairs and got my digital camera to get a picture to post on the *Cloudland Journal,* then stood and watched and waited in awe.

Before long the helicopter was right there in front of me. He was so close that I could look right into the cockpit and see the expression on his face—what an incredible bit of flying! At one point the helicopter was flying only two hundred feet beyond the edge of a gazebo that we had just built—it was a sight to behold for sure. I held up the camera and pushed the button—nothing. I had left the digital card that records the images up in the computer. I could only stand there with my jaw dropped open and watch.

Just before dark I got in my truck and drove up towards the Faddis cabin to see if I could do something else to help. I ran into a number of officials there, including a dog team, and a couple of folks that I knew. While I was talking with someone, a young lady got out of the back of a car and approached me—it was Haley's mom Kelly Zega. I had never met her before. She wanted to thank me for helping out. Good grief, I had done nothing to help out so far. I told her that my cabin was available for anything that she needed, and that it would be open to whatever, whenever. She had been attending a film festival in Fayetteville when all of this had happened, and her husband Steve had been in National Guard training in Ft. Smith. He was also on the scene now, and out with one of the search parties.

A good friend of mine, Mary Woods, drove up and asked if anyone had checked out their little hunting cabin that was located down in Dug Hollow, a half mile away in the woods, on the opposite side of the ridge from where Haley had been hiking. I had not been down to that side of the hill at all, so I offered to hike down and take a look.

As I approached the cabin, which is well-hidden in the dense forest, up against a hillside, I thought that I heard a child's voice off to the right. The sound was out there in the wind, which was blowing strongly. That sound stopped me in my tracks, and I strained to hear more. Nothing but the wind. I ran, or rather scrambled down the steep pitch to the bench below, calling out Haley's name. I began a methodical search of the area around the cabin, walking my own little grid pattern. I realized that before long I was *screaming* out her name at the top of my lungs, trying to overcome the sound of the wind. My heart was pounding, and I was breathing heavily. The initial rush of enthusiasm that it might have been her slowly gave way to desperation and finally dejection. It must have been the wind that I heard. There was no sign of her at the cabin either. (Haley later said that she never called out during her entire ordeal.)

I returned to the trailhead where I had seen Kelly and the others to file my report, and found only empty vehicles—everyone had gone into the woods to the point where Haley was last seen, and would not return until after dark. At this point I felt sort of helpless. The authorities were conducting sweep searches with a growing number of volunteers, had teams of dogs working, and two helicopters were flying their grids. This was turning into a very large and extensive search. It was getting dark, I really did not know what else to do, so I returned to our cabin.

Chapter 2
THE FIRST NIGHT

As darkness fell on this first day of the search, my spirit went flat. It would be tough on Haley out there all alone at night, but also a strain on the searchers that were scouring the wilderness looking for her. One thing that brought hope was the helicopters, who were still working. I stood on the back deck and watched.

The helicopters were flying a grid pattern, this was really something to witness, with their flashing lights against the darkening night sky. They would fly slowly all the way from one end of the ridge to another, then turn around and move over a couple hundred yards and fly to the other end. A few minutes later they would return to this end, turn around, and fly back.

A little while later I drove up to the Faddis cabin to see what was happening. There was a truck parked at the end of our driveway, blocking the road. A man from the Hasty Fire Department was inside the truck, talking on a radio. His call sign was "Hasty One." This was the first contact I had made with the official search folks—I had been isolated out there in the woods doing my own search, and had no way of finding out what was happening. Until now. I could hear a lot of activity going on, mostly chatter between search and rescue (SAR) teams. There were SAR teams out all over the place, even though it was dark. Vehicles were positioned along roads in a number of locations and were supposed to be there all night, keeping their lights on in case Haley came out of the woods. This truck was parked across the road so that its headlights would point out across a field near the Faddis cabin. I had turned on all of the lights in our cabin and office before I left, just in case.

I found out that one team of searchers had spent several hours covering the long bluffline down below us, both from the top and the bottom. They were utilizing a wooden ladder that goes down over the bluff near our cabin to get up and down the bluff. There had been a ladder of some sort at this location for more than a hundred years. The locals used it to get up the bluffline along a trail that connected several homes along the Buffalo River to the Cave Mountain Church up on top. This church used to be a one-room school house, and it was a *long* hike to get to school, with more than a 700 foot vertical climb! The ladder and trail have been used in modern times to access the wilderness, although government officials have removed the ladder a couple of times trying to keep people from using the wilderness (locals have always replaced it though—trail structures are allowed and perfectly acceptable in wilderness areas). It was a good thing that ladder was still there now—that spot was the only safe access down through the bluffline for a very long ways in either direction, and it would be used a lot in the days to come by SAR teams.

There was complete darkness now, and the guy from Hasty and I stood next to his truck watching the helicopters working, listening to the radio chatter, and discussing where Haley could be. Then we heard what sounded like someone yelling down below us. The choppers were not in the immediate area at the moment, so we were able to hear pretty well, although the wind was blowing a bit. It did not sound like a child's yell, but rather that of an adult. The more we talked about it, the more we figured it was just members of the SAR team down there trying to communicate with each other.

Hasty One wanted to see if it was indeed the SAR team or not, so he tried to get them on the radio. There was no response. I could tell that he was getting more and more concerned as time went on, as much for the fact that he could not talk to the searchers who were probably within a few hundred yards of us as anything. It became apparent to me at that point that very few of the SAR teams out there could actually talk with each other on their radios. Hasty One complained about this, and talked about how bad the communications were between groups.

He was able to finally get through to the command post that had been set up at Cave Mountain Church. All he really wanted to do was find out if the SAR team had been yelling, trying to relay a message to them through the command post. Someone on the other end of the radio transmission, however, misunderstood what he was saying, and soon we were hearing a great deal of excited people on the radio announcing that there were "Screams for help at the Faddis cabin...screams for help at the Faddis cabin!"

Oh brother, did the emergency wheels get put into motion with that announcement! Within a few minutes we were covered up with SAR teams, both on foot and in vehicles. As we were all standing around trying to figure out what to do, some members of the SAR team that had been down along the bluffline began to appear at the truck. This group emerged tired and dazed as they hiked through the darkness. They had been in the woods for several hours, covering some pretty rough and rugged terrain. After a few minutes of intense questioning, no one could determine if it had indeed been this SAR team that Hasty One and I had heard yelling. It probably was them, but they could not be sure. So one of the SAR teams that was there headed out into the night to check the wooded area below us to see if they could find anything.

I have known a number of SAR people over the years—most of them are volunteers—and have always been quite impressed with their absolute dedication to every detail of a search. They simply refuse to leave a single leaf unturned. It gave me a great deal of hope knowing that the woods were filled with these people.

There was a bit of stress showing through in this group that had gathered around though. As a helicopter passed overhead, one of the team leaders commented under his breath that he wished the "blankety-blank helicopters would go home!" They were making quite a bit of noise, which made it difficult for the SAR teams on the ground to hear. We were told the helicopters were utilizing night vision scopes and special heat-sensing equipment, so it seemed like they were a valuable asset to have working. I eventually got used to the chopper noise day and night, and rather expected to hear it as time went on.

The SAR teams dispersed, and it was just Hasty One and me again. Eventually he had to leave and go up to the command post. He asked me to stay at his post until he returned—with my headlights turned on. He drove away, and I put my green SUV across the road just like he had done with his truck, with headlights shining across the field, hoping to see a small child come running towards me.

A little while later Landon Woods drove up (he is of the Woods Boys clan, who owns the little hunting cabin that I had checked on a few hours before). There was a deputy with him, and they said that they needed to go down and search our cabin. That was fine with me, although it did feel just a bit odd to have someone that I didn't know (the deputy) going through all of my things without me being there. It turns out that searching every structure in the area at regular intervals is one of the many procedures that is done during a SAR mission of this magnitude. That made perfect sense to me, especially when searching for a child who may be looking for a place to hide. (Several months later, Landon was bitten twice by a copperhead while hiking deep in the wilderness. It took his brother Billy more than six hours to get him out. He was in serious condition, but came out of it in pretty good shape after spending a couple of days in the hospital.)

A number of folks were milling around and coming and going from the Faddis cabin. I spent a bit of time conversing with them, trying to rack our brains about where Haley would be, where could we go next to look for her, etc. At one point the phone rang in that empty cabin. I picked it up and

Crow Johnson, a famous and very talented folk singer was on the other end. How in the world did Crow get this number? She was asking for someone who just happened to be standing up on the hillside and who had just arrived—great timing I told Crow.

I returned to my post to wait for Hasty One to return. Soon a National Park service truck drove up. A ranger got out and began to interrogate me. I'm not saying that he asked me a few questions—he was really *interrogating* me and seemed agitated that I was there. He wanted to know who I was, why I was parked there, and what I was doing. It didn't seem to help matters when I informed him that he was standing on my land. I told him that Hasty One had asked me to stay there until he had returned. Boy, that really got to him, and he told me that it was *his* post, and that he would get to the bottom of it! I'm not sure what he meant by that, but he drove off and I never saw him again.

There seemed to be plenty of activity and lights on at the Faddis cabin, and after waiting at my post for another hour, I decided to go back to our cabin. It was after 10 p.m. I sat down at the computer to try and get some work done, then heard a vehicle drive up. It was *very* dark outside, but I recognized one of the people in the lead vehicle—it was Mary Woods. She said that her husband Billy and about a dozen others had just started a sweep from the church and were going to search the woods above the bluff on the south side of Dug Hollow.

Moments later a couple of folks with shell-shocked faces who accompanied Mary made their way up the front porch steps—it was Kelly and Steve Zega, Haley's parents. Kelly was clutching a pillow. There were few words spoken, if any, and I led them into the cabin. Kelly headed to the big couch in the living room, but I directed them into my daughter Amber's room instead. These people were obviously grief stricken and wrung out and needed to just get away from it all for a little while. I was absolutely thrilled that they sought refuge at our Cloudland cabin.

But then, just as I turned on the lights for them in Amber's room, I was horrified—I realized that Amber's stuff was everywhere, and could not believe that I had been so insensitive as to put them in a room filled with a little girl's things while they were trying to deal with the potential loss of their own little girl. I began to apologize profusely, explained that this was my new little girl's room but was abruptly cut off by Steve who, without really saying anything, let me know that they were grateful for *any place* to be right then. This room would turn out to be where they would spend much of the next 42 hours, some of that time in a great deal of pain and agony.

It was very quiet at the cabin, and Steve and Kelly were up and wandering around, just trying to figure out what was going on. I felt *so sorry* for them, especially since there was absolutely *nothing* that I could do for them. I had very little food here, and basically had been caught totally unprepared for guests. That, of course, did not matter one bit to them.

Steve was still in his camo gear from National Guard training and was exhausted from participating in the search. Both were drained emotionally, yet could not sleep. Then Kelly got an idea to call a psychic and wanted to know if I had a phone book. She must have detected a slight hint of skepticism in my face because she looked right at me and said, "at this point I am willing to try *anything!*" At 11:08 p.m. she placed a call and spoke briefly with a psychic. This would be the first of over 200 phone calls that went out from our cabin over the next couple of days.

"She is lying down next to a stream and is unhurt," the psychic said. Without any further information, that was all she could tell them. As it turns out, this information was exactly correct. Of course, there were dozens of streams in the area, so the information did not help locate Haley. It did provide a great deal of hope and comfort to Steve and Kelly.

The cabin got very quiet again. Steve returned to the bedroom. Kelly was sitting on the couch when my dog Aspen came over to her. This dog had not left her alone since she first arrived. Aspen is the sort of dog that begs for attention, and won't allow you any peace until he gets it. Before long Kelly had him rolled over on his back and was rubbing his belly. I think that was a good bit of therapy for her, which she really needed at this point. That, along with the promising words from the psychic, gave Kelly just a moment or two of mental relief from the most despairing period of her life.

I really did not know what to do. Should I go to sleep, stay up and work, offer them something, *anything?* There really was nothing to do; I could not sleep, or work. I felt quite helpless.

Kelly will never know how much this meant to me, but at one point later on she came out of the bedroom and sat down at the bar and asked if I had any crackers (we have a long bar that is glass-topped and contains maps of the area). She had not eaten a thing all day but was not sure she could get anything down. This would turn out to be the *only* thing that Kelly or Steve ever asked of me during their entire stay here—a couple of crackers. And lo and behold, I produced not one, but two different types of crackers! I felt so relieved that I was able to do *something* for these wonderful people in their time of great need.

Kelly seemed to be doing a little bit better, and while still a bit dazed by it all, there was color in her face and a bit of brightness in her eyes. I looked at her and could not imagine what her little girl was going through, out there in the darkness, all alone, and scared to death. Kelly said something to me then that I will never forget. She said, "You know, when all of this is over,

I am going to call the social organizations that I am involved with and tell them that I have a new priority in life—I am going to be spending my time with my daughter now, and will not be able to work with them as much."

I ended up back at the computer and managed to type a few words and post them to the *Cloudland Journal* web page. This posting would turn out to be the first that many people would hear of the search and would be their link to what was going on here.

Steve and Kelly spent some time in Amber's room and some time in the living room. Few other words were said. None were needed. They finally returned to their room and turned the lights off, and I went up and laid down in my own bed. A little while later I thought that I heard something. I got up and looked out the window. There were two guys out there in the darkness, both in full camo gear. I had not heard them drive up. I got up and went outside. They were good friends of Steve's, from his National Guard unit and didn't really know if they should knock or what to do. I led them into the cabin where Steve and Kelly were still obviously wide awake.

One of the guys was the chaplain from Steve's Guard unit, Wes Hilliard. He would remain in close contact with the Zegas and play an important role throughout this entire ordeal, spending a lot of time at our cabin. The other Guardsman was Vixon James. It turns out that Vixon played an important role in all of this too—it was he who not only got his dad involved in the search, but suggested the area where his dad and good friend would eventually look. His dad was Lytle James, and he and William Jeff Villines would eventually find Haley in one of the areas where Vixon suggested that they look.

Later, a police officer knocked on the door and delivered some prescription medicine for Kelly, having had to get a pharmacist out of bed in Harrison to fill it. Kelly excitedly told the officer about the news from the psychic. I was thinking to myself that I doubted this information would ever be passed on, although I later saw a note in the sheriff's log in Jasper that the comments from the psychic were indeed radioed in.

Another knock at the door was Steve's mom, Julie Videtto, and her husband, Al, and their friend, Lynett Vinson. That meeting turned out to be somewhat of a clash of states of mind. Steve and Kelly were both physically and mentally exhausted and needed some rest, while Julie and especially Al were fresh on the scene and anxious to know everything and do something to help. After a short period, Steve and Kelly returned to their room, while I stayed up and showed Al the map of the area. We talked for a while about where they had been searching, why they had not located Haley yet, and where she might be. As it turned out, Al had a pretty good feel for it all, and correctly predicted that she would be down along the Buffalo River. (Al would later end up in the hospital in Harrison after suffering a kidney stone attack. He was at the same hospital that Haley was transported to after her rescue.)

At some point in our conversation, as Al and I were rehashing everything that had happened once again, Steve appeared, and he was not too happy. He explained that the very reason he and Kelly had come to our cabin was to get away from all of that discussion, to be out into clean air so that they could think and reflect. He kindly asked us to be quiet!

There were enough beds and futons down in the basement for these new guests, along with Steve's brother and sister-in-law, Joel and Karen Fineberg, and his step-father, Ken Fineberg, who arrived a short time later. It wasn't uncommon for a dozen or more folks to spend the weekend at our Cloudland Cabin, although most of them slept on the floor or out on the decks. We were bursting at the seams now, but still holding together.

Each time new guests would arrive, they were escorted by another vehicle with someone in the lead who knew me. Most of them were either Woods brothers or related to them. Mary Woods, Billy Woods' wife, would end up making dozens and dozens of trips down to the cabin during this ordeal, to bring people, food, water, and do all sorts of wonderful things—she is one of the many terrific souls who worked non-stop for the cause.

Once during the frenzy that always followed a new arrival, Mary Woods pulled me outside. "They think they have found her," she told me, not wanting Steve or Kelly to hear. She explained that several of the search dogs had "hit" on a hot trail at the same spot—a trail that led right over the edge of the big bluff. The dogs had to be restrained to keep from going over the edge. They had sent SAR members over the edge with ropes to see what they could find. That was very grim news—Haley never could have survived such a fall. Fortunately, the trail was a false one, and no body was found. But it reinforced the gravity of the situation, showed what length the SAR teams were willing to go to find this child, and indicated how dangerous it was out there in the dark looking for her.

Sometime in the wee hours of the morning, Colleen Nick arrived, along with her assistant, Chip Hurst. This was a very big deal. Colleen is the mother of Morgan Nick, the little girl who was abducted near Alma, Arkansas, a number of years ago and was never found. Colleen organized the Morgan Nick Foundation, a group that works to locate missing children, no matter what the situation. She sat down with Kelly and talked, letting her know that she was here, and intended to stay with this case until it was resolved.

At one point later in the night, I went out to the back deck. The wind was blowing and there was a chill in the air. Steve and Kelly were in their room and quiet, and the basement was filled with people trying to get some sleep. I found Colleen and Chip out on the deck. They had left their car at the command center and had been driven down to our cabin. I asked them if they needed a ride back up to the center, and they said no, "we will be here as long as we are needed." I have no idea when these women slept! They were involved with nearly everything that went on here and up at the command center, at all hours of the day and night, right up until a few minutes before Haley was rescued. I was quite moved by their dedication.

One reason why I had ventured out onto the deck was because we had just built a new 50 foot long deck across the western side of our cabin, and there was no railing up around it yet. The drop-off of one end of the deck was about 16 feet. We had no lights to shine on this area, and I was really concerned that someone wandering around out there might not see the edge and fall off. Colleen and Chip helped me drag some deck furniture over to block off the access.

While I was out there I took a moment to stare out into the wilderness, which was lit up a little bit by the half-full moon. The helicopters were silent, waiting for the cooler temps of early morning before going back up to search. I had never realized how vast and remote our little wilderness area was until that moment. There had been a hundred wonderful people out there looking for Haley, yet she had vanished without a trace. Where was she at that very moment? Curled up under a bluff somewhere? Standing under a tree, shivering from the cold, and crying out for her mother? I wanted *so bad* to know where she was, to find her, and bring her back to her parents. How in the world would I be able to cope if it was my own daughter that was lost? I am not a religious man, but I raised my eyes toward the moon and said a prayer or two—a prayer not only for the safety of Haley, but that Steve and Kelly would be given the strength to handle all of this and to continue on, no matter what the outcome.

I returned to my bed and tried to sleep, but it was no use.

Chapter 3
DAY TWO

Monday, April 30, 2001. No need for an alarm clock—the sound of the helicopters overhead broke the early morning silence well before dawn. I laid in bed wide awake until I heard the word "toothbrush" being whispered. And then a bit of panic hit me. Neither Steve or Kelly had expected to be spending the night—they didn't have time to pack bags anyway. A person can do without many things for a number of days, but a toothbrush is not one of them! I quickly got up and rummaged through my bathroom drawers looking for one of those extra toothbrushes that you get from the dentist. I always try to keep at least one new toothbrush at the cabin for unexpected guests, but there were none today. Funny how something as minor as a toothbrush can become major.

It was 5:30 or 6 a.m. when I heard Steve and Kelly drive off to go check with the command center at the church. Colleen and Chip were with them. These two ladies spent what was left of the night on the back deck, or on a couch downstairs in the living room, but I never heard them.

When I have a cabin full of guests I normally am prepared for them, and try to lay out some sort of spread for breakfast. But I was caught off guard this time. Pam and I had eloped just a month before, but I was still basically just a bachelor, without much food in the cabinets.

I got up and fixed a pot of coffee—there really wasn't much else here that I could feed a crowd. As long as you have coffee, that will usually be OK. There must have not been any coffee drinkers in the group though, because the pot sat there untouched all day (of course, it could have been my bad coffee!).

Steve and Kelly soon returned from the command center, and would remain at the cabin until the end, except for one quick trip out on Tuesday to make a statement to the press. The cabin would indeed become a refuge for them, their own little command center, a place where they could make and receive phone calls, fax things, send and receive e-mails, eat, sleep, and be with friends and family, away from the hoards of folks that were gathering up at the command center. We made the decision early on that no press would be allowed down at the cabin. This was a huge relief to Steve and Kelly. They are savvy enough to know that none of these search efforts would happen without the incredible job the press would do, but it was best for everyone concerned that Steve and Kelly be out of sight so that the press and the workers could do their jobs.

It didn't take long for vehicles to begin arriving, mostly friends of the Zegas, and SAR officials. The cabin quickly filled with people, and a steady volume of chatter began. Someone brought a container of little frosted donuts, which began to disappear in a hurry. That was about all of the food we had for a while, but before long the machine kicked in, and the cabin was filled with food—namely pizzas from *Pizza Pro* in Jasper, which were a *big hit*. A steady stream of stuff from that point on arrived, sent down by the Red Cross from Harrison (donated food and supplies had begun to pour into the command post from all over the region).

I spent a good part of the morning at my little office computer that was tucked away in a corner of the main floor of the cabin, writing and posting another update to the online *Cloudland Journal*, and answering a batch of e-mails that were beginning to come in. The phone started ringing—this would continue until long after everyone left. We have two phone lines at the cabin. One of them is a published number and our incoming line, while the other is mostly for internet connections, faxes and outgoing calls. That second line would turn out to be a great help since the incoming traffic continuously tied up the main line. In addition, I had a hard-wired cell phone in my vehicle that did work out here some of the time (three full watts of power instead of the .6 watts that most hand-held phones are). That cell phone in the car would be my only way to contact the outside world much of the time.

Every time that I ventured into the kitchen, someone was there directing traffic. Often it was Kelly's best friend Rebecca Wood (no relation to the Woods Boys clan that played such an important role in all of this). Rebecca quickly would take charge of many situations that came up at the cabin, and I often turned to her for help, confirmation of facts, or simply to have a neutral personality to bounce ideas off of. She seemed to be a voice of calm and reason in a sea of chaos. And she kept the dishes clean!

I remember one time when Rebecca came to me looking for a broom— with all of the traffic in and out, the cabin was getting a bit dirty. Cloudland has always been a shoe-free zone, but I removed the "no shoes" sign as soon as folks began to arrive. It would have been impractical to have everyone remove their shoes. "Don't worry about the floor, I'll get out the vacuum cleaner," I told her. What I did not realize was that while the floor certainly did need sweeping up, what Rebecca really wanted at that point was something to do. A physical activity that would take her mind off of the events surrounding her. A bit of therapy for a weary mind.

Looking back, I really missed a golden opportunity to get a lot of work done around the cabin. At times there were perhaps 50 or more folks in the same frame of mind as Rebecca—wanting to be close to Steve and Kelly, but needing to do something, *anything* to keep them occupied and take their minds off of Haley (they had been encouraged by the SAR folks *not* to participate in the searches). Heck, I had just the right chore for all of them— a meadow full of small stones that needed collecting! All I had to do was issue everyone a bucket and point them in the right direction. But that thought never occurred to me. The cabin remained filled with worried folks with nothing to do, and the meadow stayed full of rocks.

There was a point during the day when I realized that the best thing that I could do was simply step out of the way and let everything happen. I turned over the mental control of the cabin to whomever happened to be there, and that was certainly a good thing for everyone. Besides, I also felt quite helpless because I was at the cabin and not in the woods searching. I had heard that there were so many folks gathering at the staging area that you had to sign up and wait a while before being assigned to a search team. I really did not want to be a part of all of that, but still wanted to help. So I got ready to set out on my own and cover an area that had not been searched before—the area from the cabin down towards Dug Hollow. This area was basically outside of the search area. Everyone was saying that there was no way this little girl could go that far, but I just had this gut feeling about it, so I decided to head into the woods.

Just as I was leaving, a group of family friends showed up that included Tom McKinney. Tom had wanted to go visit one of the areas that had already been searched dozens of times, so I suggested that he go with me. We spent the next several hours searching, crawling around, looking up and down and in and out, and stumbling around in the thick brush.

Once we got below the bluff, I took the high route as we worked our way around the base of the big bluffline that towered over the Buffalo River far below. It was slow going, and once again my route would take me through an area where I really did not want to find Haley. If she had gone off of this bluff, it would have been tragic. Just before we left the cabin, someone pulled me aside and, with a grim face, said to be sure and watch for buzzards.

Tom took a lower route, walking along the far edge of the bench below the bluffline. Even though we were often within a couple of hundred feet of each other, the brush was so thick that we seldom saw one another. I would move along the base of the bluff, then stop and visually search everything above me.

Tom was going slower—the terrain down there was *really* rough—which gave me extra time to scour my area, climb up on top of boulders, crawl back into bluff overhangs to check every dark corner, and look for tracks. There is usually soft earth or even powdered rock under these bluff overhangs, which is a great place to look for footprints. If Haley had been through the area, she probably would have gone under the bluff at some point. This was all virgin territory—it had not been searched by anyone—so it was very important that we do a thorough search. Once again though, my state of mind was on high alert. Quite literally each and every step could bring an end to the search, either with tragic results, or celebration. *"Please* be under this overhang Haley." "Oh God, *don't* be at the bottom of this dropoff!" The mental tug of war was exhausting.

"Hey Tom, how's it going down there?"

"Nothing here but a giant timber rattler and lots of poison ivy."

It was hot and humid and the air was thick with pollen. Every bush that I brushed up against produced a green cloud. And when I had the misfortune to time it just right, my head would be hung low and taking a big gulp of air just as the pollen cloud was rising. I did a lot of coughing trying to clear my lungs.

We made our way around a point of the long ridge and headed up into Dug Hollow to a split in the bluff that is called "The Gap." It was here that we crossed the path Haley had taken just the night before, although we never realized it. We gathered together at a spot just past The Gap, a place that I call Magnolia Canyon. It is a beautiful spot that I visit often. Haley had just spent the night down below us at the bottom of Dug Hollow, and was, at that very moment, making her way farther downstream to the Buffalo River. The forest was so dense that she would have never heard our cries from up above where we were searching. We were the closest that anyone would come to her until Lytle and William Jeff found her.

Tom asked if there were any waterfalls nearby—knowing that Haley liked waterfalls so much—so we continued our search along the base of the bluff until we came to Robert's Falls (named after Doc "Robert" Chester). This was a cool and refreshing oasis out there in the middle of the jungle. There is a spot next to the waterfall where we climbed a series of small ledges and made our way up and over the bluffline.

Once on top we split up again, and began a search of the two benches directly above the bluffline—these would lead us all the way back to the cabin. Some of the first part of the benches had been searched the night before by the Woods Boys in the dark, but it never hurts to check again. This time Tom and I did not keep in good contact with each other. I was on the lower bench, narrow and thick with brush and boulders. Tom was above me, searching along a broad and more open bench. At some point he thought that he heard me yelling for him, so came down to my bench to see what I was up to. When he got down to the lower bench, he heard more yelling lower down, below the bluff—this was actually a search team working the area below the bluff on horseback and mules. I'm not exactly sure where Tom ended up, but we did not see him back at the cabin for several more hours. I do believe that he knows this area of the wilderness quite well now!

I returned to the cabin a bit dejected, but actually happy that we had not found anything at the base of the bluff. That big bluffline had been nagging me all night, and I really wanted to make sure that Haley had not gone off of it. My head was a little clearer now, although my lungs did not appreciate the pollen.

The cabin was a hub of activity all day long. Family and friends of the Zegas were coming and going—many staying. Food and supplies were coming in. Teams of searchers were passing through constantly. Helicopters were buzzing overhead and up and down the valley below. Many of the SAR leaders stopped by just to go out onto the back deck and gaze out into the wilderness—it was certainly the best place to get a genuine feel for exactly what type of terrain they were dealing with. I guess our cabin became an important part of the rescue mission in many ways.

I must stop here for a moment and say a word about thank you's. There were hundreds of folks, both here and via e-mail and phone, who went out of their way to thank us for opening up our cabin to the family and others during this crisis. I quite frankly could not understand why they were thanking us for anything—who in the world would *not* open up their home in this situation? It just seemed perfectly normal to me and absolutely nothing that I needed to be thanked for. My main concern was that I did not provide a thing to these people (not even a toothbrush!), and I was embarrassed about that many times.

Just about the time we had the most people at the cabin, the water monster struck—the well went dry. I had been concerned about it from the very beginning and was holding my breath. Our tiny well only produces 65-70 gallons a day, which works out to about 28 flushes. The water actually lasted much longer than I had ever expected. But now we had dozens and dozens of folks at our cabin and *no toilets!* I sent word out that water was needed, and before long jugs of water began to arrive—at first just small water bottles, then eventually gallons. Mary Woods brought several gallon jugs of water, and we went up to the well and poured them in. When the National Guard began to arrive up at the command center, plans were made to bring down a "water buffalo" (a tank of water on wheels). It would be after dark before that would happen.

Much of the discussions at the cabin centered around the incredible amount of support that was pouring in from all over the region. The generosity of everyone who was participating in the search efforts—from the volunteers who had taken off work to be out in the woods, to the people and companies in distant cities who donated goods and services—was overwhelming. Steve and Kelly were moved by all of this and didn't know quite how to handle it.

The activity level at the cabin remained high—both phone lines were constantly in use, as was the computer. Scores of folks were sitting/standing around talking, planning, telling stories, hugging, and crying—there was a great deal of crying. Many folks just stood around not really knowing what to do or how to act. Every hour that passed lowered the chances that Haley would be found alive, and this was something that simply was not discussed with family or close friends. Several times Steve would curl up on one of the couches with a dazed look on his face. We all felt that way, only I think it was hitting him harder than anyone else.

I got to help with a couple of important projects during the day. Matt McGowan and Scott Davis from *The Morning News* had been visiting the Zegas at our cabin. They needed to get a copy of Haley's picture sent to their newspaper office. All that we had was a little wallet sized photo of her, but that would work. We spent an hour up at my main office scanning and tweaking the photo, then sent the digital file out over the internet. Net access way out here at the end of the phone line is dismal at best—often only 10k. It was a very long upload, but the file did finally go through. This little scanned photo of Haley would become the image of her that was broadcast across the country and printed in every newspaper in the region.

There happened to be a large gathering of "dowsers" taking place at the Crescent Hotel in Eureka Springs (a dowser is someone who locates people and objects using alternative methods—like a witchhaze l branch to find water for example). Crow Johnson help set up our communications with this group. They needed an accurate map of the search area, so I pulled a topo map of the area out from under our map bar at the cabin, marked the necessary info on it, cut it down so that it would fit into the fax machine, and faxed it to the dowsers. Several hours later they faxed the map back with a possible location marked on it.

Kelly continued to speak with psychics, and we faxed them maps and latitude/longitude information. I found the mix of modern technology and spiritual activities quite interesting. Haley being near water and safe were two common themes from most of the psychics' predictions.

My office is located several hundred yards up the hill from our cabin, connected by a narrow trail through the woods. I made the trek up that trail many times that day, going back and forth to fax things, find a map, or look up something on the computer. On one trip back down to the cabin I ran into Steve, who was on his way up to the office to sit and wait for an incoming fax they were expecting. When I told him that I would be happy to sit and wait on the fax for him, he grasped my arm, looked me in the eyes, and said that he really needed to get away for a few minutes and my office was just the refuge that he needed—it was quiet, and there was no one else up there.

Later, Chaplain Wes Hilliard also would use the office as a place for quiet reflection. As anyone who visited the office soon found out, it was not nearly as neat and tidy as our cabin had been when first occupied. Hey, a messy desk is a sign of high productivity, right?

One thing that puzzled everyone was the fact that not a single bit of evidence of Haley was being found—no footprints or anything. She literally had disappeared into thin air. When word filtered down to the cabin that a hiking stick was found in the prime search area, and that Haley's grandpa Jay had identified it as hers, there was a jolt of hope in the air. I saw Jay later in the day and asked him about it. He didn't say much, just shook his head and said "no." Haley had picked up and used several different "natural" hiking sticks during the short hike before she got lost, but this particular one could not be positively identified as one of them.

There had been so many stories of the huge crowd and developing mini-city that was springing up at the staging area near our mailbox that I just had to drive up the hill and see for myself. I also had heard that a couple of friends of mine, Mark Clippinger and George Stowe-Rains, were two of the incident commanders and basically running the SAR operations. I wanted to see them and say hi and see if there was anything that I could do to help.

Before I reached the main road where all of the activity was going on, I would pass a small army of people and vehicles—most of them SAR teams either heading out or coming back in from a sweep. I pulled off to the side of the road as several pickups approached. They stopped and unloaded 20 or 30 volunteers who were to begin a sweep of the woods from the dirt road down to the bluffline. This area had been searched several times before, but they wanted to search it again. One of the team leaders was a friend of mine, Jeff Montgomery. We spoke for a moment. The optimism and determination in his voice was quite refreshing, an attitude that I suspect was shared by most of the searchers. "We are going to *find* that little girl today!"

I also passed Mark Clippinger, who was on his way down to the cabin for a meeting that Steve and Kelly had requested. The SAR leaders were giving them regular updates, so Mark was puzzled as to why they had wanted to see him now. I also passed my friends Dan and Deborah Coody (Dan was the new mayor of Fayetteville, Arkansas, and had visited Cloudland and hiked around the area many times). They had just come off of a sweep search and were headed back to town but wanted to stop and say hi to Steve and Kelly first. Just another example of how far reaching this mission was—having the mayor of a major town (major for Arkansas!) take time out of his busy schedule to come out and help search.

One of the vehicles that I had to pull over to let by was a National Guard Humvee. I'd never seen a Humvee up close before, and they take up a lot of room on a narrow road.

The reports had been correct—it was a zoo up at the main road. The large field near our mailbox was filled with tents and vehicles. People everywhere! A large part of the field was flagged off as a landing spot for the helicopters. One was there being refueled as I drove past.

When I came to Cave Mountain Church I found another small city, but there was a distinct difference here—most folks wore uniforms and badges, and the parking lot was filled with police and other law enforcement vehicles. A small trailer had been moved in to use as the incident command center, and there were folks coming and going from it constantly.

I got to speak with George Stowe-Rains briefly, and he too was concerned about why the Zegas had called a meeting with them. "Are they wanting to call off the search?" he asked. Boy, I had no idea, but I definitely did not have that impression. Why had they called the meeting? Being sort of right in the middle of all this, I decided that I wanted to get back to our cabin and see what the heck was going on, so I left and returned to our cabin, stopping several times to allow vehicles to pass.

When I arrived at our cabin the circle drive in front was absolutely filled with vehicles—including the Humvee, so I had to park up the hill and hike back to the cabin. There was a small group of individuals huddled outside near the wood pile—Steve and Kelly, Mark Clippinger, and Colleen Nick. The conversation was tense and quite serious. I slipped on by and went into the cabin.

It turns out that Steve really just wanted to make sure that everything possible was being done to find Haley. He wanted specifics as to what areas were being covered and wanted to make sure they were not thinking about calling off the search (they weren't). They also talked about establishing a reward fund, how it might affect the search efforts, and when the right time to announce it might be.

Once the meeting broke up, the activity at the cabin was elevated to an entirely new level. A well-oiled machine fired up as Kelly, Rebecca, and others began the process of setting up a reward fund, typing up the exact wording, and constructing a framework to get the word out to the largest number of folks possible. This had to have been a tremendous boost to

Kelly. It gave her something to focus on besides the fate of her little girl—a project that would require a great deal of thinking and action on her part. I could only sit back and watch.

Chapter 4
THE
SECOND NIGHT

As darkness fell for a second time, many hopes were dashed. Haley probably would be fine in the woods for one night, but two nights without food or shelter would be another matter. The temperature was a bit cooler, dipping down into the upper 50's. I, for one, had all but given up hope that she would be found alive. That was a difficult thing for me to deal with, especially being around all of Haley's family and friends—I could not let any of them see the despair and doubt lurking inside me. More than once I had to leave the cabin and go outside to deal with those feelings on my own. I got in my car and drove up to a small field here called Aspen's meadow. The moon was partially hidden by haze and thin layers of clouds. I called my wife on the cell phone. Her reassuring words were a great deal of comfort to me, although she was very frustrated at not being able to be here in person to help with everything.

Back at our cabin, I mingled with the others, trying to make small talk. Everyone was doing their best to stay focused on the potential rescue and avoid the alternative. At one point, while I was standing back in a corner of my cabin (my usual haunt when there are a lot of people around), I realized that I did not know a single person there before all of this started, and even now I only knew a few of their names, yet I felt as close to them as I ever have to anyone. While no one ever wants to be a part of such a grave situation as we were in, these events do tend to bring out the raw, genuine, and wonderful goodness of human beings.

Suddenly, the front door burst open and someone yelled, "The water buffalo has arrived!" That was really good news. The National Guard had come through with a tanker of water for our empty well. It took them an hour to siphon 100 gallons of water and fill the well—that would be enough for 40 more flushes (we *really* needed to find Haley soon!).

When I was trying to get the cap off the well, I accidently loosened the rope that was holding the submerged pump suspended a few feet above the bottom of the well. A couple of hours later we discovered that the water coming out of the tap (and into the toilets) was something akin to liquid red clay. The pump had fallen down into the muck at the bottom of the well, and was pumping it into the water system. I hustled back up the hill to the well and raised the pump, and the water eventually cleared.

There was no official sit-down dinner—or a real meal at any time for that matter—just a lot of food. Folks helped themselves whenever they wanted. Rebecca and others washed a lot of dishes, and dealt with a growing mountain of trash. People were on the couches, standing in small groups anywhere they could get, and many more were outside on the decks. One group was over in the small office area typing away at the computer, making phone calls, and using the fax machine that I had moved down from my regular office up the trail. Mostly it was quiet, with a hushed murmur as background noise. The television never was turned on (we can't get any local stations out here). We only used the stereo once, just to add a few new-age sounds to the air, but I don't think anyone ever noticed. There was no party atmosphere here. It was rather subdued and business-like. Helicopters were grounded, waiting for the cooler temperatures of early morning, so it was quiet outside.

Folks eventually drifted off to wherever they had found to lay down for the night. Many were downstairs in the basement, others on the couches or chairs (there were seven couches), Steve and Kelly were in Amber's bedroom. Sometime after midnight Mark Clippinger came by to brief the Zegas on the current status of the search operation. Finally, the lights went out, and an eerie silence settled in.

Even though I was mentally drained and physically exhausted, sleep came slow for me. So many images kept racing through my head, none of them pretty. And then I realized that someone was crying. It was Kelly, the only one among us that had remained solid as a rock through all of this terrible ordeal. Pure granite she was, and I could not believe how in the world she could have held up so well for so long. But she had finally had enough, and it was all coming to the surface. She was not crying out over the potential loss of her only child though. Her words were ones of hope and encouragement—"I feel even *stronger* now than ever that Haley *will* be found alive. I am *certain* of it!" Her sobbing brought me to tears once again—I doubt there was a dry eye in the cabin (if only we could have funneled all of that moisture into the water system!).

It was a defining moment for me. If this woman—the one person who had the most to lose—could be so optimistic in one of the darkest hours of her life, then heck, I could be that optimistic too! I think it is fair to say that Kelly had that sort of impact on most of the people around her, and it was her optimism that kept everyone going. Yes, we would find Haley. She would be OK. Somehow.

Chapter 5
DAY THREE

T uesday, May 1, 2001. Once again the alarm clock this morning was a helicopter. We had come to expect that particular sound they make; and when we could not hear them, we scanned the skies to see if we could find one anyway.

Everyone was still asleep when I got up, or at least they were very quiet. While I was in the kitchen making a pot of coffee I heard someone giggle—that was an odd sound that I had not heard in the cabin for a while. I walked around the corner and saw John Goodwin in the over-stuffed leather recliner in the far corner of the little office area. Aspen had jumped up on top of him and was licking his face to wake him up. Good dog!

Aspen was a treasure to have around during all of this. Even though there were hundreds of strangers coming and going here at his house, he only barked *one* time at any of them (when a group of searchers on horseback rode through). Somehow he was fully aware of the situation and spent most of his time walking around trying to console everyone—and of course getting a ton of affection in return.

Within a few minutes most folks were up and milling around the cabin, the fund-raising ladies went back to work at the computer and phones, others wandered out onto the back decks and sat down, and the discussions of Haley's whereabouts continued in small groups throughout the cabin.

The map bar and kitchen counter tops were completely covered with food, and the refrigerator bulged with milk, juices, and plates of all sorts of things. There were coolers with even more food and drinks. These coolers were all over the floor and out on the front porch. The volunteers up at the staging area were sending down loads of food!

Just as things began to get going at the cabin, I was summoned to the command post to try to deal with a member of our Ozark Highlands Trail Association hiking club who was making trouble. They thought I would be able to calm him down and get him to back off of some demands he was making. "I will be up there as soon as I can," I told them. "The ultimatum that he gave us expires in a few minutes," I was told.

When I reached the staging area there were hundreds of people all over the place. Vehicles were parked wherever they could find space. This was more activity than the area had ever seen, even though it actually used to be a community with a post office and a number of residences. The post office was located exactly where the check-in tables were set up, at the edge of a field.

I walked over to the check-in desk; and even before I got near it, folks were yelling at me, wanting to know who I was and telling me that I needed to check in. It sounded like they were getting pretty serious! I heard someone in the crowd yell out to the SAR worker at the desk, "*you should have to check in with *him*!*" There were long tables of food set up, a number of mules tied to trees, a tent city in the large field behind a fence, and an area roped off with orange tape where the helicopters landed and were refueled. There were three helicopters on the ground, one of them with its rotors going.

I asked one of the hiking club members that I saw near the check-in desk where our troublemaker was. Jeff Montgomery, who had led one of the search teams the day before, came over and told me that he was down at the command post trying to get orders to go out on another search. Like many of the volunteers who had come out to help, this guy was tired of waiting around and was demanding that he and a group of hikers be given an assignment.

By the time I had arrived at the command post, they had already taken care of him. I asked George Stowe-Rains, one of the incident commanders, about him. He told me they were going to load the group of hikers into several helicopters and fly them deep into the wilderness to make a sweep search. I guess that was one way to handle him, and that is exactly what they did! The group climbed into the waiting choppers and flew away.

There seemed to be a different feel in the air as I stood there with George. Many more state police folks were running around, along with many others wearing guns and badges. George pulled out an updated map of the search area and talked with me about possibilities (they had a color printer in the little SAR trailer that they had set up, and this map was very impressive). "Where could she be?" he asked me.

"Do you think she was abducted?" he asked. "Nope." That was a question I was getting a lot more lately. Many folks were thinking that since many of the search dogs had followed a hot trail out to one of the dirt roads—and then that trail ended—that perhaps Haley had made it to a road and had been picked up by a passing vehicle. I refused to even consider that as a possibility.

As I left the command post and headed back toward the cabin, I met many more law enforcement vehicles and frustrated volunteers. We had been hearing lots of stories about volunteers being told to go home, or, if they were accepted, having to wait many long hours before getting to participate in any search. Even some locals who knew this country well were not too happy about being asked to sign in and wait for an assignment. The frustration level was reaching a high point, both with the volunteers who came a great distance to help, and with the SAR folks, who were being overwhelmed by a hoard of ill-equipped volunteers.

A young lady showed up at the cabin and said that she was a masseuse and had come to offer massages to Steve and Kelly. She set up her padded table in their room and worked on both of them during the morning. Later Steve came out and commented how wonderful it had been and said that she was willing to give anyone a massage that wanted one. She also had one of the powerful cellular bag phones, which she let folks borrow when both phone lines in the cabin were being used. I had thought that she knew Steve and Kelly, or that someone had called her out to the cabin to help, but that turned out not to be true. She told someone that she simply heard about Haley and wanted to do whatever she could to help, so she loaded up her table and headed for the cabin. To this day, even after extensive questioning, I have not been able to find out who she was.

Many people were milling around outside on the back decks, watching the helicopters work. There were four helicopters now, and they made quite a noise. I remember standing in a corner of the deck with Jay, Haley's grandfather, who had been with her when she was lost. His eyes were glazed over and staring out into the vast wilderness. "Where could she be?" he echoed the thoughts of everyone. Few people had put more energy into finding Haley than this man. And while I knew it must have been tearing him up inside, he remained focused.

More new faces arrived at our cabin. One of them was Mike Shirkey, who I knew from his popular "Pickin' Post" radio show on *KUAF* that we listen to at Cloudland on Saturday nights. I had made a comment to a group of the people standing outside that a regular *Cloudland Journal* reader (Nanette Ward from California) had sent an e-mail suggesting that we go search a hand-dug well that was located at the bottom of the hill near Whitaker Creek (I had mentioned the well in the *Journal* a year before). The SAR folks had pretty much discouraged family members and close friends from participating in the search efforts, but Jay could not stand around any longer, and both he and Mike Shirkey jumped up and declared that they wanted to go down and search the well. Deborah Batson and Chris Johnson spoke up and wanted to go as well. I gave them instructions on how to find the old well, loaded them up with water, and sent them on their way.

I didn't quite make the connection until much later, but many of the folks who were at the cabin were part of two very distinct groups. One group was Sierra Club folks—Jay and Joyce are very active members. The other large group were friends of Steve's—lawyers. We had lawyers up to our eyeballs at the cabin! Had I known we were being overrun with lawyers, I might have kept the doors locked! Just kidding!

Mary Woods brought a large cooler filled with fried chicken strips. The cooler was lined with foil, and the strips were hot. I piled a plate high with them and ate it all. We thanked Mary for the lunch, and she said, "No, no, that is not lunch—they have two big cookers set up and will be sending down BBQ for lunch—all you want!" Later she brought a 20-pound container of BBQ brisket, two large pans of beans, coleslaw, and on and on and on. Truckloads of food were arriving at the staging area, and the Red Cross and others were there to prepare it. And the National Guard had set up complete kitchen and serving facilities. The food machine was indeed in full swing.

Kelly Kemp from *KFSM TV 5* in Fayetteville had called and wanted to do a live telephone conversation with me on her noon news program. I had worked with her many times and was happy to do it. The biggest problem would be to have a phone line free at the right time. We had two different 2-line cordless phones set up at the cabin, one black and one white. This worked out great. We were able to carry on a couple of private conversations at the same time on the two different lines. However, after the phone calls ended, the phones were set down wherever the conversations stopped, making it tough to locate one to use. "Has anybody seen the white phone?" could be heard many times echoing throughout the cabin.

I was able to secure one of the portable phones in time, took up a spot on the floor of the loft, and waited for the interview to begin. I was a little bit apprehensive about doing this interview—I had been so darn emotional through all of the ordeal so far, and I certainly didn't want to break down and weep while on the air. Some big tough wilderness man I would be!

The interview went very well, I never broke down, nor gave out any confidential information. It was a good glimpse of the general mood of the family and friends, as well as some inside info about how the searches were going. When I hung up the phone, I heard someone say "That was a very good job!" It was George Stowe-Rains. He had been sitting at the top of the staircase that led up to the loft listening to every word.

George was here to brief the family on the status of the mission. But there seemed to be something other than just the standard briefing going on. For one thing, they wanted a location where they would not be disturbed, so I sent them to the guest room down in the basement. Colleen Nick and Chaplain Wes Hilliard went in with Steve and Kelly.

George emerged from the basement a little while later and told me they had to end the meeting because the emotions were getting out of hand. He also told me that Steve and Kelly had decided to make a statement to the press, and asked if I would drive them to the remote hunting cabin where the press would be gathered. They did not want a circus, nor any other family members or friends to be involved. I gladly accepted.

I loaded Steve and Kelly up and drove away, leaving the cabin-turned-bee-hive behind. We had actually been given a couple different sets of directions to the remote hunting cabin, and I was unclear as to exactly where it was. Once we got to the main gravel road, we were stopped by a road block. The volunteer manning the stop gave us yet another set of directions. We drove on to the first location, then the second, and finally the third one—all located along that main gravel road. We did not see any large gathering of press. While it really was kind of a desperate situation—the entire world waiting to hear the first public words from the grieving parents—I sort of got the feeling that Steve and Kelly were enjoying the drive, and the fact that for once the focus was not on Haley, but rather *on us*, being lost! I eventually located some neighbors and asked them if they had seen anything. They told me where a cabin was surrounded with press vehicles—yep, that had to be what we were looking for! The cabin belonged to Wesley Sparks, and he had loaned it for use during the search.

The yard in front of the little cabin was indeed packed with vehicles, but they had left one spot for us to park. Television cameras were everywhere—along with one or two men wearing guns. I felt as if I were escorting some criminals—security was rather tight. We got out of the truck and were met by Colleen, who embraced Steve and Kelly with a big bear hug that lasted for a full minute. I got out of the way of the television cameras and went up to the cabin.

Steve and Kelly were led into a *tiny* room in the cabin, then placed on a couch. There were quite a few television cameras encircling them, with several other reporters packed in. No one said a word, nor made a sound. It was quite eerie. And it was obvious that the Public Information Officer (PIO) had everything under control (Kevin Thomas from the Arkansas Game and Fish Commission). Colleen spoke first and basically said that they had wanted to make a statement to the press to thank the public for everything that was being done for them. She stepped aside and Steve began to speak.

He began by reading a list of the many agencies that were involved with the search and how much he and Kelly appreciated everything that they were doing. Next he talked about Colleen Nick and what her participation and influence had meant to them. And then he said my name and talked about all I had done for them. That was a big surprise to me. Heck, all that

I did was to leave the front door to our cabin unlocked! His voice was beginning to break as he continued:

> The people of Newton County have been amazing, they have broken these woods with their feet and their legs and their hands to look for our daughter—THANK YOU! We want to thank our family and friends who have all stopped their lives, come from all over the state and country to be here, and have left their own jobs and families, and have just been here to hold our hands. Thank you all. We love you. Haley loves you. Everything that you have done for that little girl. We love you. Thank you. Pray for us. Thank you very much.

By the time Steve finished I was just about to lose it, and I know many others in the room were too. But then Kelly began to speak, while clutching Haley's blankie, and she was choked with emotion and nearly sobbing:

> I also want to thank *you all* (the media) because our message could not get out there like it has without your assistance, and we know that everything you are doing is in the best interest of this beautiful little girl.
>
> We know that all of you who have seen her precious face know that she is a little girl who is going places. She's smart and she's tender, and she's an angel here on this earth. We know that we are blessed to have her in our lives.
>
> This is her blankie, and she can't suck her thumb without her blankie, and I bet right now probably the best thing to make her feel better would be to suck her thumb, and I don't think she can do it without this blankie.

Just when it appeared that Kelly might not be able to go on any longer, she reached deep down inside herself and found a new burst of strength. Her voice changed and she went on with a new level of determination:

> And so, if anyone knows where this baby is—I don't care how you know, how you find her, why you have her, where she is—it doesn't matter to us. We just want her back. She is the most important thing to us in our entire lives, and we would give up everything that we have to have this baby back in our arms, and to put this back in her hands. And I would just plead that you would put her back with us.

Before Kelly had finished, I did lose it and had to leave the room, covering my eyes so no one would see. I also wanted to bring my truck up close to the cabin so that Steve and Kelly could make a quick departure. The deal was that they would arrive, make their statements, then leave without taking any questions.

This had to have been one of the most difficult things the media folks had ever filmed. And I must say that they all acted with the utmost dignity and respect—none of them ever said a word, or tried to poke the cameras in their faces. It was obvious that the media who gathered out here in the wilderness to cover this event had a great deal of class. How in the world Steve and Kelly ever faced those cameras and made their statements I will never know—I would have been a babbling idiot the first ten seconds.

No one knew at the time, but while they were making this emotional plea, Haley was at that very moment being rescued, although it would be several hours before they knew anything about it.

As we drove away Steve and Kelly embraced each other and talked quietly as only two best friends and parents could do. It was quite a touching moment, and I was very proud to have been able to help and be there. "I love you Zega." "I love you Kelly." Steve was in the front seat and Kelly in the back, but they did the best they could to reach out to each other, obviously torn apart by what was going on.

As we drove on I was searching for something to say to them, *anything*. And then a thought came to me. I had been working on a guidebook to many of the scenic waterfalls in Arkansas. One of the waterfalls that would be in the new guidebook is the one that Haley had wanted to go see just before she got lost. Like most of the waterfalls in the hills out here, this one did not have an official name (although press reports were calling it Double Falls, which was not correct). And then it hit me, and I turned to Steve and Kelly and told them about the book. "What's the name of that waterfall?" Steve asked. I told them, "Well, up until this moment it did not have a name. And please note that this has *nothing* to do with the outcome of Haley's predicament, but the official name of the waterfall from now on will be HALEY FALLS." I replied. When one draws maps and writes guidebooks to unnamed locations like I do, you get to name them!

There were few moments of joy for these two people during this terrible ordeal, but I think this was one of them. We all shed a tear. And then a smile or two. That bit of news seemed to bring just a little calmness to them.

Later on, Steve turned to Kelly and said "I am *so* glad that you asked me out!" That brought more smiles all around. Through all of the gloom and sadness it was easy to see that these two were very much in love. When one looked at Kelly and wondered where she got the strength to stand up and carry on through all of this, one only had to look at Steve, and the immense bond they have, to find the answer. A person can make it through a great deal in this world if their lifemate is by their side.

After we returned from the press conference, I spent the next couple of hours watching the drama unfold in the wilderness below, along with dozens of others at the cabin. At one point there were four helicopters circling in the big Buffalo River valley below. One by one the choppers touched down on a small patch of gravel in the middle of the river and let out police officers and dogs. It was easy to see all of this through our telescope.

Steve came out and watched it all through the telescope too. "Hey, those are my dogs!" he said. In an ironic twist to all of this, Steve had been involved with the training of one of the teams of search dogs for the Lincoln Police Department. Now his friends were out there on the ground with those very dogs, looking for his daughter.

The group returned from their trip to the bottom of the hill to check out the well. They all were exhausted and sweat-soaked. You really can't get an idea of just how big these mountains are until you take a hike down to the bottom of the valley and back. It's 700 feet to the valley floor right here in back of the cabin. "Hungry?" I asked. Out came several more plates of fried chicken and BBQ brisket. I listened as they told the story of their trip. This is a scene that would be repeated many times on the deck today—tired and hungry searchers stopping at the cabin for food, water, and conversation. The cabin became a destination point for volunteers today, more so than at any other time. Fortunately, we had plenty of supplies for them.

As the afternoon drew to a close, I decided to make good on a promise that I had made to my wife Pam. She had asked me to go visit a special place of hers that was nearby in the woods, where I had built her a wooden bench that looks out over an open forest of maple trees. She had asked that I just go sit there for a while—for her. There was some sort of peace that came over me while sitting there. The forest was so beautiful, quiet, and serene. I thought about my new bride, our lovely daughter, and how great our life would be here together, once they moved in.

That silence was broken when a couple of gun shots rang out across the way, up the hillside on the other side of the Buffalo River. I had no idea what was going on. (I suspect now it might have been one of the teams of searchers who had heard over the radio that Haley had been found.)

I walked back to the cabin half expecting to hear some news, but everyone was milling around just like normal. There were dozens of folks out on the decks and in the yard, plus the cabin was nearly filled with people. Someone showed up with a case of beer and set it down on the deck. Then the phone rang, and I answered it.

"Is it true?" the caller asked. "They are reporting on television that Haley has been found alive!" she said. "What? Are you sure?" I asked the lady on the other end of the line. "What exactly are they saying?" She said that it had been confirmed by two different sources that Haley had been found alive—no further details. I thanked her and said that I had to get off the phone to verify.

My first thought was to find Rebecca—she had been my source for any news, but I did not see her. I did see Kelly nearby, so I grabbed her and asked her to step outside. It was just the two of us on the front porch. "Kelly, do you *know* anything?" I was trying to find out if she knew about any false reports that had been circulating. She gave me a puzzled look and said, "no." "OK," I said, "this is not confirmed, but I want you to know that the television stations are reporting that Haley has been found alive." Kelly gasped, and raised both hands to cover her mouth. She immediately went to find Steve.

I began to yell, "Where is the yellow pad—we need to talk to the command post!" There was a yellow pad on a clipboard that had served as the official spot to list any important phone numbers—including the cell phone number for the command post. I found Rebecca and she said that the cell phone simply did not work—we had no way to confirm the television reports. (I found out later that the phone company had hooked up a land line to the command post just hours before, but no one had ever told us about it.)

The next minute seemed like an eternity, as news of the television report spread through the cabin, and we frantically tried to find some way to contact the command post.

Just then, a police car drove up and parked a hundred feet up the driveway. Steve Whitmill (Washington County Sheriff) and Chaplain Hilliard got out and walked briskly towards the cabin. I was out on the front deck with Steve and Kelly and about 50 others. Both men had frowns on their faces those first few steps. My heart sank right down to China. My first thought was that Haley had indeed been found, but that the television reports were wrong, and the news they were bringing was grim.

Soon Sheriff Whitmill broke into a wide smile and said, "We have a little girl up there who is looking for her mommy and daddy!" Needless to say, the place erupted—it was sheer pandemonium—unlike anything I had ever witnessed before. I guess everyone had been holding their collective breaths for the past three days, and now they were finally able to let it all out. People were jumping up and down, running all over the place, hugging and crying. Screaming for joy! I tried to find Steve and Kelly, but they had other things to do—like go find their daughter. They jumped into the patrol car and drove away (after Kelly ran back into the cabin to get Haley's blanket).

Man, I really wanted to go with them and witness this incredible reunion. I noticed that Jay had jumped into the back of a pickup truck that was leaving. He was family, I thought, and they would let him in, and perhaps me too, if I was with him. I ran over and said something to him, and he shouted "Get in!" I did, and we began to drive off. Then a couple of things entered my mind. First, I had no business being a part of that reunion, and secondly, I had a cabin full of people to deal with. I also wanted to make a post to the *Cloudland Journal* so that the world would know Haley was safe. I looked over and saw Aspen chasing the truck—that did it! I jumped out of the truck so that Aspen would not run all the way to the main road.

What an incredible rush those first few moments were! The shouts of joy are probably still echoing through the wilderness.

The next hour went by really fast. No one at the cabin knew a single detail about the rescue—where she was, who found her, or anything. But it really didn't matter. She was alive and safe and the mission was a success. I tried to make a quick post to the Journal, but the phone lines were jammed—lots of people calling in, and many calls going out too (Rebecca was doing her best to notify all of the press). I finally got an open line and made a very simple post—HALEY ZEGA IS FOUND ALIVE (in bold, red, flashing type). I put that on my main Cloudland web page as well as on the regular May *Cloudland Journal* page.

It was kind of an odd scene at the cabin—no one really knew quite what to do. The remaining people sort of wanted to hang around with everyone, yet there was really no need to do so anymore. It was clear that Steve and Kelly were not coming back to the cabin. A party atmosphere soon emerged. I heard someone say, "Too bad we don't have any champagne." I quickly produced a *chilled* bottle of champagne, popped the cork, and passed it around. Hey, our Cloudland cabin may be located in the middle of the wilderness, but we *are* civilized!

Finally someone began to load up the coolers, which started a mass exodus. Within 30 minutes, many folks were gone. But there were still dozens left, and we were all out in the front talking and laughing and digging into some very fine beer that Art Evans had brought with him.

Jay returned, along with Mark Gieringer. Mark had been at the cabin the day before and was coming back today with a truck full of supplies when he came across Lytle, William Jeff, and Haley, just as they were coming out of the wilderness and getting to the dirt road. Mark would be the one to deliver Haley to the command post. We all stood around and listened as Mark and Jay told their stories of that pickup and the reunion at the command post. Finally, we knew the facts and could put an exclamation point on the end!

The lady who had been giving massages drove up. I did not realize it but she must have overhead me earlier in the day saying that what we really needed at the cabin was a bunch of ice, because there was so much food that it was going to start going bad if we could not cool it. Well, she drove off on her own, found a little store somewhere, and raided all the ice they had—17 bags in all! While it was a wonderful thing that she had just done, I felt bad because we no longer needed the ice.

One of the helicopters flew by, emitting a very strange siren sound of some sort—it reminded me of the sound that a blue jay makes when it is sounding an alarm. Then we heard muffled voices coming over the loud speaker. The chopper was obviously telling any SAR teams that Haley had been found and to return to the command post. It was very surreal.

Before long there were only a few of us left at the cabin—Jay, Mark, Rebecca, Tom McKinney, Art Evans, Mike Shirkey, plus a couple of others. There were strong hugs all around, and then all of a sudden, I found myself standing in the middle of an empty cabin (surrounded by sacks of potato chips).

It was more than just empty—there was a vacuum. It felt like all of the life had been sucked right out of the place. This was absurd, of course, as I had just witnessed one of the greatest life-giving events of all time. I had been through such deep emotional horror in the past three days, then suddenly, was catapulted up to the highest high.

I turned on the stereo and put in a CD that I had bought the week before. I turned the volume up loud, very loud, and sat there in the middle of the floor listening to the same song over and over again. It reminded me of my wife and daughter, who I was missing very much. And now it was a song that spoke volumes about Haley too, the little person who had been the total focus of my existence for three days, who I still had not even met.

"...I hope you never fear those mountains in the distance. Never settle for the path of least resistance. Livin' might mean takin' chances, but they're worth takin'. Lovin' might be a mistake, but its worth makin'..." (*I Hope You Dance* by Lee Ann Womack) It has always hits me right between the eyes when I hear this song, even today, after I've heard it a thousand times. Something about that song makes the connection between young people and the wilderness and encourages them to live life to the fullest—a lesson for us all.

Wow! It was finally over. The three most intense days of my life.

Cloudland Cabin

Chapter 6
THE SEARCH MISSION

"We are going to search until we find her. Period." Those words from one of the men in charge of the search and rescue mission summed up the feelings of everyone involved. It was a simple task after all—find a child in five square miles of the most rugged and remote wilderness in the central United States. And do it in record time, while the world watched, as hundreds of untrained volunteers overwhelmed the area, and while trained professionals and law enforcement officials argued with each other. This is a story of exhaustion, frustration, a mountain of paperwork, and of deep emotions that brought many tears, even from grown men. It was far and away the largest search and rescue mission in Arkansas history.

While doing research for this chapter I spent many hours talking with the principals involved and poured over hours of recorded tapes of those interviews. I looked through hundreds of pages of documents and watched hours of video tapes, all to try to get a feel for exactly how this mission was set up and run, why it was successful, and why there were so many problems. I must say that I came away with a huge respect for the search and rescue community, and for the volunteers that were involved with this mission. It was indeed a super-human effort on their part; and while there were indeed mistakes made, those who made them were the first to step forward and not only admit them, but challenge themselves to do better in the future. We can all be proud of the job that was done by our fellow citizens.

This is a very long and complicated story, far too much for me to try to explain it all here. What I want to do though is lay out a few of the basics: what the time line was, who was in charge, how they went about their jobs, and what some of the problems were. It is not simple, or easy to explain, so bear with me.

Let me start with a few numbers. There were nearly 80 agencies and organizations that participated on-site with this mission. That's not 80 individual people, but 80 *groups* of people. The exact number of individuals who actually went into the woods to search will never be known. So many people struck out on their own without ever signing in at the official staging area or were on the scene before a sign-in procedure was set up, but records showed that nearly 1,000 people did sign in—450 on Tuesday alone. That puts the number of people *in the woods* during the search at any one time or another at nearly 1,000, perhaps even more! That does not count the support groups or managers. Some of these people only participated for a few hours, while others were there the entire time. There is no way to calculate the total number of person-hours. A very conservative estimate would be 20,000 hours spent on-site either searching, supporting or managing. I inspected a stack of papers that were generated on-site during the mission that was taller than two reams of paper. That stack, along with documents that had already been delivered to other people, totalled close to 1500 sheets of paper. And that was paperwork that was generated *during* the search at the command post. And one last number—there were 73 separate searches or "team assignments" performed by official SAR teams during the mission (this does not count free-lancers or the early searches).

It was indeed a huge effort. A framework of professional and volunteer people had to be set up and organized within a matter of hours, out in the middle of no where, without a single facility of any kind—not even an electrical outlet.

There is no one in Arkansas who is a professional search and rescue person full-time. Everyone involved does something else for a living. Yet the people who were put in charge had been highly trained and had a fair amount of experience with SAR missions in the hills of Arkansas. None of them, however, had ever participated in a mission of this magnitude, and the only training available was on the job training—nothing could have prepared them for this.

I have heard a great deal of criticism about how this operation was organized and run. Some of it was justified. Some of it was not. After reviewing the evidence, and talking with those in charge, there is no question that the right guys were running this show. They would be the very same people that I would want to be there if something ever happened to me or a member of my family. There are five individuals that I consider to be the top "gurus" of SAR in Arkansas. Four of them were on the scene very early and remained until the end, and the fifth was en route when Haley was found. We had the cream of the crop on this search, plus most of the crop!

Of course, some say that all of the official SAR operation was a waste of time because Haley was found by two men who were not part of the search party, nor even looking within the search area. The fact is that the reason Lytle and William Jeff were searching at all, and especially in the area where they found her, was a direct result of the SAR operation. Everyone who participated was an important cog in this giant wheel.

Let's go through the time frame and a few details of the mission.

The Newton County Sheriff's department received the call from Haley's grandmother, Joyce Hale, at 12:55 p.m. on Sunday, April 29, 2001. It is generally accepted that the County Sheriff has the ultimate responsibility in any SAR mission. The first thing that the dispatcher Edd Kelton did was notify the National Park Service, U.S. Forest Service, and the Ponca Volunteer Fire Department, who all immediately headed for the remote location on top of Cave Mountain.

Jay Bullington from the Park Service and Roger Atkinson from the Forest Service were the first to arrive at the trailhead at 1:48 p.m., where they found Joyce, who gave them a quick description of Haley and the situation. A "Lost Person Questionnaire" was filled out, and Joyce provided them with a picture of Haley from her wallet:

Female, 6 years old, 4 feet tall, weighs 48 pounds, blonde hair, blue eyes.
Healthy, shy, gives up easily, occasional pouting tantrums, cries easily.
Afraid of "dark, animals, snakes, bugs & you name it."
Clothing: dark shorts, tennis shoes, gray cotton t-shirt.
Child became angry, left main trail, separated from hiking group.
Search urgency factor 10 (the highest).

Michael Smithyman from the Park Service arrived a few minutes later. A "hasty search" was organized, using the seven people who were there, led by Jay. A hasty search is basically a quick search of the immediate area where Haley was last seen.

Members of the Madison County SAR team arrived, as did a K-9 unit from the Arkansas Game and Fish Commission, and Newton County Sheriff Charles Raulston. Sweep searches were set up and run in the wooded areas near the trail. Locals who knew the area well like Danny, Billy, and Landon Woods (the Woods Boys) were called and quickly joined the search.

Soon an official command post was set up at the nearby Cave Mountain Church—there was more room there for the many vehicles that were arriving than was available at the Hawksbill Crag Trailhead parking area. There were already 40 individuals on the scene at this time.

It was decided early on that the National Park Service would be in charge of the operation, at least for the time being, and Jeff West was appointed to run the show. It is typical for the sheriff to pass on this responsibility to another agency, which often has more training and resources to handle SAR missions. Also, Sheriff Raulston was new at his job and had little experience with SAR. It was a good decision on his part to turn over the reins so quickly. The overall responsibility would remain in his lap though, and his office stayed involved until the end.

Two helicopters arrived. The only place they could find to land was in the rear of the graveyard at the church. What a bizarre scene that was! Teams of search dogs showed up and went into the woods with torn up pieces of Haley's clothing that her mother had brought from town. Things were beginning to get serious.

Calls went out to many other SAR folks, including George Stowe-Rains, who works for Arkansas State Parks. SAR teams from many different counties in northwest Arkansas were contacted. A SAR team member can be almost anyone—a volunteer who goes through many hours of specialized training year in and year out, and who is required to have a "24 hour pack" with them at all times (a backpack filled with everything needed to stay out in the woods for at least 24 hours). These teams are usually set up through county sheriff's offices or fire departments. Often, members are law enforcement officials or park rangers, but many are simply individuals in the community with a tremendous desire to help. Their work is usually all volunteer; and in fact, they typically have to pay their own way for training and equipment.

George has been involved in many searches in Arkansas, both as a volunteer in the woods and as the person in charge. He is an expert woodsman and passionate about SAR. He spends a great deal of time hiking, hunting, and exploring caves. By the time that George arrived at Cave Mountain, volunteers, SAR people, and law enforcement were flooding in, and very soon these numbers would balloon out of control. George would be asked to take charge of it all.

It was obvious that an official framework needed to be set up to manage the SAR mission. It was up to Jeff West to get the ball rolling. A group of folks who knew each other and were all SAR veterans stood around in a circle. Jeff pointed to George and said, "You are IC." IC means Incident Commander, the guy in charge of the Incident Command System, which is used for large-scale SAR missions and wildland fire fighting. With that pointed finger, George took charge of the entire operation.

Here is what the top level looks like:

Incident Commander—Develops the main objectives and oversees the entire operation.

Planning—Determines Strategies to achieve objectives.

Operations—Implements Strategies through Tactics.

Logistics—Supports all of the mission needs.

George's first duty was to appoint Jeff as Operations Chief. Together, they would plan and implement the many operations that took place in the first hours of darkness. As more and more people began to arrive, it soon became obvious that they needed more staff and more structure. George appointed another SAR veteran from Arkansas State Parks, Denver West, to handle planning. Kevin Thomas from the Arkansas Game and Fish Commission was appointed Public Information Officer (PIO) to handle the media. A logistics officer was not immediately appointed.

The parking area at the church was not large enough to accommodate the growing crowd, so a separate area was set up to handle the volunteers and SAR teams that were arriving every minute. A large field about a quarter mile down the road from the church became known as The Staging Area, or simply "staging." This is where the volunteers and SAR people came to check in and wait to be assigned to a group before heading out into the woods. These searches are set up to be very organized, with each team having at least one leader who has been briefed by the command staff about where to go and what to do. That same leader returns to the command post to debrief the command staff about what they found and how effective their search was. Everyone had to be accounted for.

In the good old days, when someone got lost you simply got a bunch of folks together and spread out to look for them. That is not the case anymore. Search and rescue missions are more of a science, with computer-generated maps, global positioning systems, and probability charts on everything. And paperwork—a ton of paperwork.

It was decided that there had to be a second management team in place to take over when George's shift ended, which would be at noon on Monday. George and Jeff worked out who those members would be: IC, Mark Clippinger from Beaver Lake State Park; Operations, Doug Gay from Benton County SAR; Planning, Sammy Lail from Buffalo National River; and the PIO, Randall Dias from the Arkansas State Police.

The teams would take 12-hour shifts. The general idea is that while the IC management team is running things, they also spend a great deal of their time planning for the next team's operations. Then, when the next team takes over, they would run the operation that the previous team had set up for them, plus plan the operation for the next team. Basically speaking, it is a giant, complicated machine that has to be run amidst high emotions and desperate people.

That first shift of George's ran from late afternoon on Sunday until noon on Monday. One thing that you learn in a hurry during a SAR operation is that sleep doesn't happen too often. Who could sleep anyway—emotions were high and the adrenaline was flowing.

Steve and Kelly Zega spent some time at the command center (after being in the woods searching for several hours), mostly just sitting around and waiting. It was a very difficult time for them, and didn't take them long to realize that they needed to be someplace else. Families are always a tough thing to deal with during a search like this one. The SAR team wants them to be available for consultation, and close by once the mission is resolved, but it is a big distraction to have them right in the middle of things. Often a family liaison is appointed to take care of the communications between the IC staff and the family. This job originally went to Kevin Thomas, but he was glad when that shifted to George, and finally to Colleen Nick, who would arrive later in the night.

Jeff West spent a lot of time in the church building debriefing team leaders as they came in from the field (someone got a key and let them into the church). Man, you should see all of the paperwork these guys generated! Each team leader would fill out a form that included such information as what they actually did, description of any clues they found, difficulties or hazards they encountered, GPS coordinates of anything significant (not everyone had GPS units), recommendations they might have, plus a map of their search area. Then Jeff would go over the map with them, noting any specific items of interest, and especially the lay of the land—bluffs, creeks, thick areas that the team could not get through, etc.

This information was used to come up with a Probability Of Detection (POD) percentage. Basically that means how much of the particular area that had been assigned was actually explored. An open field would be easy to search with a very high percentage POD. Thick woods with bluffs and boulders are an entirely different matter—20%, 30%, 40%???

Probability Evaluation of Search Areas Consensus Forms, Cumulative POD's, Search Urgency Evaluations, Team Assignment Forms, Team Assignment Debriefings, Incident Briefings—Operations, Incident Objectives, Incident Action Plans, Lost Person Questionnaires, Staging Logs, Zega SAR Sector Analyses-these are but a few of the many forms that had to be filled out.

All of the info from the teams coming in was fed into a computer, and detailed maps were generated showing the areas that had been searched, what the POD percentage was. From that, the possibility that Haley was actually still in that particular area could be calculated. It is all very complicated and takes a trained mind to interpret. Especially at four in the morning, when you have not had any sleep in a long while. They were using special Maptech brand computer-generated topo maps, with each little area being a different color. Twelve different areas were searched, so all of those colors came in handy.

At some point during the night, a trailer arrived from Benton County SAR that would serve as the command post and brief/debriefing spot for the remainder of the mission. It was complete with computers, telephones, and all the necessary equipment to run an operation like this one. A long extension cord provided electricity from the church. The church had become a resting spot for weary searchers who needed a place to lay down for an hour or two before going back out into the woods.

In the wee hours of the morning, someone from the National Guard called and asked George if he needed anything. George rattled off a long list of resources that he would like to have, including Humvees, water tanks, personnel, and showers. A little while later the guy called back to say that it all was on the way. Soon after that George was told by a higher-ranking official in the National Guard that the stuff was going to cost him $4,000 a day! The problem was that in order for the National Guard to officially contribute resources there had to be a state of emergency declared by the County Judge and the Governor.

Ring...ring... County Judge Harold Smith was ousted out of bed to meet with Sheriff Raulston to sign the papers, and the process of declaring an emergency was begun. It would be later in the day before the declaration was official, allowing the National Guard to "bust loose" the resources. Everything but the showers had already arrived by that time though—the National Guard was way ahead of the game! Judge Smith would make several trips to the command and staging areas during the mission.

Vixen James from the National Guard had already arrived at the scene during the night to be with his buddy Steve Zega. His dad Lytle had been there Sunday evening and met with Steve and George, asking them if there was anything that he could do to help. Lytle went home convinced that there was nothing he could do at the time. Vixen kept a close eye on things and was privy to the search area maps and plans for future searches. He began to realize that there were areas that probably needed searching that were not being addressed. His close contact with the IC staff would later allow him to direct his dad into the area where they found Haley.

As daylight arrived on Monday morning, things at the command center were going smoothly, and plans for the second shift that would take over at 11 a.m. were being finalized. It was an entirely different matter down at the staging area.

The numbers of new people who were showing up and wanting to help began to increase. Michelle Viney from the Benton Country SAR team was assigned to sign in everyone. Most of them were untrained in SAR, and many of them ill-equipped to head out into the woods. There were 100 of them. Then 200. Then 300. And only one tired SAR volunteer to check them all in and make assignments! The numbers began to swell out of control. With the increased numbers came long wait times before volunteers could be assigned to a team with trained SAR people and sent out into the woods.

There were two different types of frustrations surfacing. First, the volunteers were being told, well, they actually weren't being told much at all other than they had to wait. And wait. And wait. Secondly, the command staff had no idea what to do with all of them. They simply could not send untrained and ill-equipped people out into the woods. They would end up having to search for the searchers and rescue the rescuers! So the plan was to put the untrained volunteers in teams with SAR folks. But there were just too many people and the process was slow. Plus, there were others that simply did not belong in the woods at all—no one knew what to do with them.

There are two very distinct sides to this issue, and there is a great deal of merit in both. It is pure human nature to want to help your fellow man—especially when it is a little girl lost in the wilderness. So what many people did was drop whatever they were doing and head for Newton County to see if they could help. Some did not stop to think, or even realize, what a remote and forbidding area it was, what their job might be, nor what supplies they would need. They just had to come help. The vast majority of these volunteers had never heard of Haley Zega. How can you fault anyone for being so generous and wanting to help? So they arrived and were eager to contribute, but were told to wait, to sit around and do nothing, and stay out of the way. Some of these volunteers got so frustrated that they struck out on their own. While that may have eased their own frustrations, they were actually interfering with the ongoing search by contaminating potential evidence.

The command center staff had a specific plan of where to search and how to search it. In this sort of operation you have set guidelines and you have to follow them or the system breaks down. One very basic part of all that, is being able to read a topo map. Most people simply cannot read a topo map, even veteran hikers. Some of the searches consisted of lining people up a few feet apart and walking in a straight line, but most of the activity was much more advanced than that. The terrain was extremely rough and rugged, and the proper equipment was necessary—including a good pair of hiking boots.

"When your house is on fire or you've just been mugged, you don't call your neighbors to help—you call the trained professionals," said George. "If we had only trained people they would know that we were overwhelmed and would have kicked back and waited for an assignment instead of getting frustrated at the staging area. Untrained people were simply unaware of what we were trying to do."

By the time George's team turned it all over to Mark Clippinger's team at noon on Monday, things were getting ugly at the staging area. This situation would turn out to be the biggest problem the command staff would face and took a great deal of their time away from running the search mission.

The problem was not that there were so many volunteers showing up—that was almost an act of God that would not stop—the problem was that the command staff was not prepared to handle them. Thinking back, George knows exactly where to put the blame for the mess. "We didn't get big enough, quick enough. We needed to expand our own resources—we only had enough to handle about 50 people. We should have put three or four guys in charge of staging. That is where we broke down. We needed a staging team to handle it all, and not just one or two people down there." George goes through speciality SAR training throughout the year, often three days a month, including many mock search and rescue missions, but nothing could have prepared him for this.

But still, things *were* going quite well. The transition with the new command staff went like clockwork, and Mark was implementing the plans that George's team had laid out for them. Mark Clippinger is the superintendent of Beaver Lake State Park, a veteran of many SAR missions, and is one of the most experienced and talented SAR people in this part of the country. I know that a lot of folks were glad to see him on the job. Mark and George had worked many successful missions together.

Not much was being found out in the woods. The mood of each new team of searchers that went out was optimistic, but their moods were gloomy as they returned empty handed. The staging area was filled with the long faces of hungry and exhausted searchers. As the day continued, more and more facilities were being set up; and when the National Guard arrived, things really got going. Tents were erected where searchers could grab an hour or two of sleep, or at least rest. Food was plentiful. Many private tents were being set up in the field as well. Vehicles were parked everywhere. The dirt road that ran in front, between the staging area and command center, was crowded with traffic. Volunteers from the Newton County Rural Fire Association used water trucks to keep the dusty road watered down—that was a big help!

Part of the large field where the staging area was set up had been roped off for use as a landing area for the helicopters. An Air Operations Director was set up to help manage all of the air traffic. Having the choppers right there was handy, but an accident so close to the crowd of searchers would have been a disaster. There were three helicopters flying now—from the State Police, Baxter County Sheriff's Department, and the Benton County Sheriff's Department. They had night vision goggles and sophisticated Forward Looking Infrared Radar (FLIR). The general principle behind this radar was that the heat signature given off by a human would be a lot warmer than that of the surrounding vegetation, and that heat signature could be spotted on their screen by a trained observer. One problem with the FLIR was that it was really too warm for it to work at its best—the difference between the human signature and the vegetation was just too close. Flying in the early morning hours before daylight, when the air was cooler helped some. Also, the many free-lance searchers out looking tended to complicate matters. Another big problem with the FLIR was that since the tree canopy was so thick, it wasn't able to get through to the ground in the first place.

One mistake that George said he made was to not turn his radio off once he and Jeff West piled into his jeep to get a few hours of sleep (throwing a blanket over the windshield to keep sunshine out). Every time something interesting would come across the radio, they would jump out of the jeep and run over to the command trailer to see what was going on. These guys needed a mental break from the mission and could have used the sleep too. They didn't get much of either.

There were so many volunteers just sitting around at staging, a massive sweep was organized. They lined the road just a few feet apart from the staging area down to nearly our cabin and went into the woods, walking slowly side by side, until they made it to the top of the bluffline. This type of a sweep with people so close is called a "Frankenstein" sweep. No clues were found.

Somehow word had gotten out that only SAR members who had reached a certain level of training would be used from that point on. Many of the SAR team members did not have this high level of training, and they began to get frustrated at the thought of going home. It took a while, but eventually the word got around that it was purely rumor. Another problem with the staging area was that those sitting around waiting to go into the woods were not told what was going on. It would be Tuesday before a "Sit/Stat" (Situation/Status) board would be set up to dispense information, along with someone to answer questions and dispel rumors. Many of the volunteers told me that was one of the biggest factors contributing to their own frustration—simply not being told what was going on. Mark gave a general briefing at staging on Monday night, which was the first one given.

One good thing was happening—darkness was approaching, and things usually calm down when that happens. To most people, nighttime is a bad thing in a search, but to trained SAR folks it is the time of day they prefer. Mark explains, "The best time to search is at night. What does the lost individual do? They generally sit down and stay put, which is the most important thing that they can do. Once they stay put, we have a much better chance of finding them."

Another rumor that had been going around was that only National Guard troops would be allowed in the woods after dark. This even got out to the press. It was not true, and no one could figure out how that rumor got started.

A new problem had emerged. All searchers that went out needed flashlights, and at least two of them (one light to see, and one to act as a backup in case the first one fails). SAR team members normally carry three lights, but many of the untrained volunteers didn't even have one. Mark told me that he was really surprised when an entire group of police officers showed up equipped with only a single small rechargeable flashlight each—they should have known better.

At 11 p.m. George and his team entered the command trailer and began an hour of transition with Mark's team. It went like clockwork, and at midnight the transition was complete. Mark made a quick trip down to our cabin to let the Zega family know what was going on, then tried to get a few hours sleep.

Both Mark and George agree that the team transitions were very smooth, and in fact, most of what went on at the command center worked very well. It was just that darn staging area and the hoard of people there. I heard the term "cluster" used many times to describe the situation at staging.

George's second shift went well through the night, although he admitted later that, "When things calmed down at staging, it gave us a false sense of security that everything was OK, and we were doing things right. We put the problems with staging on the back burner." By daylight a new surge of volunteers began to arrive, and the situation at staging would mushroom out of control. The State Police had to be called in to handle it.

The State Police had been on-site from early on. They were conducting an investigation involving the remote possibility that Haley had been abducted. None of the SAR folks in charge believed that was much of a possibility. Colleen Nick's feelings were the same—"Predators don't operate in remote areas." Yet that is always a consideration in any missing child case. And the fact that a team of search dogs had hit on a hot trail that led out to and ended on the county road gave them more reason for concern. The State Police kept busy following a number of leads, including tracking down hikers from another state who had been on the trail that day.

The Governor and Attorney General kept in close contact with what was going on through the State Police. County Judge Harold Smith told me that Governor Huckabee talked with him as well, and told him he was praying every day that Haley would be found alive.

The Washington County Sheriff's Department brought out a Winnebago that was set up at the command center. The SAR trailer was for the SAR operation, and the Sheriff's Winnebago was for the criminal investigation. George and Mark told me that both camps worked well together, and that the investigators did not interfere with the SAR operation. Carroll County Electric Coop installed a power pole next to the church that would provide adequate power for the trailers.

Tuesday morning, at Incident Command's request, the State Police issued a notice to everyone in the staging area that they would be arrested if they attempted to enter the woods to search without being part of an official search team. "Free-lancers" as they were known, were becoming more of a problem all the time.

George and Mark were highly complimentary of the locals who came out to help—the ones that knew the area and were equipped and able to be in the woods. The Woods Boys went out on many searches, and even led a number of them. Even that very first night, they were out there with flashlights and a team of volunteers, sweeping areas where no one had been. Mark said that he, "didn't care *who* finds her, as long as she is found. But we need everyone to go down to staging and check in."

The Sit/Stat board was finally set up at staging, and along with it Mike Higgins to answer questions and deal with rumors. No doubt this helped out a lot, but the numbers of volunteers showing up were still swelling. There was a road block of sorts set up at either end of Cave Mountain Road, and they were successful in turning away pure onlookers. Hoards of volunteers continued to flow into the staging area, some even on foot.

While Mark was waiting for his next shift to begin, George sent him down to the spot where Haley was last seen. Shirley McDaniel went with him. While Shirley is one of the regular Benton County SAR team members, she also has some unique "intuitive skills" as Mark puts it. She is not a psychic, but has been described by others as a "clairvoyant searcher." They went down to the trail and waterfall area. She did not "feel" anything down at the waterfall or below it (this was one of the main theories—that Haley had crawled down to see the waterfall, then continued on down the hill below it). Within minutes Shirley was moving along the trail *away* from the waterfall, back towards Hawksbill Crag. Before too long she was heading on the primitive trail past Hawksbill Crag and ended up just below our cabin, stopping at the downed tree across the trail there. This was the very same route that I feel certain Haley took.

After taking a look at the area around the waterfall and the Crag, Mark was convinced that Haley was not in the immediate area. Yet this was still where a great deal of the focus of the search was. By early afternoon on Tuesday, that 155 acre area had a 98% POD, which was almost unheard of outside of a golf course (that means they had looked at all but 2% of every square inch of it)! "We have searched and searched and will search it again," the PIO Kevin Thomas told the media. The search area had been expanded several times, and now totalled nearly 3,000 acres (almost five square miles).

The State Police began to get uneasy about the duration of the search efforts. They felt like IC was considering giving up and calling off the search, and met with George about it. "We are here until we find her," he told them, and that seemed to set their minds at ease. As the noon hour approached, George's team was not ready to turn it over to Mark, not just yet. They felt like they were finally getting into the flow of things, and were coming up with plans to greatly expand the search area.

There were two things that George was quite confident about. First, the SAR system being implemented seemed to be the right one—especially with the new plans his team was coming up with—and that they would eventually find Haley if they kept going. And secondly, he was quite sure that Haley was still alive. "Unless she fell off the bluff, she was out there, still ticking. The weather was good, and no critters were going to eat her. Her personality was just right—she was feisty, and it would have taken a lot to get her down. Her survivability rating was on the high end of the scale." That is one thing common to most SAR people—they are confident of their ability to find someone—if not, why would they be out there in the first place? It makes you feel good to have someone like that searching the woods.

Since George was sure Haley was still alive, and probably had not been abducted, his team began planning to expand the search area. They also wanted to make absolutely certain she was not within the current search area. Their general game plan would be to first define the extended search area and then send qualified teams into every bit of it and search until they had a 90% POD for all of it. They estimated it would take about 72 hours to complete this, still within the survival time frame for Haley.

In the meantime though, George had to deal with the other big problem he was having, and it was one of his own doing. It is always good for the Incident Commander to have some contact with the actual family—so that they know things are being well run by a confident individual. George went down to brief the family a lot, however, that much contact will get you into trouble. "I did not do as good a job as I should have managing this mission because I got too enthralled with the family. Having too much contact with them was effecting me emotionally, and was drawing me away from what I needed to be thinking about. That pulled me away from my job, and I allowed that to happen."

George made one last trip down to our cabin to brief the family around noon on Tuesday. He had Colleen and Chaplain Wes Hilliard with him, and they met with Steve and Kelly in a secluded room in the basement. One of the things that George told them was that a cadaver search dog was being brought in. At the same time, he assured them that he felt that she was still alive and that they would find her, and that she had probably not been abducted. Colleen was a giant help, although this was a very difficult meeting for all concerned. On the way back to the command post, George told Colleen that it would be his last briefing with the family, and that she would be doing it from then on, which was what should have been happening all along. There is no way to measure the importance that Colleen played in all of this. All of the SAR folks were very glad that she was there.

While the press conference was going on, both IC teams and law enforcement personnel were meeting in the Winnebago, where George laid out his plans for expanding the search area. There was some concern from the other members—not so much for the expanded search area, but for wanting to re-search everything else, and why it was taking so long for George's team to complete these plans.

Then one very important bit of hard evidence came in from the woods— a free-lancer was reporting that he had found a small footprint down along the Buffalo River, between Whitaker Creek and Dug Hollow. Chances were very good that this print was indeed Haley's, although a SAR team would need to be sent down to confirm. At about the same time, this free-lancer's camouflage tent was discovered right in the middle of the central search area. Along with a number of other items, there was a "men's" magazine inside the tent. That fact seemed quite odd to many, and the State Police took a very good look at this evidence, but quickly dismissed it as nothing more than the free-lancer using very poor judgement.

Some relief from the terrible communication problem came when Tri-County Telephone Company came out and hooked up a hard-wired land phone line to the new power pole next to the church. At last the command center would be able to make and receive phone calls—cell phones had worked poorly, if at all, and could not be relied on.

Things were now beginning to happen quickly. A team was being assembled to helicopter into the river area and check out the footprint report. Another high-level meeting was taking place in the Winnebago with all of the main people and agencies involved. There were three people down in staging now, so it was running more smoothly. The new plans were taking shape, and a few ground rules were being laid out to implement the new plan for the extended search area (they would no longer use any untrained volunteers, and no one in the staging area would have to wait more than an hour before being sent out). A special Blackhawk helicopter was on the way from Oklahoma, and would use their FLIR technology to search the area between 2:30 a.m. and 4:30 a.m.—the best time for the FLIR to work.

There was another group of National Guardsman on the way; and the showers, which still had not arrived yet, were almost to Cave Mountain! As part of the expanded search area, it was decided that two teams from the National Park Service would go down into Boxley Valley and come upstream, one team on each bank of the Buffalo River. And it was agreed that George's team would turn it all over to Mark's team in less than an hour at 6 p.m.

One of the most experienced and talented SAR people in the region was in another helicopter en route to the area—Guy Howe from the Benton County Sheriff's Department. He had trained and worked with both George and Mark on many missions. Guy has a sixth sense about searches, and his intuition has led to a number of successful missions. He had already told George to "get down off of the bluff—she is not there." And, of course, he was exactly right. Guy is also a great "man-tracker" and was going to be put into the woods immediately to go to the river and look at the footprint. So the stage was set for an even larger and more intense search effort to get underway, with a renewed level of confidence.

At 5:18 p.m., on May 1, 2001, just a few minutes after this meeting broke up, came the news over the radio that Haley had been found. Needless to say, two of the happiest guys on the planet were Mark Clippinger and George Stowe-Rains.

It did not take long for the command post and staging areas to be vacated on Tuesday night. In fact, it was down right spooky to me when I drove up there for the first time after the mission ended—the miniature city that had been erected had vanished in a matter of hours, with hardly a trace left behind.

A couple of days later, Christy Comstock from the Washington County SAR team invited me to go with her to help locate the exact spot where Haley was found. While we did not find that spot, we did locate a set of Haley's footprints that was farther downstream than anyone thought Haley had gone. That was a very strange moment—obviously Haley had been found safe and sound and was back home—but both of us got rather emotional when we came upon her tracks in the sand. We never did locate the footprint that had been reported by the free-lancer much further upstream.

Several weeks after that, I returned to the river to make another attempt to locate this now historical spot. This time I brought several snapshots that Lytle James had taken of Haley at the time they found her to use as reference. It was pouring rain, and it took a friend of mine, Roy Senyard, and I nearly an hour to scour the banks of the river looking for the rocks that matched the photos. We did find the spot, and once again a rush of emotion came over me. That spot was nearly a half-mile farther downstream than we thought.

After the dust settled, I sat down with both George and Mark and talked with them about the search mission (a large debriefing was held later for all groups involved). Both of these guys took their IC job very seriously, even more so I suspect because the mission involved a child, and both men have children. "With a child, you take it to heart. You are *it*. You are responsible, the ultimate person. And if you don't find her, it's *your* fault," George told me.

Obviously the problems with the staging area that resulted from the onslaught of untrained volunteers was the number one problem. Mark addressed the situation. "I applaud everyone who came out to help—it's tough for them to take off work and leave their families behind. Their hearts were in the right place. But trying to manage that many people and get them paired up with qualified people and into the field safely was a huge job that took away from our normal duties." Both men agreed that their own management teams were not ready to handle this situation and that they needed more training in order to be able to handle it.

"We simply don't have enough trained SAR people in Arkansas," Mark said. "One of our biggest challenges is to get more people trained and qualified in SAR. If we don't have large numbers of people in the communities who are willing to give up personal time to get trained and participate in their local SAR team, then we are going to end up having more searches like this one where so many of the people are untrained."

Mark also brought up another major problem—the fact that a perimeter was never set up and maintained around the search area. "Setting up a confinement barrier around the area is one of the very first things that needs to be done. This keeps the subject from moving out of the search area. But how do you do that in a remote location like this one where there are no roads? Certainly we talked about this a number of times, but the fact is that we never did anything about it. We probably should have taken some of the untrained volunteers who were sitting around looking for something to do and put them out into the woods to secure the perimeter. But that involves sitting someone down in the middle of a creek or along a bluffline and having them stay put. That is not a very glamorous part of the mission, and people get bored easily."

The fact was that every time search area boundaries were expanded, she had already moved beyond those boundaries. "We were always chasing her, one step behind," Mark said. "The greatest fear that you have is that you have missed her, that she may be down and hurt, so you want to keep looking in the same places over and over again. We did too much of that. Once we had covered an area to a 60 or 70% POD, we should have moved on."

There were many positive things that happened also. Mark commented that "the coordination between the different agencies was amazing!" George said that overall he felt the management teams, "did a better job than they had ever done before." It was obviously a tremendous opportunity for the SAR teams and individuals to get a great deal of real time training with a search effort this size. "We've never had to call in the National Guard, have an emergency declared, or even had to set a utility pole before." George said. And, of course, both men recognized and were grateful for the tremendous outpouring of support from the people of the state of Arkansas and surrounding areas. Let's hope and pray though that they never require as much support ever again!

Cave Mountain Church—the Command Post Location

Chapter 7
THE RESCUE

While the world held its breath and hundreds of volunteers and professionals from around the region scoured the wilderness for Haley, two local men from the nearby community of Mt. Sherman saddled up their mules and rode off to find her. Lytle James and William Jeff Villines scooped Haley up and brought her back to civilization. Lytle's son Vixon James (who was in the National Guard with Steve Zega) was at our cabin many times during the search, and I asked him to tell the story of how his dad came to saddle up that morning to go look for Haley.

Steve and I were at Fort Chaffee doing our two week annual Guard training when the call came in that his daughter was lost in the woods. When I heard where they were hiking, I was more concerned than if it was somewhere else because the country was so rugged there. After Steve headed out, I started calling the Newton County Sheriff's Department to find out any news. I called my Dad and told him what was going on. I asked if he could possibly go out to the search area and check in with Steve to see if there was anything that he could do to help.

The Battalion Commander discussed the possibility of Chaplain Wes Hilliard and I going to Cave Mountain to take care of Steve and to see if we needed to send other soldiers or equipment. I knew if the search continued, Steve would need some counseling support. I also could offer Mom and Dad's beds, showers, food or whatever— or other local residents' facilities in the area as well. When they did not find Haley by 9 p.m., Chaplain Hilliard and I headed out.

On the way to Newton County, I called Dad. He said that he went up and checked on the situation. He talked to Steve and some of the other search and rescue officials and had offered his services. He said based on the number of people that were there, he was not needed and probably would not come out on Monday morning to help, but to let him know if I thought he was needed. He said he would be prepared to bring his mule and other mule riders if necessary.

Chaplain Hilliard and I got to the mountain about midnight. We went to the command post and talked to Kevin Thomas, who was helping brief the Zega family. He was very glad to see us and immediately gave us an update on the search and rescue operation and condition of the family, and asked if Chaplain Hilliard would be part of his family liaison team.

I began to coordinate the support provided by the Arkansas National Guard, which was part of my normal duties. I was staying around the command post and got a crash course in their search and rescue methods. I looked at the map showing the search boundaries and areas with the percentage of POD (probability of detection). I also spent some time in the staging area on Monday. I was trying to get a feel for other things that might be needed for an extended operation and to get a feel for how many horse and mule riders were there. I was kind of concerned that there were not very many. I talked to what few riders were there, asking them what area they had been in and how their stock was handling the terrain. Most said that they were staying close to the top of the ridges and near the trail.

Monday evening the Chaplain and I decided to go to Dad's to take showers and make some phone calls to our superiors. Because there were not many riders out searching, and considering the limited areas they were covering, I was also intent on getting dad out there. Based on the search and rescue maps and their POD's, which were very low in some of the outer areas of the search area, I suggested that Dad search along the Buffalo River and Whitaker Creek. Also, because of the chaos he saw when he was up there on Sunday, I knew Dad was not going to sign in at the staging area. He agreed to go help search, and said that he would probably enter at the lower end of the wilderness and travel up the river and search the lower portions of the area.

—Vixon James

Lytle (age 64) had hunted in the vicinity of the search area many times and knew the country well. He knew it was extremely rough and rugged there, and did not want to go in alone. In fact, while on a squirrel hunting trip into the area some time ago, he promised his dog that he would never return again!

Lytle called up his good friend, neighbor, and riding buddy William Jeff Villines (age 51). William Jeff knew the area even better than he, and had made many a coon hunting trip by mule there. The history of the Buffalo River area is filled with the family name Villines. They were some of the first white settlers in the area, and also some of the more colorful characters. Lytle and William Jeff were used to riding together and made a good team.

They struck out for the trailhead early, and by 8:30 a.m. were saddled up and headed into the woods. They chose a spot along Cave Mountain Road to begin their journey, just uphill from the parking area for the famous Bat Cave. This cave had been used during the Civil War to mine bat guano (used in making gun powder). There also had been a skirmish with Union troops at that very location. It was also a gathering place for the community in the 1800's and early 1900's and now sees many cave explorers throughout the year (it is closed part of the year due to endangered bats).

Lytle and William Jeff were confident that they would find Haley and made sure to pack along snacks and treats for her. This is something that even most of the more experienced search and rescue folks didn't do. Lytle also threw in a camera, just in case they actually found her so that he could document the event.

Their general plan was to search along the base of the sandstone bluffline that runs through the entire wilderness area, then look along the river on the way back. This was the same bluff where she was last seen, although several miles away.

The terrain under the bluffline was extremely rough and difficult to travel through. Lytle and William Jeff were forced down on foot many times, even having to retreat to the benches below to make it around some areas. They made slow progress throughout the morning, working their way along the bluffline and heading toward Dug Hollow.

Lytle was riding his mule, "Copper," and William Jeff on his mule, "Big Momma." Copper was about normal size for a mule, but Big Momma was *huge* by any standards. Both were sure footed and comfortable in the rugged terrain, although they too had trouble negotiating some of the land below the bluff.

The two men had hunted all of their lives, from small game like squirrels and rabbits to larger game like deer, black bear, and elk. Their approach to hunting for Haley was much the same as if they were hunting game. While most other searchers were simply looking for Haley, Lytle and William Jeff looked for *sign*. "You won't find the game if you don't have any sign," they told me. Sign can be anything from tracks to scat to pawed areas in the dirt, or even broken branches where an animal—or a little girl—had passed.

As they entered Dug Hollow the terrain got even rougher, and they were forced to take a route well below the bluffline. Before long they came across what appeared to be "sign" that someone had made their way down the steep hillside on foot. There were bent weeds and disturbed brush. According to the information that they had, this area was at the outer edge of the search area, probably where no one had looked before. It was fresh sign, and got them excited.

They worked their way down the hillside towards the Buffalo River below but didn't find anything else that seemed encouraging, so they continued their push upstream, under the bluff, towards Whitaker Creek.

The upper reaches of Whitaker Creek was where Haley got lost, and that area all the way downstream to the Buffalo had been and was being heavily searched by teams of volunteers on foot and on mules, tracking dogs and helicopters. Lytle and William Jeff wanted no part of all that, so they turned back downstream once they reached the Whitaker Creek drainage.

Their return trip would be down along the Buffalo River. They made their way down to the river, rode along the banks and even rode right down the middle of it when they could. When the water levels are high, this stretch of the Buffalo River is a wild ride by kayak or covered canoe and is called "The Hailstone Run." It is 16 miles of wilderness whitewater with no access other than at either end. If you get in your boat at the upstream put-in point at Dixon Ford, you must do the entire run to the takeout point at Highway 21 in Boxley Valley (unless you wreck and have to hike out!). This run really isn't worth doing unless the water at Ponca is not only *over* the low-water bridge there, but *rising*! It is certainly not for the faint of heart, nor the inexperienced.

Lytle and William Jeff continued their ride downstream. They crossed the river and came to a beat up, twisted wreck of a canoe up on the East bank. No doubt those folks had quite a story to tell of their float on the Buffalo River.

Just below the wreck, they came to the mouth of Dug Hollow, where they found a small set of tracks in the wet sand. They could not really tell if those tracks were Haley's or those of a small bear. Nor could they tell which direction they were pointing. But somewhere in the back of their minds, they matched these tracks up with the sign that they had found high on the hillside above.

Lytle and William Jeff searched downstream, then back up to Dug Hollow again, but found nothing. It had been a tough day of riding so far, and they stopped and dismounted to have a bite to eat around 1:30 p.m. They knew that it got dark early down in this deep canyon, and the ride back to their rig would be a long and tough one. Their search was about up; and while they had not given up yet, it was time to "head for the house."

They got back into the riverbed and rode downstream. Before too long they came to a spot on the river where they could see for quite a ways downstream. Lytle saw it first. "Why, there's that little girl," he said to William Jeff. He was looking at a lump of clothing several hundred feet away, piled up on a rock on the opposite side of the river. William Jeff commented that it was probably just a shirt or other clothing that had washed up on the bank.

The mules continued downstream, slowly. It soon became apparent to the riders that it was a pile of clothes, a pile with Haley inside. There was no movement or sign of life.

Once they reached a point directly across the river from Haley, they stopped their mules. Lytle could see that her legs were blue and feared she had a broken leg. If she was alive, they did not know what frame of mind she would be in, indeed, if she would even get up and run from these two grizzled old men on mules. So they did not immediately get off the mules and run over to her—a very smart decision on their part.

"You're the little girl that everyone has been looking for," Lytle said in his soft, reassuring voice. Still no movement. Lytle said that her eyes were open though, and that he would never forget the blank stare that drilled holes through him.

Haley was perched on a slab of rock about the size of a coffee table at the edge of the river, with one foot in the river, and her head carefully laid down in her hands. A wild hazelnut tree arched low overhead.

"Haley, your momma and grandma sent us to look for you, and they are waiting up on the road to take you home." Those were the magical words. Haley sat up and looked right at them but still no sounds.

Both men dismounted and walked their mules through the shallow river on over to Haley. Lytle approached first, wanting to examine her to see if she was injured. "Can I hug your neck?" She nodded, and he carefully put his arms around her, checking the back of her head for injuries. Lytle has a five-year-old grandson, so he was used to handling children, and did so with great care.

She appeared to be OK, but rather shell shocked and exhausted—understandably so. She perked up when the men began to pull snacks out of their saddle bags. A plastic bottle of Diet Coke was first. Then chocolate pudding, Milky Way bars, and Vienna sausage. Lytle and William Jeff knew she was extremely weak; and since they still had a long and tough ride out to civilization, they wanted to get some energy into her so that she might be strong enough to make the trip.

Haley seemed to really want the chocolate pudding, but there was no spoon to eat it with. Lytle reached over and cut a branch from the hazelnut tree and quickly whittled a little wooden spoon for her. Haley was not immediately impressed with this, but agreed to try the "spoon" after Lytle told her that his grandson ate with a wooden spoon all the time.

"Do you like Life Savers?" Lytle pulled a roll out and began to unwrap it. "What color do you like the best?" Haley answered with the very same answer as most kids—"Red!" As Lytle broke off the other colors and laid them on a rock, trying to get to the red one (how come they just don't make a roll of *red* life savers!), Haley told him, "You know, I like the red ones the best, but I like them *all*." William Jeff had already been reaching for the other colors, but now they belonged to Haley.

(Lytle gives her a roll of life savers every time that he sees her now—"She thinks that I'm a candy machine.")

She began to talk a little bit about her ordeal. She said that she had slept on top of a bluff the first night, in a cave the second night, but she could not remember where she had slept the third night (she had only been out two nights). She was soaked from head to toe, and commented that she had fallen into the river several times while trying to scramble up a steep bank. She only had one sock, which was over her left hand and wasn't sure where she had lost the other sock. She was also clutching a hair scrunchie. "I think she was about to give up—this was her last stand," William Jeff said.

Lytle dug out the little camera that he had brought along and snapped a few pictures of Haley and William Jeff.

William Jeff, Haley, Copper, & Big Momma at the rescue site

William Jeff with Haley—her first drink in three days!

Haley, Lytle, & Big Momma

After about 30 minutes, it was time to go (around 2:30 p.m.), and they put Haley on Big Momma for the ride out. William Jeff said that her body was limp, and he had to hold onto her tightly to keep her from falling off. Haley said later that riding Big Momma was like "doing the splits."

Lytle and William Jeff decided to try to make a quick exit by heading downstream, following the river into Boxley Valley and Highway 21 where they would be able to find help. They rode out in the middle of the river where they could.

Haley "doing the splits" on Big Momma, with William Jeff, & Copper

At one point, they heard a helicopter approaching—it was making a sweep of the river. Both men waved their hands excitedly to get the pilot's attention, but the craft continued on without changing speed or direction—they apparently had not been seen. A few minutes later the helicopter returned. Their moment of hope vanished as the craft once again disappeared without seeing their frantic movements below.

The going along the river got rougher and rougher, and downright impassable at times, so Lytle and William Jeff decided to climb back up onto the benches above and try to reach Cave Mountain Road and get back to their rigs. Haley was very weak and slept much of the way. She rode on Copper with Lytle for a while, and he gave her his shirt because she was cold. The day was growing long, and everyone was getting tuckered out—including both mules, so they stopped for a rest. Haley went fast asleep on top of a rock. When she awoke a little while later, she said that she wanted her mommy and daddy. Lytle said that at about that point he wanted his mommy too! They were still a long way from the road, and the terrain was very rough.

William Jeff thought it better to walk instead of ride so he carried Haley through the thick brush, while Lytle led the two mules. Finally they reached Cave Mountain Road. As soon as they emerged from the woods, a vehicle appeared with three folks inside. The vehicle stopped, and everyone jumped out and ran towards the men yelling "Haley, Haley-bug!"

One of them was Christy Lunsford, who had been Kelly's assistant when Kelly worked at the Arkansas Alumni Association and knew Haley well. The others were Mark and Dana Gieringer, and they were heading for our cabin with fresh supplies of water and other goodies for the family and volunteers.

It was obvious that these people probably knew Haley, but Lytle and William Jeff could not be sure exactly who they were and were not too happy about giving her up to them as requested. They finally did turn her over to them when they realized that it would still be a while before they reached their rig, loaded up, and could get Haley to a hospital. Just about that same time, Roger Atkinson from the Forest Service drove up and said he would accompany the group to the ambulance back at the incident command center, so they felt OK about handing her over.

It was 5:18 p.m. when Roger radioed in that Haley had been found and that they should get an ambulance ready for her arrival. The location of where all this took place on the road was close to the Bat Cave parking area. Some TV stations reported early on that a park ranger had found Haley walking down the road near Bat Cave—at least they got the important part correct, that Haley was found alive and well!

Here is a note from Christy Lunsford about the event:

I jumped out of the vehicle yelling Haley-bug! Mark asked the men if anyone knew that Haley had been found. No one did, because the men had no radio. The men had planned to ride on down the mountain to their rig and drive back up to the command center. We convinced them to go ahead and let us, as friends of the family, take Haley up there ourselves. Her Mommy needed to hold her and kiss her and see for herself that she was okay as soon as possible. On the way up the mountain, I was able to hold Haley and talk to her. She was very exhausted and hot. She wanted ice cream and her mommy and daddy. She said that it had been lonely out there. On the way up I explained what was going to happen when we got to the headquarters, hoping it would help her not be so scared when people started crowding around and wanted to examine her. Haley is one tough little girl—a survivor! I stayed by the back of the ambulance with her until Steve and Kelly arrived. As they ran up, I backed out of the way and witnessed true beauty—the most blessed, beautiful event in my life! Praise God for answering the prayers of so many.
—Christy Lunsford

"Well, that was that," Lytle and William Jeff thought—yeah right! Little did Lytle or William Jeff know that their own ordeal and fifteen minutes of fame was just beginning. What they had just accomplished would make them heroes and local celebrities. They would spend the next days and weeks hounded by the press, with microphones stuck in their faces, cameras pointed at them everywhere they went, and phones ringing off the wall. Lytle took it all in stride and made numerous public appearances, as did William Jeff at first. But William Jeff eventually grew tired of all the attention and avoided any further press, that is, until *Dateline NBC* persuaded him to return to the spot where they had found Haley.

When Haley arrived at the command center, the area around the ambulance had already been cleared of bystanders, and they were able to get her inside just fine. Meanwhile, Washington County Sheriff Steve Whitmill was on his way down to my cabin to tell Kelly and Steve, who had no idea that she had been found. Their reunion was captured on film, and eventually the word got out to the entire world that Haley had been rescued.

Lytle and William Jeff made it back to their rig, loaded up and were about to go home. Neither of these guys were in this for fame or glory— they just wanted to find a lost little girl and return her safely to her parents' arms. They decided that they had better go ahead and drive up to the command post to make sure everything was OK. When they got there, they were met with less than a hero's welcome. Lytle told me that as he was trying to pull his rig into a parking area near the church someone in uniform came running over waving his arms yelling, "whoa cowboy, you can't park there!" It took them a few minutes to explain who they were, only then were they allowed into the inner circle. The heroes would be identified at last!

It was widely reported that Lytle and William Jeff had been turned away from the official search, not allowed to participate, and that they had even taken their mules up to the staging area and had to sit around and wait all day. While Lytle did go to the search area on Sunday and talked with Steve and others, he was not turned away. He simply decided to go out and search on his own with William Jeff on Tuesday, after his son, Vixon, had asked him to. He did not, however, want to be a part of the obvious chaos at the staging area.

Another story that made the rounds was that our heroes were going to be fined by the National Park Service for riding their mules in a wilderness area, or were going to get a ticket because they did not sign in at the staging area. Neither was true. First off, it was perfectly legal for them to ride mules into the wilderness area. And secondly, they were not inside the official search area most of the time anyway, so fining them was not applicable. Obviously everyone was thrilled that they were successful and found Haley—no one more so than those running the official search mission. The only comment from the SAR folks was that they wished Lytle and William Jeff would have checked in so that they could have been issued a radio. If these two heroes had been given tickets, there would have been a public outcry!

There were many more wild stories out there, including one that both of their mules had died from the trip. Hardly. Just go stand next to Big Momma and tell her that!

Many folks also have wondered about the reward money. A reward fund was setup for the purpose of buying information in the event that Haley had been abducted—it was never intended to entice more people to get out and look for Haley, nor pay someone who might have found her. The money that had been collected was either returned to donors or given to the Morgan Nick Foundation, as directed by the individual contributors. Some other groups that participated in the search received private donations as well. Lytle and William Jeff did receive some funds from the family, although these two are the kind of guys who had to be persuaded to take the money—their greatest reward was seeing a lost little girl sit up and show them that she was alive.

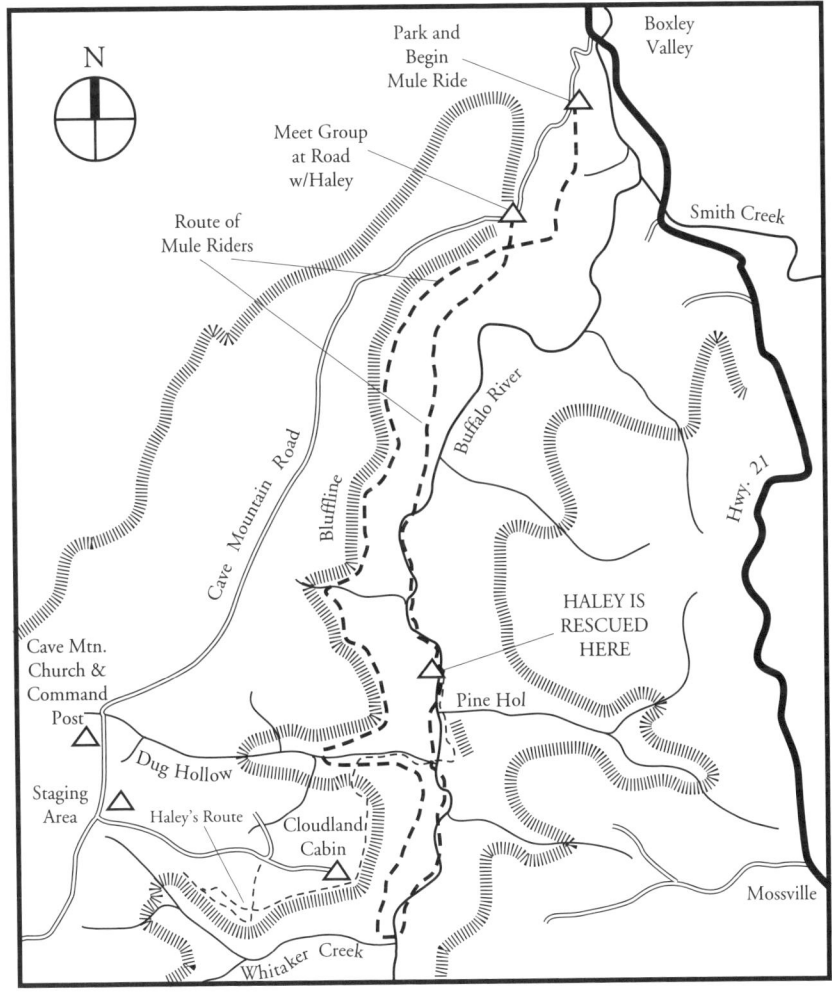

Map of Lytle and William Jeff's Route

Chapter 8
HALEY'S HIKE

It has been several months since Haley's Hike. Since that time I have spent hundreds of hours trying to figure out exactly what route she took, how she got away from her hiking group and out of the search area so fast, and eluded hundreds of searchers, dozens of tracking dogs, and four helicopters that were all scouring the wilderness looking for her. If you looked closely enough, there were many clues, and I have devoted this past summer to finding them all. I poured over countless news reports, looked at maps from the search and rescue folks, spent a lot of time walking the woods and talking with the two men who rescued her. I spent time with her grandparents, searchers and law enforcement officials, not to mention speaking with Haley herself. And finally, I spent many long hours in the woods following routes that I thought she might have taken. And, oh yeah, I was there while it was all going on too, and have always had my own ideas. After all of that, and just before I sat down to write this book, I finally figured out where she went and why she did what she did. It all made perfect sense to me. What follows is my description of the route that she probably took as well as the things she might have seen and had to overcome in order to make her way through the woods. Some of it is conjecture, but it all fits together out here in the wilderness like a giant jigsaw puzzle. No one will ever know the exact route she took, but here is what I think happened.

It was a warm and sunny day when the group set out for a quick hike down to Hawksbill Crag and a nearby waterfall. With Haley were her grandparents Jay and Joyce Hale, their friends Dennis and Michelle Boles, and Clay Bass. The Boles knew Bob Chester ("Doc"), who owned the property at the Faddis cabin where they parked. Folks used to park at this private trailhead before the Forest Service built an official trail out on Cave Mountain Road. The trail into the Crag from this point is less than a half mile (it's 1.5 miles from the main trailhead).

Haley was dressed in a grey Kennedy Space Center t-shirt, black shorts, and black and white tennis shoes. She was not wearing a daypack or fanny pack, nor carrying any food or water, but she did have a little walking stick that Joyce had picked up near the trailhead.

They stopped for a moment to chat with Doc and Tom Triplett, who were cutting up a downed tree with a chainsaw, then headed down the trail towards the Crag just after 10:30 a.m. It was an easy downhill hike, and soon they were all standing out on Hawksbill Crag, enjoying the morning. This spot is one of the most recognizable and photographed wild spots in Arkansas and is visited by hundreds of hikers throughout the year.

Haley was not comfortable with the 100-foot dropoff at the edge and was very cautious about getting too close or looking down into the wilderness below. The group sat out on the rock for a short time, but soon moved on before Haley had gotten at ease with the height.

Next the hikers headed towards a waterfall that Dennis knew about, located about a half mile farther along the trail. A primitive trail leads along the top edge of the sandstone bluff between the Crag and the waterfall. This route provides some spectacular views down into the Whitaker Creek drainage, as well as of the bluffline itself. The dropoff maintains an average fall of 90 to 100 feet.

The group stopped to inspect a neat pine tree that had fallen over ages ago but was still growing. They took a few pictures. Haley posed next to a tall rock outcrop for another picture. The trail through this area was grown up a bit (it is not maintained by the forest service), yet is mostly level and was easy to hike along.

Eventually the trail came to a small stream that poured over the upper part of the bluffline—this was the waterfall they were looking for. Jay climbed down over the bluff to one side of the falls to get a better look, using a small hickory tree growing next to the bluff as a fire pole (about an eight foot drop). There are actually two parts to this waterfall—the upper fall that is visible from the trail, and a second and much taller drop just out of sight below. The waterfall did not have an official name, and is marked in the *Buffalo River Hiking Trails Guidebook* simply as "the falls." Some folks have referred to it as the "double" falls because of the two drops. (This fact would become a confusing point during the search efforts because there is a waterfall named "Double Falls" in the same drainage, but at a different location. And while this trail is actually part of the Hawksbill Crag Trail, many press reports called it the "Double Falls Trail," which does not exist.)

At about 11:30 p.m., after having a quick look around below the upper drop, Jay returned to the group and decided that it was time to turn around and head back to the trailhead. They had planned to eat lunch back at

Doc's cabin and later drive a short distance to join a wildflower hike hosted by the Newton County Wildlife Association at the other end of Cave Mountain at 1 p.m.

Haley liked waterfalls, and really wanted to go down where her grandpa had just been to have a better look for herself. She was not happy when told there was not enough time for this—she *really* wanted to see those falls!

As the group turned around to head back, the first part of the trail was mostly uphill. By this time Haley had grown tired, and began to ask about being carried up the steep slope. "Come on, you can do it yourself," was the reply—certainly a typical response from a parent or grandparent. Clay volunteered to carry her, but Haley and her grandparents began a contest of wills. The adults headed back up the trail towards Hawksbill Crag and on to their vehicles back at the Faddis Cabin. That would be the last time Haley would lay eyes on another human being for 51 hours.

The next few minutes of the hike were extremely critical. I asked Joyce to tell us exactly what happened, and here is her eye-witness account:

Jay moved on ahead to catch up with Dennis and Michelle, who were headed back towards the Crag. Clay and I remained at the back of the group to deal with Haley. She stayed seated on a rock step in the trail for a few moments and then came slowly up the trail. She grew madder with each step, still wishing that she had been allowed to see the waterfall. Clay and I slowed down and kept an eye on Haley from a distance. Several times we moved forward to a point where an obstacle or bend in the trail kept us from seeing if she was coming. Each time we would stop and visit while Haley slowly came into our view. The third glimpse was of Haley, walking stick in hand, starting around a bend in the trail. We walked on a few more feet, stopping just out of sight to wait for her to catch up. We continued our conversation for a couple of minutes.

Concerned that the group was being delayed, I told Clay to go on ahead with the others and that I would go back and hurry Haley along, or carry her if needed, in order to catch up. As I went back I realized for the first time that there was a path that split off the trail we were on. It led a short distance uphill and intersected another trail that was parallel to the one we had used coming in. It suddenly hit me that Haley could have become confused about where to go. I had simply been following the group as we hiked in, not looking for landmarks, so didn't really notice the other trail until now— Haley was in the same situation. Suddenly the options of different directions created anxiety. I decided to return to the falls, just in case Haley had gone back to see it on her own.

I hurried down the trail, calling out her name, and briefly checked the place where she had seen Jay go to the fall's lower level. I convinced myself that Haley would not attempt to go down on her own. Now I was running to make up lost time, and returned to the cutoff in the path that led uphill, near where we last saw her. I realized that the concern in my voice might make Haley think I was mad and prevent her responding. So I softened the tone—then worried that it probably wasn't carrying very far.

When I returned to the trail intersection I started up the hill into unfamiliar territory. Soon the short section of path joined another major trail with more options. Going right would place me on a path above the rest of the party. Choosing left was unknown. Since the unknown path led father away from our group, Haley would not be seen by them. I decided to hurry forward on this path to the left and cut Haley off if she were going in the wrong direction.

Soon this arcing route crossed the stream which fed the falls and joined the main trail from the official trailhead. There were two hikers coming in. I was relieved to see other people, and quickly gave them Haley's description. They had not seen her but would start looking. One asked if she had any water or food, and I said no, so he left some fruit, chips, and water on the trail, just in case Haley might find it. Another man, also in their party, joined us. They split up to check the bluff and began a sweep. I was grateful for the help and felt that at least one side of the area was now secured and that no one had seen Haley moving in the wrong direction. This freed me to hurry back to check the upper parallel trail.

After a few minutes along that parallel trail I came to a downed tree. Worry was starting to build and my voice was giving out from calling. I decided that I had to get back to the others in our group and let them know what was happening. Running and calling for Jay, I first came to Clay. We were very close before he ever heard me—sound did not appear to carry well in the dense forest. Soon we organized and split up to keep looking. Clay began searching between the two paths, knowing people were on the lower one, and I returned to my last point at the downed tree.

By this time Jay decided to come back, wondering why the delay. He met two women with dogs who had hiked in from the main trailhead. They were the ones to tell him that Haley was missing. As Jay started back to the falls he saw me on the upper trail calling for Haley. He decided not to delay my search, and continued on, where he ran into Clay. They split up to search separately. Jay returned to the falls and climbed back down the short bluff at the hickory tree, thinking that Haley might have done the same thing. He didn't see any footprints. We continued the search.

—Joyce Hale

It has been widely reported that Haley stomped off in a huff, ran away from her grandparents, and even might have been hiding from the searchers, ignoring their calls. The simple fact of the matter is that while Haley was indeed upset at not being able to go down and see the waterfall and was miffed that her grandparents would not carry her, it is obvious now that she simply took the wrong trail while trying to catch up with the group—something all of us who hike very much have done many times. In fact, I have stood at that very same trail intersection near where Joyce last saw Haley, and became confused, not knowing which way to go myself. It was a simple matter to get lost in the maze of trails in the area.

Haley did indeed take the wrong trail, which led her up to the upper trail. When she came to this next intersection, she turned right, and continued hiking on the level path towards the direction she thought the adults had gone. She was now hiking back towards the Crag alright, but above and out of sight of the lower trail where Joyce and Clay were waiting for her. By the time Joyce went back to look for her, Haley was already too far along the upper trail to be able to hear Joyce calling out her name—remember Joyce was headed back along the trail towards the waterfall in the opposite direction.

Haley hiked along this easy trail, but somehow missed the spot where the main trail left the level bench (which goes down the hill to Hawksbill Crag). She continued on the level and followed a lesser trail that goes to a small primitive campsite just above the Crag. At this point the trail ran out, and Haley was faced with crossing the level bench without the aid of a trail.

Walking through the woods without a trail had to have spooked her a little, but she eventually ran into another trail, and all seemed well. This trail was not running along the level bench, but rather came down from a steep hill to her left and went down the hill to her right. Since she had hiked uphill a little after leaving the group, it only made sense to take the trail downhill to rejoin her group. This trail was actually the same one that they had hiked on at the very beginning, and turning left and heading uphill would have taken her right back to the Faddis Cabin and their vehicle.

Soon the trail she was on came to an intersection. If she turned right, she might end up right back at the waterfall, so she turned left, and hiked the level trail along the top of the bluffline. This seemed correct because the trail between the waterfall and the Crag also took the same general path. At this point she was a mere hundred yards from Hawksbill Crag.

Up to this point Haley had been hiking very close to her group and on the maze of trails in the immediate Hawksbill Crag area—no big deal. But now she was headed away in the opposite direction from the group, and the trail would soon take her out of what would become the immediate search area. None of this was obvious to her, of course, and all she knew was that she was hiking on a trail, trying to catch up with her group.

This trail was even more overgrown than the one she had hiked to the waterfall though. At one point a cedar tree forced her to the edge of the bluffline where a crevasse only inches from her feet opened up into 75 feet of thin air below. This spot made enough of an impression on her that she described it perfectly to one of the incident commanders a couple of days after her rescue. It was one of the few landmarks that she could remember clearly at the time, and became the first piece of hard evidence of her route.

She continued along this primitive trail, which runs basically level across the same bench she had been on for most of her hike so far. She was simply following a trail, and on the level, and there was no need for her to become alarmed and panic.

Before too long Haley came to a sign along the trail. She did not remember seeing this sign until she was talking to her kindergarten class about it a week after being rescued. She told her class that she came to a sign that read "PRIVATE P——." She was unable to read the rest of the sign. This became another piece of the puzzle because there is only one sign like that in the area. It is a sign that marks the beginning of our property here at Cloudland. It reads "You Are Entering PRIVATE PROPERTY. Hikers Are Welcome. Please Respect the Rights of the Property Owner." "Private Property" is in very large letters. This recollection would become another valuable piece of the puzzle to help me locate her exact route.

Soon after she passed the sign, a log cabin came into view. It was up on the hillside, just barely visible through the trees. She described the cabin as being "pink and purple," which must have had something to do with the angle of the sun and time of day. This was our Cloudland Cabin.

The trail continued straight ahead, on the level, and so did she. As she got closer to the cabin, she could not see any cars, nor even a driveway, so she figured that no one was at home and kept on hiking (from the trail you can't see all of the cabin, nor the driveway). It was still pretty easy walking along the narrow trail; she hadn't even thought about being "lost."

In all likelihood my wife and I were inside the cabin as Haley passed it, and in fact we may have been talking on the phone to Doc about her being lost at the very moment she was walking past the cabin.

It was now about 12:30 p.m., and she had arrived at the end of the long ridge. The trail made a gradual turn to the left, following the bench, where it came to a large tree that had fallen across the trail. The tall bluffline just below her made the very same turn. Just above her, behind a wall of brush, was a wooden gazebo, twelve feet in diameter, 16 feet tall, and topped with a copper weather vane of a running fox. Even though she passed within 50 feet of this gazebo, she never saw it because of the thick brush and steep hillside.

A trail of sorts continued on the other side of this large tree, so she climbed up and over the tree and continued on. The trail led off on the level through a small opening that allowed her to look up and see the cabin once again. This time she could see a second, and much smaller cabin right behind the first one, which she also reported to her kindergarten class (actually a log-sided workshop building).

She did not realize it at the time, but she had just left the hiking trail, and was now on a game trail, barely ten or twelve inches wide. It would be the last hiking trail that she would see on her journey. She had already traveled more than two miles—nearly half of her long journey. It would take her two days and almost a lifetime to cover the next two miles.

The game trail continued along the level bench through the thick forest. The hillside both above and below were extremely steep; and while the game trail was difficult to find and follow at times, it was really the only way that she could go.

The underbrush got really thick, and the trail disappeared altogether, but she pressed on along the level bench. There were many hidden rocks covered with leaves—she stumbled a lot, and the going was rough. And the fact that the ground cover of Virginia creeper and poison ivy was so thick that she could not see the ground—nor the rocks or small crevasses between them—made it just plain tough to hike.

Right in the middle of the thickest part of the forest, she came to a fence. It was rusty, although not barbed wire. She looked around for an easy spot to climb over the fence, following it to the upper part of the bench, and then back down to the dropoff below. She never found a break in it. So she simply picked a spot, climbed over the fence and continued on her journey.

Soon the forest opened up a bit, in fact quite a lot, and the ground was a lot easier to hike on. Many of the bigger trees in this area were maple trees, and they don't allow as much underbrush to grow, which created a nice open forest.

She passed by several rock outcrops that were on the slopes above her, some with inviting overhangs or caves that would make a great place to spend the night. Having to spend the night in the woods was the farthest thing from her mind at this point, so she hiked on.

There was no game trail to follow, but the bench that she was on was still mostly level, so it only seemed natural to continue along this route. When you hike this way without a specific path, you end up wandering back and forth a lot, actually covering more mileage than if you were on a trail. This bench was about 50-feet wide, with steep hillsides, both above and below.

The big trees changed back to oaks and hickories, and once again Haley found herself in a thick Ozark jungle of tangled underbrush and tricky rocky footing. She came to a giant boulder that spanned nearly the entire bench, and just beyond it, another huge oak tree that had fallen across her route. She would have to climb up and over it, then face more jungle ahead.

All of this climbing around and negotiating through the thick brush would take a toll on her—it is tiring for anyone, much less a young child who, at this point, had been without food or water for several hours. She was getting weak. Daylight would soon begin to fade.

The bench that she was hiking on made another turn back to the left, and with that turn she entered an area with many bluffs just above her and lots more below. This spot marked the beginning of Dug Hollow, a steep and treacherous area that is probably one of the most rugged locations in all of the Ozarks. She would soon hike right through the middle of it.

Another large, fallen tree blocked her path, although she would hike around this one without too much trouble. Just beyond the tree, she came to an enchanted area where there were many "block" boulders sitting right there on her bench. These blocks were simply chunks of sandstone that had rolled down from the nearby bluffs above.

Alecia

At some point during her journey, an imaginary friend came to Haley. Her name was Alecia, and would become somewhat of a guardian angel in the difficult times ahead. The drawing at the beginning of this chapter is of Alecia. Here are a few thoughts from Haley's mom about Alecia:

Alecia came to Haley as soon as she knew she was lost and left as soon as Lytle and William Jeff found her. Haley says Alecia "went home" then. When I asked where home was, she said that she didn't know, but that Alecia knew where she came from. Alecia had long black hair which was pulled away from her face, brown eyes, and wore a red sweatshirt with purple sleeves and blue jeans. She was four years old.

Haley says they slept curled up together, they played games and told jokes, sang songs, etc. Haley also said that when she came down the toughest part of the climb, she did so crawling on her back, and Alecia went down in front of her with her arms outstretched upward so that if Haley slipped, Alecia would stop her from falling. I have a feeling Haley slipped and slid quite a bit from the looks of her back and bottom (as well as a couple of bumps on her head)...but she says she never fell far! Alecia also had a flashlight, although she would not share it with Haley. It made them both feel better at night just knowing the flashlight was there.

I really believe that she was most comfortable with a younger child because then Haley could feel like she was still the "leader" and could advise someone else, which might have made her feel better and more in control of an out-of-control situation, yet Alecia was big enough to "help." Haley has always been really great with younger kids—maybe this was a really wonderful coping mechanism.

I find the whole thing overwhelming; Haley is extremely literal about everything and has never had any inclination toward having an imaginary friend. When she mentioned Alecia for the first time on our way to St. Louis on the first Friday she was back with us, Steve and I both were quite stunned and amazed.

And telling people about this story has probably produced nearly as many tears from the listeners as the whole ordeal and Haley's rescue did. It has, in fact, inspired the last chapter of a religious book that was already underway, written by a gentleman in Hot Springs in cooperation with the Second Baptist Church of Hot Springs. I've also had a significant number of moms talk about how this gave them the chance to illustrate the meaning of guardian angels to their own children. I have to think that angels could be one of two things—perhaps a real person, but more likely to me, the manifestation of exactly the person we need to guide us when we need it most. Haley needed another child to make her feel safe—someone non-threatening, someone who wouldn't seem so much like a stranger, someone who could empathize...if only we could all call upon such a person all the time!

—Kelly Zega

Alecia was the perfect companion for Haley, however, she might not have been so imaginary after all. While doing research for this book, I came across some information that sent chills through all of us who contemplated it. It turns out a little girl was murdered 25 years ago by members of a small cult. She was beaten to death, stuffed into a five-gallon bucket, and buried. The gruesome murder happened in April, very near where Haley first got lost. The little girl's middle name was Alana (mighty close to Alecia), and the age, dress, and general appearance of the two girls was strikingly similar. A group of dowsers who were meeting at the Crescent Hotel in Eureka Springs spent some time focused on Haley during the search. "We got quiet and did some dowsing to see what info we could come up with...we got that she was in a ravine and was scratched but not seriously hurt...we felt a female presence with Haley but couldn't tell if she was physical or in spirit."

Could Alecia have been the spirit of Alana? The head of the cult (all were prosecuted and sent to prison) had died in jail just a few days before Haley got lost—did his death set Alana's spirit free to wander the wilderness, just in time to help Haley? Could Alana *really* have been with Haley? I am personally not a big believer of such things, but this is just too spooky to discount entirely.

Up to this point in her hike, there was no real reason for Haley to have tried to find a route down through the bluffline. Since the country both above and below her was steep, and the bench that she was following was nice and level, staying on it was the obvious choice. And it was a good decision, because an attempt to hike down through the bluffline below might have resulted in a fatal fall.

Just past this enchanted boulder block area, there was a way down through the bluffline. It is called "The Gap" by the locals. It is the only spot along the bluffline for many miles where an animal, such as a mule or deer, can get down to the bottom of the bluff. There was a mule trail through this spot back in the late 1800's that connected the communities of Ryker and Mossville. This trail has not been used in many decades and in fact there really isn't much of a trail there anymore. The hillside sort of funnels down to a spot in the bluff where the bluffline has broken down to nothing. A game trail used by deer is about all that remains—this trail would lead her down the steep hillside to the bottom of the bluffline.

The route down through the bluffline was not easy. In fact, it was downright tough because the hillside is extremely steep. It is mostly dirt-covered with a thick layer of leaves and small sticks. I'm sure she spent a lot of time on her rump, sliding down the hillside (as I have on many occasions!). Alecia was there to keep her from falling.

On the lower end of the bluffy area, there was a short switchback on the old mule trail, which led her down to the base of the bluff. She had been hiking along the top of this bluffline for more than two miles, and now, all of a sudden, she was below it.

At the base of the bluff she was met with a near solid wall of *jungle* all around! The brush was so thick that you could hardly penetrate it at all.

There was really no open area to her left or right along the base of the bluff (nor any reason to go there), so she continued her trek downhill, into the thickest part of the jungle.

The next half mile would be the worst of the entire ordeal. She left the bluffline and headed down into Dug Hollow proper, facing that wall of jungle. Overhead umbrella magnolia trees blocked out most of the sunlight and blue sky. Down at her level she found a tangle of grape vines—some as big around as her legs and even larger—poison ivy, and stinging nettle plants, waist-high on her. Heck some of these ground plants were even over her head.

The ground itself was not really ground at all but rather loose stones and rocks that had fallen from the bluffline above. Most of these rocks were covered with moss and a layer of dead leaves. Often when Haley placed her foot on a seemingly solid object, it would move under her weight, sending her off balance and sometimes rolling down the slope.

There were also tons of ferns growing all over the place—many were delicate maindenhair ferns that often twist back and forth when you brush up against them. Lots of Virginia creeper, poison ivy, green brier, and other forest plants covered the slope. She seldom saw her feet on this trip down the mountain.

I have hiked down this very route many times and always dreaded it. No other area in the Ozarks is as thick with vegetation. Loose rocks underfoot make the going even tougher. Haley no doubt spent a lot of time on her backside coming down this slope! The terrain is *very* steep, making balance a problem—it is sort of a controlled fall, grabbing onto small trees to keep from falling down.

Eventually Haley could hear the sound of rushing water—it would be the first water that she had seen since early in her hike. That excited her and gave her hope. Her pace quickened. The steep terrain around her gave way to a more level bench—that water sound was just beyond the edge of this bench.

She ran across the bench and peered over the edge. It was a wonderland of large, smooth boulders, with water spilling over them and splashing all around into little emerald pools. This was the creek that runs through the heart of Dug Hollow, and it must have been a wondrous sight for her indeed.

She remembered what everyone had always told her—"don't drink the water!" That must have been a difficult thing for this six-year old to do—to be *so* thirsty, yet not reach down into the crystal clear water and scoop up a handful. Heck, I probably would have dropped right down to my belly and sucked it up direct. It took a great deal of restraint on her part to resist the temptation to quench what must have been a terrible feeling in her throat.

By the time she had reached this point in her hike, it was getting late in the day. She was exhausted, hungry, with an extreme thirst that she had never known before. She decided to stop at this beautiful oasis and "bivouac" for the night (bivouac is a term used to describe camping without shelter). The temperature was beginning to drop, and those big boulders were radiating stored heat gathered from the warmth of the day. Haley got her feet wet splashing through a pool of water, then managed to climb up on top of a warm boulder and curled up to rest.

During the night she was awakened several times by helicopters. She was very familiar with them prior to her journey and had always been quick to point them out in the sky. Now she was confused why there were *so many* of them way out in the woods. Haley had thought that they might be looking for her, which was another reason she choose to sleep on top of the rock—they possibly could spot her out there in the open. For whatever reason, their heat seeking sensors never did record Haley's presence. Perhaps the warmth of the boulders masked her own heat signature.

When she was awake, she could see a light somewhere out there in the darkness. This light was more than a mile away, at a farm house across the big Buffalo River Valley and up on the far ridge near the community of Mossville. None of the cabins in the search area had outside lights, although we had turned on all the lights inside our cabin just in case. That light, along with a half-full moon shining down, must have been some comfort to her.

Obviously we did not know it at the time, but Haley's mom and dad and a growing number of family and friends were spending a worrisome night within a mile of this very spot.

As daylight began to filter into the forest, Haley was faced with a major decision—where to go next. "Downstream, always hike *downstream*." Haley had heard that somewhere. And that is where she headed—to follow this lovely stream down the hill and see where it led her. She had no idea that if she went upstream instead she would eventually walk right into the command post with hundreds of stunned searchers (located at the head of this hollow at Cave Mountain Church). It would have been impossible for her to have climbed up and over the bluffline where it crossed the creek (a very nice waterfall that she would have enjoyed was located there). What? Did I say that Haley could *not* do something? She was about to prove that she was capable of just about any feat in this wilderness.

The creek took her down through some of the most rugged terrain of all. Those pretty, smooth boulders grew larger and were very slick to walk on. She got her feet wet a time or two. That felt good at first—nice and cool—but walking all day with wet feet gets uncomfortable in a hurry.

As she hiked/stumbled/slid her way down along side the watercourse, the sound of helicopters bounced off of the canyon walls above; but by the time they got down through the tree canopy to her, they were nothing more than muffled sounds that she did not recognize. In this thick jungle, a helicopter hovering directly overhead would have little chance of seeing her anyway, even if she could look up through the trees and see it.

The terrain remained steep, rough, and rugged, but she pressed on, stopping often to rest next to small waterfalls and quiet pools. She had been without food of any kind now for 24 hours. The body can certainly function without food for long periods, but your energy level drops a great deal. Even though Haley was proceeding downhill most of the time, it took a lot of her energy simply to keep herself upright as she made her way through the thick brush and slick boulders. She was growing weaker with each step.

By early afternoon the hillside around her had leveled out somewhat and the walking was easier. And then she heard a different tone in the falling waters of Dug Hollow—a more hushed sound. A few moments later she stepped out onto a flat slab of limestone rock and into bright sunshine. She had arrived on the banks of the Buffalo River and could see the big sky above her for the very first time since being lost. It was a wonderful sight, and her spirits soared.

Even though it was springtime, we had not had much rain lately. The river was running less than normal for late April. This would be a good thing for Haley, for if she tried to cross the river at normal flow for this time of the year, she might very well have been swept downstream and drowned.

Fortunately, the river was not running too hard or loud. She rested there at the mouth of Dug Hollow for a while, then wandered around a bit just to see what she could find. The going was pretty tough no matter which direction she hiked, and she was forced up onto the bench above the river. (The two men on mules who rescued Haley would later find tracks in the dirt in this area that they thought might have been hers.) She did not realize it, but she may have walked right next to the grave of my faithful springer spaniel and hiking companion for 14 years, Yukon. He is buried on that bench overlooking a nice pool in the river.

There is no telling how far or long she explored this area, but a single footprint was found upstream several hundred yards. She eventually returned to the river and found a good spot to cross—it *had* to be easier hiking on the other side! The rocks were slippery, and she fell in the water a time or two. No worries—it was a warm spring day in the mid 70's. In fact, since she only had shorts on, her legs had gotten pretty scratched up and itched a lot. That cool water felt great on her legs.

On the opposite side of the river, there was a sandy beach of sorts—a welcome pad underfoot for her wet and tired feet after several miles of rocky slopes. She had traveled more than three miles since the beginning of her hike.

There were more sandy beaches downstream, so she headed that direction, following an open corridor next to the stream. At one point a helicopter flew overhead. She still wasn't sure exactly what these "big birds in the sky" were, or if they were looking for her, but just in case she reached down and tossed handfuls of sand up into the air, hoping someone would see her. With her muted clothing she would have been nearly impossible to spot from the air. The helicopter slowly moved on and out of sight.

Haley followed that open corridor next to the river, leaving footprints behind in the sand. These very prints would later move me to tears when I found them a couple of days after Haley had been rescued. Finding them meant as much to me as seeing those first footprints on the moon on TV. They would also give the search and rescue folks a clue that Haley had gone downstream much farther than they had first thought.

It was easy hiking through the open corridor, although she was still tired and hungry and getting weaker with each step. The day was also growing long; and in fact, it had begun to get dark. The moon was just over half-full, and was hanging high in the sky overhead.

It was hazy up there, which produced a ring around the moon. She had been told by her parents and grandparents that any time the "moon is walking in water" like it was tonight, that there was a good chance it would rain before dawn the next day. She certainly did not want to get rained on. She remembered passing a number of small bluff overhangs back up in Dug Hollow, but that was too far away.

As luck would have it, the open corridor that she had been following veered over to the right and ended near the base of a steep hillside. From this point Haley could look over and see a bluffline. There just through the trees, was a bluffline that contained several small caves. In fact, from the end of that open corridor you can actually see a couple of cave openings without getting any closer to the bluff.

She was tired—exhausted really—it was getting darker, and it might rain tonight. She headed toward the dark spots in the bluffline. The first cave opening that she came to did not look very good to her. It was easy walking along the base of the bluff, so she continued on to see what else she could find. Eventually she came to another cave opening—right there at ground level. There were actually two caves—one went off to the left and the other to the right. She checked the one on the left and found it a bit too rocky, but the one on the right had hardly any rocks at all, so she crawled in.

(Hum, the first cave was toooooo hard. The second cave was toooooo soft. The third cave was just right!)

She looked around and discovered that she was not alone in this little cave—she saw pairs of eyes looking back at her—crickets! She was not afraid of them. A little while later a caterpillar crawled into the entrance of the cave. Haley reached out and picked it up. It was small and fuzzy and seemed friendly. It had two white spots on its head, so she decided to name it White Spot. This little critter would keep her company during her second long night in the wilderness.

Haley's shoes and socks were wet from the river, so she decided to take them off. She put one of the wet socks over her hand and used it to replace her security blanket. Every night since she was a tiny baby, and during times she felt frightened or worried, her blanket was a comfort. Now at her greatest hour of need, and with no one to console her, she created a "blankie" substitute. Rubbing the knit material together and sucking her thumb would have to do in this emergency (perhaps she got a bit of water from the wet sock too that helped dampen her parched mouth).

She was getting chilled from the night air, which would drop down into the upper 50's before the night was over. No telling where she picked up this bit of lore, but she decided to gather up some of the many dead leaves that were piled up at the entrance to the cave. They were soft and would help insulate and keep her warm during the night. She also stretched out her t-shirt over her knees, removed her shorts to wrap around her feet so that they might stay warmer, and curled up in a fetal position. This was actually a great position to be in because the blood can circulate better and keep you warmer. So there she was, all curled up in the leaves, with her new friend, White Spot. She was so worn out and exhausted that sleep would come quickly, although the chill of the damp night air would stir her awake several times during the night.

It did not rain, but being tucked away inside that little cave with all the leaves kept her body core warm enough to avoid slipping into a hypothermic state. Her decision to seek out this cave may have saved her life. A person can develop hypothermia at surprisingly warm temperatures and die quickly—it does not have to be the middle of the winter for this to happen.

When she awoke, Haley was faced with yet another missed meal, more time alone in the woods, and still no end in sight. Every bone and muscle in her body ached, and she didn't have much strength. But somehow she pulled it all together—both mentally and physically—and crawled out of that cave and into the new day. Sunshine in the treetops above had begun to warm the air, so it felt good to get out. She put her shoes on but didn't bother to put her socks on. One sock would remain on her hand, but the other one has never been found—it probably remains there in the leaves somewhere near the entrance to that little life-saving cave.

Haley returned to the river where she had been the night before and was faced with a tough decision right away. The river ran into the steep hillside that came down from her right, and the river bank ahead was filled with large boulders. She either had to cross the river once again—and the river was wild and dangerous at this point—or climb up the steep bank to avoid all of the boulders. She choose to climb up the bank instead of getting wet again and risking injury in all of that thrashing water.

She climbed up the bank, and it leveled out a bit and came to a small stream—this was the mouth of Pine Hollow. This is a beautiful stream course that tumbles out of the wilderness above and is filled with large boulders. Crossing it was tricky, but at least it was level where she was.

She made it across Pine Hollow safely, but her luck was about to run out because the route ahead was extremely steep, no matter where she went. She eventually ended up back down the hill, next to the river, looking for a better way. But this area also was bad, and she would end up falling into the river several times as she scrambled up the steep bank trying to make her way downstream. The water there was deeper than it had been in other places, but it was calm, actually a very nice emerald pool.

While she did not know it at the time—and certainly could have cared less anyway—Haley left the Ozark National Forest at this point and moved into the Buffalo National River, an area administered by the National Park Service instead of the National Forest Service. This new area was also a wilderness area, and had the same name as the one she just left—Upper Buffalo Wilderness Area. All of this gets a bit confusing!

After what must have seemed like an eternity, Haley made it past the big pool with the steep banks. The terrain leveled out, and she found an old road to follow. This was actually the original pioneer road that runs through the entire wilderness area from Boxley Valley up to Highway 16 near Red Star. Much of this road trace is so grown up with lush vegetation and trees that it can no longer be traveled on foot or horseback. Luckily, the stretch of road she happened to be on was mostly open and easy to hike.

While on the old road, Haley passed below the opening to a very famous cave—Tom Watson Bear Cave. I have heard several stories about it from the old timers in the area (all of them involving a ferocious bear and some poor soul). It is one of the longest caves in the wilderness; and while the entrance to it is a belly crawl, the passageway opens up into several large rooms.

The pioneer road was level and open, providing easy hiking, but Haley was about at the end of her rope, so her pace was slow. Then suddenly the road ended—she was looking at a raging river right in front of her, filled with slippery boulders and an extremely steep bank off to her right. She did not want to attempt either, but the river did seem the lesser of two evils, so she began to hike upstream looking for a better place to cross.

The river was much wider upstream and a lot calmer. She would attempt a crossing there. More than fifty feet later, and no telling how many slips and falls, she finally reached the far bank. But that was about all she could do. She didn't even have the strength to get completely out of the water and collapsed on the first dry thing she got to—a flat rock that connected dry land and the river. She put her hand with the sock on it down on the rock, laid her head on it, and fell fast asleep, one foot still dangling in the river. She had hiked only a half mile this day, but she had nothing more to give.

At some point in her dreams she heard voices. "Haley..........Haley." And then a short time later, "You're the little girl that everyone has been looking for." Her mind was shut down and not really comprehending. And then she heard, "Haley, your momma and grandma sent us to look for you, and they are waiting up on the road to take you home." Those words were just too real—she sat up and looked into the eyes of Lytle James and William Jeff Villines, the good samaritans that had come to rescue her.

While Haley still had quite a bit of rough traveling to do before being reunited with her parents, she was safe for now, being fed chocolate pudding and coke and life savers and Vienna sausages! She had been alone in the wilderness for a total of 51 hours, missed a dozen meals and snacks, and lost about five pounds of body weight. Her entire hike spanned 55 hours from start to finish. She was in remarkably good shape considering what she had just been through. And while she was covered with a hundred scratches and had several bumps and bruises, she suffered no major injuries.

It wouldn't be until nearly three months later that anyone returned to this spot and plotted the exact location on the map. I had to use photos that Lytle had taken when they first found Haley in order to match up the rocks and trees and locate the exact spot of her rescue. This location ended up being farther downstream than anyone had first thought.

After hiking the same general route several times that Haley had taken (with a GPS unit in hand and plotting it all on a computer topo map), here are a few numbers that I came up with: If there had been a trail the entire way, and she did nothing other than hike down the middle of the trail, she would have walked nearly five miles. Obviously she had hiked much farther than that as she negotiated the rugged and trail-less terrain—perhaps twice as far. I later had Haley walk several level stretches for me so that I could measure the length of her stride, then extrapolated the minimum distance she could have hiked. At the very least, Haley took 20,000 steps in the wilderness on her little springtime hike in the Ozarks!

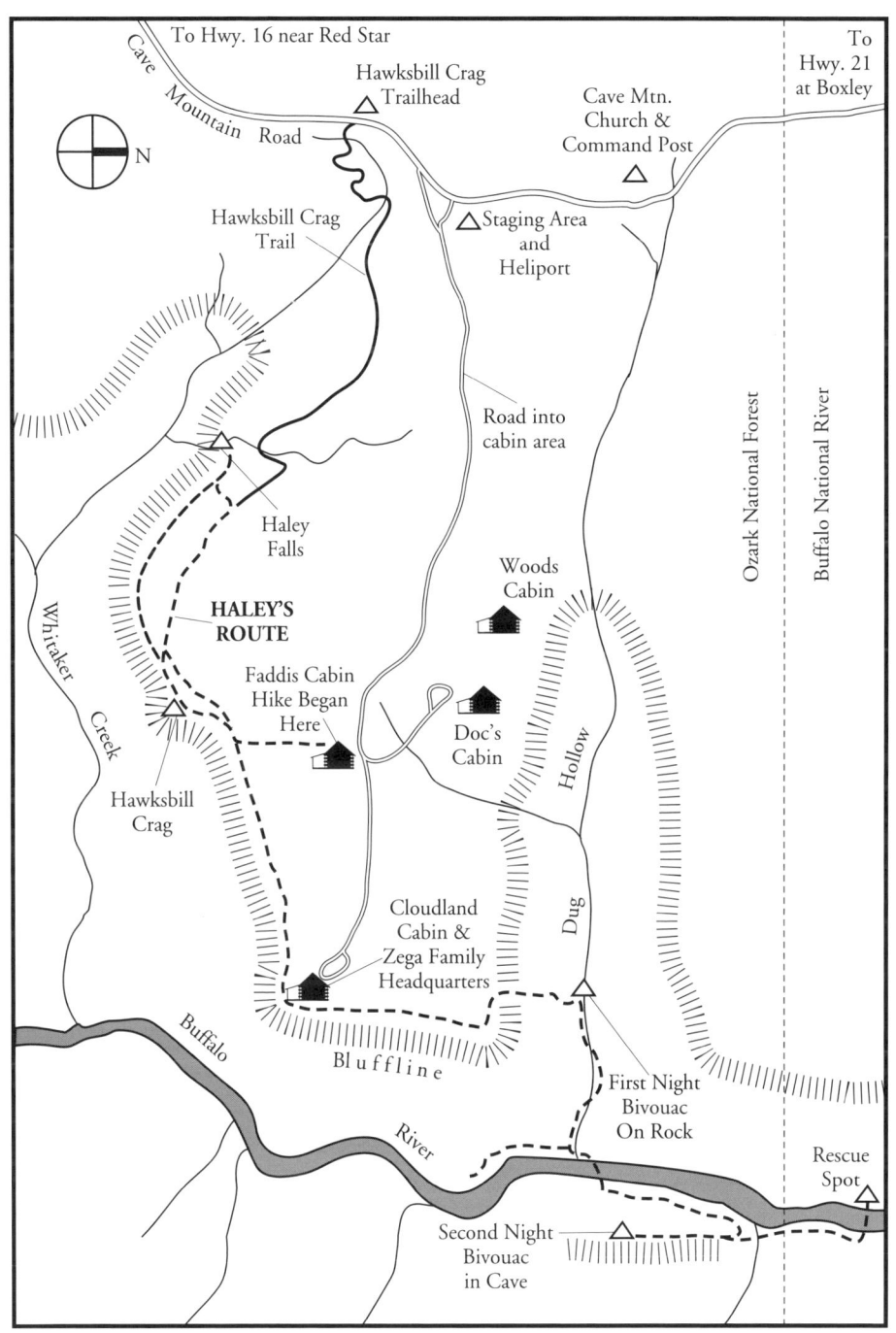

Map Showing Haley's Route

Chapter 9
VOLUNTEER'S STORIES

*M*ost of the hundreds of great people who searched for Haley were volunteers. They dropped everything and put their lives on hold because, well, there were many different reasons. Some knew Steve and Kelly well, many had small children of their own, while still others simply wanted to do anything to help, and often that meant coming to Newton County to join the search efforts. A majority of the agency officials and other SAR people were volunteers too.

Volunteers are the very best sort of people. They will work to exhaustion, put their own lives at risk, and ask nothing in return.

Much has been written and said about how the untrained volunteers may have hampered the search for Haley. I guess that is akin to being showered with so many gold coins that you cannot carry them all to the bank. And while it is true that pound for pound a trained SAR person might be more efficient in the woods, I know that the tremendous outpouring of support by the volunteers was indeed a great help and much appreciated.

Soon after Haley was found I began receiving e-mailed accounts from volunteers who wanted to tell their story. I was not working on this book at that time—they simply had to put their thoughts down and tell someone. Later, I asked others to write down their own thoughts. A number of those stories are included here, plus several that were published in newspapers.

Some of the stories were written by close friends of the Zegas, including a fraternity brother of Steve's and one written by one of Kelly's best friends, who was a major confidant of hers during the ordeal. One is by Haley's kindergarten teacher. Another is from a member of the law enforcement community. Others are personal accounts from friends of the family who volunteered, and several were simply strangers who had to come out and help find a lost child they never knew. A couple were sent in anonymously. All will give you a unique perspective into what it was like here. And while some of these narratives run several pages, I think you will find them worth your time. They are not in any particular order.

The words belong to each individual author—they have not been edited for content or accuracy.

The following is from a veteran newspaper man who helped search all three days. He told me that it was interesting how the SAR groups changed as time went on. He worked with just about every type of searcher—both volunteer and professional, including local good old boys, trained SAR folks, a search dog, regular hikers, and government employees. Here are his comments, taken mostly from his personal journal.

Charlie Allison

I spent the beginning of my vacation helping search for a six-year-old girl lost in the Upper Buffalo Wilderness near Hawksbill Crag.

Normally, I play the role of a city editor for the *Fayetteville Morning News.* This particular three days, though, I got to eschew the role of journalist and become a search and rescue volunteer.

I happened to be at the Fayetteville Film Festival when Kelly Zega found out her daughter was lost. I left the film festival, got things ginned up at the newspaper for a new lead story, gave my topo map of the area to reporter Matt McGowan and told him how to find the site. Then I called Ron and Rebecca Wood, who are close friends of the Zegas, to see if they wanted to go over with me to help.

We didn't arrive until nightfall, just about the time that many of the members of search-and-rescue teams from Washington, Benton and Madison counties had arrived. Volunteers had already walked the upper and lower edges of the bluffs and not found Haley, which at least relieved me that she might have fallen.

I got assigned quickly to a crew of mostly locals who were going to cover the south side of Dug Hollow, just in case Haley had come over the ridgetop, crossed the dirt road, and wandered downhill. We worked about 40 feet apart, keeping each other within flashlight range as much as possible and sweeping the contours. I kept an eye on the lights to either side of me while also trying to track my general direction from the moon to the west.

Several times, we had to pick our way through trees felled by the ice storms of winter. I managed to fall through a surfeit of fallen wood, luckily landing on my feet in the creek of Dug Hollow.

The guy in charge of our group, Billy Woods, had a cabin back in the dark woods, at which we stopped to grab sodas. Next to the front porch was a dead copperhead. Don't know how many live ones I stepped over during the night.

Listening to the guys who lived thereabouts reminded me of Vance Randolph's writings about Ozark dialects. At one point, a guy named Marty said, "We need to swing downhill, or we'll end up in that thicket of sarbrar." It took me hearing it a couple more times to realize he was saying "saw briars."

Later, Billy asked whether we should continue around to the "pour-off." I caught on pretty quick that a pour-off was a waterfall, and not so bad a description from someone who lives on a ridgetop farm above the bluff line and who sees much less frequently the water falling from above than where it pours off to below.

We finished our designated search area at about 2 a.m. I could occasionally hear helicopters as we walked. They were supposed to use infrared sometime during the early morning hours to see if they could pick up indications from Haley. There were no signs of anyone having walked any of the old paths or logging roads that we covered, no footprints around the couple of ponds we checked or along muddy spots on the trails.

Groups had been working the Whitaker Hollow side of the ridge, too, but no luck there either. On one of the radios, I occasionally heard mention that tracking dogs were getting hits near the creek where she had last been seen and near the double pour-off where that creek goes over the bluff.

I returned to Fayetteville with Ron. Rebecca stayed with Kelly and Steve.

Early Monday morning, I drove back over to the staging area and got assigned to work with a dog handler named Connie Scott who also lives in Fayetteville. Her dog, Delago, is a lean rottweiler trained for air scenting and cadaver searches. Jeremy Scott of the *Arkansas Democrat-Gazette* staff (no relation to Connie) joined us as a working press photographer. Being on vacation, I had the luxury of not having to decide whether to be a journalist or a volunteer searcher. Jeremy, who has training in search and rescue operations, clearly wanted to be searching but was stuck being a photographer for the day.

My immediate job, since I knew nothing about canine tracking, was to be a pack horse for Connie and Delago. In my hip-bag, I carried a Zip-loc bag that held clothing with Haley's scent, water for both trainer and dog, and a two-way radio in case we hit on a scent trail and needed to call in searchers.

We walked the Whitaker Point Trail, Connie giving commands in her native Swiss, and Delago giving head checks where Haley had last been seen. Delago took us down the Lower Fork of Whitaker Creek to the bluff's edge, still giving head checks to the breeze coming up the valley.

Head checks, if I understand it, are not necessarily strong indications of scent but more along the lines of, "this seems right, what do you think?" We eventually went below the bluff line but Delago seemed at that point to lose either concentration because of the rough terrain or scent because of the dead air beneath the bluff. Maybe both. Soon, though, Delago was too tired to continue tracking, so we returned to staging and were debriefed at the command post. We showed them where we had taken Delago, or more accurately where Delago had taken us. Their maps were split into sectors for searching, mostly broken up by geographic features such as the bluff line and the creek. Various colors showed the level of intensity that a particular sector had been searched.

I returned to staging and grabbed a sandwich and water. By now, at least 120 people were gathered waiting for assignments. Some had been waiting quite awhile and had little information about how the search had been proceeding so far. I stopped and talked to a small group, showing them on a map where Haley had last been seen, what had been searched, what hadn't. No one had given them any information, and they were glad to hear what had been covered.

While talking to them, I looked up and saw Sarah Fenno, now Sarah Jones, whom I had not seen in 10 years. She and her husband, Casey, had come over from West Fork to help. Casey hooked up with another canine crew, and Sarah and I talked while waiting for a next assignment.

Two guys near us were tired of waiting and said they were heading to the Boxley bridge and were going to walk up river. I told them it was a six to seven-mile bushwhack to get to a point less than a mile from us, but they seemed undeterred. Some pasty-faced guy checked in at staging and was being belligerent about not having been given an assignment on the spot. He had served two years in Special Operations, he let everyone know, and shouldn't be stuck at staging. He and his beer belly wanted to be out searching until the girl was found. That's what he wanted.

The command post was changing strategy, and that was what had held up assignments at staging. Part of the problem was too many volunteers for not enough team leaders. If I understood it right, command was planning a more intensive search on the area above bluff line and wanted to make sure enough people were on hand to do it right, but it meant not sending out small teams for the moment.

Finally, the 120 or so of us at staging were split into groups of 20, then we lined the ridge road and line-walked south down the mountainside to the creek, then shifted down creek and walked back up the next swath of hillside, eventually covering the whole south-facing side of the ridge above the bluff line.

Sarah and I spent most of the afternoon together line-walking. Like so many volunteers who had come over from the Fayetteville area, she was a trooper. We finished up at Tim Ernst's cabin and hopped a ride back out to staging.

Late that day, the command center sent word that they would quit sending out volunteer teams and instead use the National Guard through the night, so I headed home again to take care of the dogs and grab some sleep. Next morning, after fixing a flat tire, I headed back to staging and found Kirstan Conley, another journalist, helping check people in. She had helped search through the night and was hoping her work supervisor wouldn't make her return to cover the Rogers Planning Commission. No luck.

Quickly, though, I got myself assigned to a group of seven guys—me, three from Springfield, Missouri, two from the National Forest Service, and another guy from Fayetteville—to do a more comprehensive search of Dug Hollow. Another similarly-sized group was covering the upper bench of Dug Hollow, and we would cover the lower bench to the bluff line. It was good work that morning. The seven of us were matched evenly in skills and physical ability and covered our territory pretty thoroughly. The guys from Springfield had heard about the search and came down because they typically hunted in the area during the winter. All three of them were outfitted with walkie-talkies, global-positioning systems and first-aid kits. None of them had formal training in search and rescue, but you couldn't have asked for better-equipped, more knowledgeable searchers.

After a return to staging to grab some lunch, we regrouped and met up with another eight-member group to do a similar search on the east side of Cave Mountain Road to check the drainage of Edgemon Creek. Haley had been missing for two full days at this point, and I remember thinking that we should have found her by now. I wondered how far the search area had been expanded.

While eating lunch, I remember seeing the Special Ops guy come stumbling into staging, his fat belly leaning farther and farther out. He asked for a bag of ice. I think his words were that he had been carrying a knapsack with more weight than he was accustomed to. I don't think the weight of the knapsack was the problem! He sat down in a canvas chair and shoved the bag of ice behind his lower back.

Our crew headed across the road and into the woods. I chose the left flank because I knew it would swing farthest into the Edgemon valley. A Forest Service guy named Terry Hope was on the far left, and I kept him in sight as we plunged down the valley. Looking back up the hill, I could see another Forest Service ranger named Carol, but the underbrush was too thick for me to see the next person except on rare occasions.

We hit bluff line at some point, and Terry walked it while I followed a contour about 30 feet uphill. The forest floor along this hillside was much thicker than what we had encountered in Dug Hollow, and the terrain was considerably more rugged. We moved slowly around the point while Terry checked breaks in the bluff line.

After another half hour of hiking, the radios crackled with the news that Haley had been found. There were lots of cheers and whoops off in the woods, lots of smiles, and lots of hugs and moist eyes.

I think I started laughing and crying at the same time.

After hiking out of the valley, I got back to the command post at just about the same time as the two mule riders who found Haley. She had already been whisked away to Harrison, and I don't guess I ever did see her. Journalists who had left for the day to file stories were arriving back on the scene to update their stories in time for their deadlines. Rhonda Justice did a stand-up in front of Cave Mountain Church. Laura Kellams and Jeff Niese frantically asked questions of the mule riders, the Forest Service personnel, anyone who had an account of how Haley had been found.

I left them there and headed off to start my vacation in earnest, just hoping to avoid more sarbrar.

—Charlie Allison

Joy Caffrey

My story starts midday on Monday. I was at Washington Elementary School. The kindergartners sang a song in the assembly that day. Haley would have been up on stage if she wasn't on a different path, so to speak.

Kay Gober, the office assistant and friend, mentioned that Haley was missing and my whole body responded. I didn't know Haley or her parents. My kindergarten daughter, Serena, is in the room across the hall. Nonetheless, as a mother of a kindergartner and an experienced hiker, I put two and two together and my heart was aching. I spoke to parents and staff at the school, and I realized the strength of my reaction. All of my "mother bear" energy was coming to the surface and there was no crossing mother bear. Every bone in my body cried for me to go out there. In the school office I heard some people were being turned away from the rescue area; it made no difference, my bear energy was in motion. I told my husband Tim I was going, independent of his own decision. He chose to go with me. He had work to finish before he could go, so I went ahead and taught my evening yoga class. My meditation focused on Haley's return.

8 p.m. Monday evening: Tim and I dropped off our girls (Serena, 5 & Melissa, 12) at Kay's house and our son (Ben, 9) at another friend's. We scrambled so fast to get out of town and to the site that we didn't grab much. When we got to the dirt road off the main highway, lots of cars were coming out. An officer of some sort was at the intersection. We told him our intention of joining the search and he let us go on, saying we can join the morning search party.

Driving up the dirt road I noticed the car clock: 10:24 p.m. We first stopped at the Cave Mountain Church and checked in. I saw Colleen Nick, although I didn't know of her yet. On my first impression, I knew this woman embodied a lot of strength. We were sent down the road to the base camp.

Three guys were sitting at the check-in desk. We signed in and were told to report back in the morning.

In our rush we didn't grab our tent, nor did we take the back seat out of our Suburban. We made do; spread out our sleeping bags and hit the sack. I began dreaming of the search. I kept feeling called to be a part of the rescue efforts from Spirit. I wasn't sure in which way I was meant to be in service. I am an energy healer and intuitive. At times I felt that if I could be near Kelly, Haley's mom, I would be able to pick up information of Haley's condition intuitively.

At 2:30 a.m. there was a knock on our car window. A friend of ours, Tim Nelson, recognized our truck. We all sat up and talked. He had just come back from doing a sweep with the National Guard. He had night vision glasses. None of us could go back to sleep. He let us know that the dogs lost Haley's scent at the road. We sat and thought of all the possibilities. I couldn't understand why Haley wouldn't have heard her grandparents if the search began so soon. I realized later, during the sweep searches, that I couldn't hear someone standing 25 yards away from me. The woods are dense and absorb sound. Unfortunately, I hadn't realized that yet, and I let myself jump into the fear of a potential abduction.

So at 3 a.m., with none of us able to sleep and full of all kinds of fears and anxiety for Haley, we got up, walked past the check-in desk and said we were going to walk the road. We each had a flashlight. We began walking the road and then at the same time all our hairs stood on end. We were drawn to the other side of the road away from the trailhead. There was a ditch and we headed into the woods. It was dark; we would walk, feel, sense, search. At least we were moving, doing something. Every once in awhile our hair would stand on end again, and we would think the worst. Some areas called our attention. We found ourselves walking parallel to the road and then back to the trailhead parking lots. Before long we heard the helicopters. We made sure we were back on the road so as not to interfere with their infrared readings. Whip-poor-wills and helicopter blades sang in the dawn.

We returned to camp, signed back in, ate the breakfast provided. More and more people started gathering. It was a long couple of hours. I paced. I saw my daughter's kindergarten teacher, we hugged, I held back tears. Tim Nelson checked back in with the National Guard; they were all for adding my husband and I to their team. We were introduced to each other. I was speaking with the army guard pastor when Colleen Nick drove up to speak to the pastor. One of the captains introduced her to the group. He let us know of her connection and about the Morgan Nick Foundation. I knew Kelly was in good hands with Colleen to support her. I had a few minutes alone with Colleen. I couldn't say much—the emotions were overwhelming. I reached into my pocket and took out a card my five-year old, Serena, had made for Haley's family. In her precious five-year old way, she drew Haley under a tree with hearts above her and her parents next to her; in the clouds it said: parents found Haley. I knew I wouldn't have an opportunity to meet the parents but Colleen would be able to deliver the letter for me. Spontaneously, I also took off my necklace that had recently been given to me by a powerful healer; I handed that to Colleen also. She wrapped the necklace around the folded card. I felt a wonderful release. In that moment, I no longer felt unsure of my purpose, and felt ready to focus on the search itself.

Soon we were organized into groups, given orange vests and loaded into one of the army's vehicles.

I was one female with a truckload of men. I didn't think much of it until my bladder was full. I had been drinking a ton of water. I couldn't eat much. Before we started the sweep, I snuck off to relieve my bladder in privacy. That was the last of my privacy for the next eight hours. Before long they all knew how often I had to pee. We were doing sweeps through forest floors covered with poison ivy and sumac. Let me tell you, it's hard for a woman to pee in the woods when every inch under your feet is poison-something! And you're in a line with 15 other guys. I couldn't get my bladder to empty and thus needed to go 15 minutes later. I tried to stay focused on Haley; to hell with my bladder and their view. My husband told me later the guys were saying they should get their wives to talk to me, as they would have had to drive their wives back into town. I'll count that as a victory.

The sweep searches: our first sweep was impressively organized. Every fourth person had a radio and was called a team leader. My team leader was Captain David Harrison. He is one of the many wonderful people I had the honor to meet and walk alongside. Tim and Tim were the others in our team. All the teams spread across in a straight line. We were responsible for everything in our path. We had a mission, and it was well defined. Look under and through everything. As I said, we got into a section of woods that was covered with poison ivy or sumac. Also, this must have been an area that, for one reason or another, didn't get much wind. I've never seen such an un-stirred area before. All the undergrowth had both dust and pollen covering the leaves. Within minutes the whole line of us was profusely sneezing, coughing and gagging. A couple guys sounded really bad. Thank God I had taken homeopathic remedies for both pollen and dust before breakfast. I kept my mind focused, and I refused to go into an asthmatic attack. My appreciation for the military began to grow. As I heard the line hacking and sneezing, I knew there were many times that these guys have exposed themselves to a lot more than pollen and dust. Nobody complained.

I am an artist and energy healer and have avoided authority, linear activities, and organizations all my life. My Dad worked for a company that made things for top secret military and governmental use. He always seemed so pro-war. My Mom was a nurse. I accepted my mom's healing path. I saw her as having reverence for life. My childlike interpretation of the military was of devaluing human life. I had some broad-based judgments. It was so healing for me to be walking alongside these National Guardsmen in a positive, life-saving mission.

I felt an authentic appreciation for organization. We were an organized team out there, not only searching for Haley, but also looking out for each other. On the first sweep we made a great big door-hinge movement and headed back, covering our territory well. Then we had a smaller section on the other side of the road to cover. The captain asked which ones of us were still good. Some people hadn't slept much, if at all, because of their night sweep, and several of the men were struggling with their reaction to the poison ivy and pollen. Those of us who felt strong took the other side of the road. This side was a steep slope with a lot more sun exposure and the undergrowth was much thicker with briar and bramble. I never realized or appreciated the use of trails. I've bushwhacked before, but even then you maneuver to find the easiest path. Here we had to go straight into the thick of it all. I couldn't even see the guys on either side of me, just heard the breaking of bramble and the snags scraping against us. It was intense. Several times I felt so caught it was hard to move. But again, little complaining, we gave each other suggestions and encouragement. We ran into a man on a mule, also searching. I whispered to the mule to send the word on animal ears to protect and find Haley. The mule's eyes were deep and full of knowing.

That was the end of our first sweep. We headed back to base camp for lunch. We were told to get some rest before our next sweep. At base camp, people were quiet. Small talk. I ran into other parents from our school. Julianna, a mother, hadn't been out yet and asked if being out there searching helped me to cope. I remembered my pacing and anxiety I felt at breakfast; I told her it did. She wasn't sure if she would get assigned to a search party before she would have to go back to get her kids. So she told me she would check on my kids. I didn't know this woman before, other than recognizing her as another kindergarten parent. But now we were all there for each other. I told her I thought my husband and I would stay on, now that we were hooked up with the National Guard, and I would appreciate her calling my kids and checking in with the families they were with. I wasn't used to being out of phone reach of my own children. I've only been in Fayetteville for two and half years. Yet I felt deeply connected to the community and knew my kids would be well cared for.

Tim and Tim and I headed to the military tents. We were warmly welcomed again, and given cots to crash on. It was about 1:30 p.m., I had been up since 2:30 a.m. I drifted in and out of light sleep. I felt like I was in a M.A.S.H. scene, sleeping in a military tent, with choppers landing and taking off 200 yards away, three-wheel military vehicles coming and going. Radio communications were going on and off. I couldn't sleep any more. We felt the heat of the day; activity was picking up. I wasn't sure if we could be of any more help. There seemed to be so many official and uniformed people about, and a lot more rescue dogs. I asked my husband if we should go home. Maybe my purpose was to give Haley's parents Serena's card. We both sat quiet a moment, taking it all in.

And then as if the universe was answering us, we were called to participate in the next sweep. It was about 3 p.m. (Little did we know Haley had already been found, and was riding on a mule back to base camp.) We were introduced to the Sergeant Major who would be leading this next sweep. We weren't quite as organized and left in a hurry. No orange vests, and the Guardsmen didn't have radios. Tim Nelson brought two walkie-talkie radios. He gave one to my husband. They proved useful. Again we were shuttled by military vehicle to a drop-off point. Tim, Tim and another local named George realized we weren't at the right place, in fact we were off the topo map. They got us back on track. We had to climb over a barbed wire fence to begin this sweep. The terrain was more up and down and the search area was not at all square. We ended up breaking off into two groups; our group backtracked to catch another hollow. We followed some creeks; less poison ivy but more sloping terrain. A couple of times, we felt we became too spread out and regrouped, backtracked and tried again. We were constantly checking in with each other. We came across another barbed wire fence. I'm short; I was glad to make it over both of them without getting snagged. I found a turtle; I picked it up and whispered for it to also spread the word through the earth floor of Haley and her need for our love and protection. I myself was constantly talking to Haley. I always felt she was alive. I didn't know if she was on her own or if someone had abducted her and then let her back out into the woods. The whole time I would talk out loud saying, "Haley, we are all caring about you, I send my spirit guides to watch over you. You are being loved and protected, you are strong, hang in there"...on and on.

We followed a creek that became larger and took a 90 degree turn. I was on a steep hill and needed help sliding down. The guys on either side of me maneuvered their way over to me and each caught me as I slid as well as I could. I felt exposed—a lot of vertical movement. When I was safely down, I saw the creek bed was beautiful. Pawpaw trees overhead were in full bloom. Scott (the maverick, we nicknamed him "Snake Bite

Man," since he was bitten twice before by rattlesnakes) and Tim Nelson crossed the creek beds to check the rock bluffs on the other side. They found small footprints. George, the local hunter I grew to admire, went up and checked too. It was getting late. We were at the creek bed awhile, waiting for the other half of our troop, and waiting for the guys up the bluff. There was small talk; we talked about our families, our kids, my bladder. I kept saying that we should be getting a call that Haley was found. Knowing it was getting late, George and Scott up the bluff wanted us to go on without them. Captain Harrison simply said, "That's not how we do business." We waited, the other group caught up, and then George and Scott rejoined us. It was 7 p.m.; shadows were lengthening. We didn't have any flashlights and I was concerned about the sun setting before getting out of the woods safely. We began our sweep back. We walked up the creek bed and came upon a beautiful waterfall. From there, we had to turn 90 degrees and head up the steep incline. At that point, it was all rock, a steep wall with lots of handholds for climbing up. It was a tricky balancing act with some exposure. Everyone made it over the ledge, and we regrouped up at the top. The two Tims with the radios anchored down the far sides of the lines, and we spread out between them. Again we scanned everything in front and to the sides, and would often turn back to face where we had just walked to make sure we didn't miss anything by looking from a different perspective. Again, I was talking to Haley and feeling like we should have heard something on the Sergeant Major's radio.

George was the first to hear it, a chopper with its ambulance sirens on. He guessed they found her and were heading to a hospital in Little Rock. He insisted it was good news. The chopper sounded closer and closer. The chopper's megaphone called down to say Haley was found and to return to base camp. I heard it via shouts up the line. We were close to the road. It was dusk. Cars and pickups were heading out. Smiles, waves, and cheers greeted us as people realized we were hearing the news for the first time. We were the last group to return to the base camp. We all said it was all worth it, every bit of it. How incredible to feel a part of something bigger and with such a successful outcome. Thank you, Haley. Thank you for your strength to overcome odds, and for whatever karmic reason to pull so many people together, teaching each of us in our own way our own lessons.

Lessons and affirmations: never underestimate the willfulness of a six year old. People care. My body is strong and able. I have come a long way from my own waif-like child body. My yoga practice feeds me in so many ways; the payoffs were revealed to me. Colleen Nick has made an impact on our state. 47 different agencies and 500 volunteers can cooperate. Thank God for the locals who know their own backyard and trust their intuition.

I continue to gain a deeper appreciation for the earth, its vegetation, its animal life, and on this trip in particular, the topography. I continue to discover a deeper appreciation for my husband and am grateful for the choices he has made on his path that allowed for us to share this experience in the middle of a work week. Being away from my children gave me space to reflect on the incredible beings that they are and affirm my commitment as a parent. I soaked each of them up upon our return and cherished the spontaneous, unabashed, and genuine love my 12-year old shared upon seeing me at her school bus stop Wednesday afternoon. (We got home too late Tuesday night to pick up the girls.) The threads of connection to the community of Fayetteville weave directly into our lives. It felt so good to give back to the community that received us so well.

Thank you, Tim Ernst and Haley, for inspiring me to write, an act I haven't done creatively since high school. We are all powerful, creative beings faced with challenges that teach us to live and love more deeply. Truly we inspire each other.

—Peace, Joy Caffrey

The following is from a member of our law enforcement community.

I first heard that Haley was missing on that Monday morning. As a parent of a four-year-old girl my heart went out to her parents and thinking of Haley alone out there was enough to warrant taking some action. My wife and both of our children had just been to Lost Valley hiking the weekend before, and I thought what I would be going through if my daughter just disappeared when scrambling around the corner. I called my wife and told her about Haley being missing, and she encouraged me to call Newton County to find out if they needed help.

I have worked around and with law enforcement for twenty years and know the last thing they needed was a bunch of people getting in the way. So when I called the Sheriff's office it was with the intent of making coffee if needed. When they said come on over I called my wife again—she didn't surprise me by saying she wanted to come as well.

We were both quiet as we drove. I remember turning onto the dirt road heading up to Cave Mountain and seeing both Fayetteville police department canine units turning right in front of us. I knew these guys well. One of them was Cpl. Robin Field, one of my best fishing buddies. We've spent a lot of time in the woods and on rivers. Robin is the son of a fish and game officer, and that is who you want to be with in the back country. There was also Terry Tate and another dog handler Sgt. Mike Key, who was the supervisor of the unit, and Cpl. Darrin Wright.

When we got to the staging area a Forest Service ranger came up to me and asked my name and told me I was expected to report to the canine unit to get our assignment. Apparently the Fayetteville guys saw me and told folks in charge I was with them. I was proud to grab my pack and head off. My wife went to the civilian searchers.

We spent the next six hours working the area right below the bluff where Haley disappeared. First thing I noticed was just how impossible it was to cover the area. There were many rocks that had tumbled up on top of each other and created so many little "caves" that checking each one was a full time career.

The mayapples and other associated underbrush was out, and unless you stepped right on something you might never see it. The terrain was such that shoulder-to-shoulder search was not possible

The area was so contaminated (with so many hikers and searchers having already combed through the area) that the dogs were not able to pick up a trail, so their purpose was to find a body if the worst was true. The chance that the worst was true was something we all put out of our minds. I would find myself thinking what the girl might be going through, and it was so overwhelming it lessened my ability to be aware. So I would get my mind off it by pointing out different plants to the officers.

They assigned a Benton County search and rescue volunteer to our unit both days—this guy was the best. Tireless, with a good sense of humor. All of these experienced police officers (a couple of which are on the Swat team) showed what they were made of by having no problem deferring to this young volunteer.

We searched until nightfall with no luck and all agreed we would go home to Fayetteville and meet again at 2:30 a.m. in Durham and be good to go at sunrise the next day. None of these guys knew if their time on the search would be counted as vacation time or just part of the work day, and none of them gave a damn.

I remember the kitchen set up by the Baptist Men's organization that morning. Wow these guys were up at four in the morning and ready to feed an army!

The search area on Tuesday morning was of a more gentle topography, still rough in sections with the always present green briars. We kept a tight line, but again with no luck. I was still impressed with all of our guys. Lt. Key, a regular smoker with a few years on the other officers, never complained and always was ready to press on. Robin and I were both conflicted in that we loved being in the woods. It is what we do every chance we get when not working. But at the same time, maybe because we know these woods, we worried more than some.

I also noticed in typical Arkansas fashion, I kept running into old friends back at the staging area and in the woods. It was odd having both of my worlds collide this way... floating and hiking friends and old friends from law enforcement.

The only negative thing about the search operation was how some of the civilian volunteers were so adamant about the fact they knew best. We actually came on to folks just meandering around in the search area who hadn't checked in and were neither equipped nor experienced and posing a threat of yet another lost person. At one point it was being discussed with the State Police about arresting folks for obstruction should they not cooperate with the search authorities.

By Tuesday evening I had come back to town to deal with business chores, and found out that Haley had been found alive. What joy that brought to people who will never be thanked and don't need to be. I know that this sounds odd in a way, but being able to go help was the best time I had in a long time.

It is a neat fact that a Villines was one of the fellows that found Haley, considering that the Villines were some of the first white folks who settled in the area.

— A member of the local law enforcement community

Brad Mize

I was at work, just another day and driving in Fayetteville when my wife paged me. When I called her she sounded very worried, "Have you heard? Can you go Brad? You have to go! She's all alone out there!" I had no idea what she was talking about. I calmed her down, and she explained that a six-year-old girl was lost in the upper Buffalo Wilderness area and had spent the night in the woods, alone. We learned later that some friends of ours knew the lost girl quite well. I said, "Yes, of course," and made arrangements for my job. Fortunately, I have some flexibility and was able to go right away. About all I knew was that there was a command post set up for volunteers.

I raced home and grabbed my backpack, which was still packed from a two-day hike we had taken near Dixon Ford only a couple days before (located near the search area). I have spent lots of time in this area and knew it pretty well, so I felt confident that I could help. I have camped hundreds of times, but never alone. I knew I had to go. I called my trusty dog, Buckshot the Dalmatian, and we were off.

An hour and half later I was turning up the huge dirt hill to Hawksbill Crag (Cave Mountain Road). I knew it was a big deal immediately because I followed three huge horse trailers up the hill. There were camera crews, helicopters, and law enforcement everywhere. *Wow!* I pulled into the command center and they motioned me into a field which had been transformed into a parking lot. I tethered Buckshot and walked over to the desk they had set up and asked what I could do to help. They told me they were waiting to get another search party together and to hold tight.

I looked up at the afternoon sun and thought of my own children being out there alone. I realized that the little girl's second night alone in the wilderness was fast approaching. I knew that I could not possibly sit there and do nothing while she was out there with the bears and snakes, in the dark and with no food. I asked several people what the girls name was, where she was last seen and what she was wearing. I asked a helicopter pilot where they were concentrating the search. I had a good topo map and my GPS, so I was off.

I left the command center and pulled down the road a bit to look at the map and plan my strategy. I noticed that the bulk of the searching was over on the side where Haley disappeared, and when I studied the map I thought she could easily have gotten around to the backside of the mountain. I pulled down the road near the top of Whitaker Holler and found a small place on the side to pull off. I loaded up Bucky (he has his own pack to carry his food) and strapped on my full pack (tent and sleeping bag included) and we started down the holler.

After about 20 minutes I realized that I should be calling her name in case I passed nearby her but just out of sight. So it began, the first of thousands of times I yelled "HAAAALLLEEYYYY!" I continued to look at the map analyzing where she was last seen and all possible routes she may have taken. I decided to roughly follow Whitaker Creek; it was just a feeling I had. I saw that it was quite possible for her to come around the mountain on a bench or even come up from the river. The whole time I was confident that I was on the right track.

I never saw or heard another soul. I knew that they weren't looking too hard here (I did see some fresh footprints) after awhile. We were in the main creek bed which was running well and working slowly downstream. I would call her name, wait, listen for a reply and then walk a little more. It was getting into the late afternoon and I was starting to get discouraged knowing that this would be her second night alone out there and that the odds would go way down after that. I picked up the pace a little.

Soon, I heard a steady noise out in front of me. As I approached I saw the most peculiar thing, it was the top of a huge Magnolia Tree in full bloom, but it seemed to be at ground level. A few more steps and I realized that it was a waterfall I was looking over, and it was flowing pretty good. Bucky scared me when he ran up to the edge because I knew he had no idea it was a 50 foot drop and was very slippery. After a few minutes of awe, we started around the right side of the bluff line hoping to find a way down. It took awhile but we finally came to another creek coming in from the right which had its own waterfall. We found a way to inch our way down the smaller falls being as careful as possible. I sure didn't want to break an ankle out here.

After we were down onto the forest floor again we went back upstream to the waterfall to see it from below. Then it hit me. With bluffs all around I was terrified to realize that she could have fallen off anywhere. I carefully and squeamishly checked all around the entire area. Up one side to the falls and back down the other side. Nothing, thank God! It was getting late and I was frantically calling her name, getting somewhat desperate. There were a couple of times around this time that I thought I heard a reply to my calls. I called again and again and nothing. Finally it was too dark to travel through this jungle, even with a flashlight.

I found a smooth spot near the rushing creek and set up my tent, made a small fire and cooked dinner. Buckshot ate as much as I did. We were very tired from our trek and I fell asleep about 10:30 p.m. The next thing I was aware of was the thundering sound of a helicopter hovering about 300 feet directly overhead. The tree canopy was so thick that I could only see flashes of it through the towering trees. This was the first human contact we had since we entered the woods. I knew that they had not found her or they wouldn't still be looking. I also thought that I might be in the right area after all. It gave me renewed hope.

We scarfed our breakfast and broke camp then headed out. We continued down the holler, hollering and looking and listening (Buckshot did a lot of sniffing). About an hour later I knew by my GPS elevation reading that I was nearing the Buffalo River. I heard a human voice. It was a man calling Haley's name. I was kind of glad to see people, but they didn't seem glad at all to see me. It was an "official" search party and they had come down the Buffalo and were turning up Whitaker Creek. I asked them if they had looked in the flats on either side of the creek or upstream from Whitaker on the Buffalo. They said, "No, we're going up the creek." I practically begged them to help me search these flat areas because I had thoroughly checked the narrow holler, and she wasn't there. They wouldn't listen to me and went up the creek.

I had a strong feeling that I was close and decided to look on one side or the other. I chose the left side, thinking I could get back up the mountain easier on that side. I worked a zigzag pattern through dense brush for an hour or so, finally ending up at the river over a pool of water. We sat down to rest and then I thought...wonder if this was Tim Ernst's skinny dipping hole? I have read most of Tim's *Cloudland Journal* on the web and knew it had to be around there somewhere.

I saw a little red flag and realized that I had stumbled onto the infamous ladder trail (a historical trail that connects the Buffalo River with Cave Mountain Church). We were about beat by this time and I decided to search my way up the mountain. I cannot imagine going up this trail nonstop the way Tim does. It was very hard with a 45 pound pack.

Whenever we came to a bench, we went to the right, then back to the left trying not to miss her. We came to the ladder, and I had a new problem. Bucky could not go up the ladder. It seemed to freak him out, so after lots of pushing and pulling I got the pokie-dotted thing up the ladder. It was very difficult.

I looked over to the right and saw an amazing view of the river valley, complete with tiny helicopters zigzagging across the valley. I turned around and there was the Cloudland Cabin, with a number of people standing on the decks outside. I later learned in Tim's journal that it was the place where the Zega's were staying—glad I didn't disturb them!

We worked around to the left of the cabin and up the driveway and across a meadow and finally out the dirt road to the command center. We were tired, hungry and thirsty, and the nice folks at the center took good care of us. I was sad that I hadn't been of any help, but I had to return to work so we headed down Cave Mountain road to the truck. A lawman then informed me that I would be arrested if I returned out there alone, which really left a bad taste in my mouth, but I got over it. A young man gave me a ride to my truck and we unloaded. About this time a green SUV came down the road. I recognized it to be Tim Ernst, and he looked me in the eye and nodded in appreciation. He had a couple of people with him, which must have been Steve and Kelly returning from the press conference.

We pulled out and left the back way rather than go by the command center again. Then a police car came racing towards us down the road. Then another and another, and soon a dozen more. I knew then that something had happened, and that it was probably all over. On my way home my wife paged me that they had found Haley alive and well. Until that moment I felt like a failure, but for some reason I felt better after that—like I had helped after all. I only wish that I would have searched longer, and perhaps found her sooner.

—Brad Mize

Dr. Terri Coats

My husband, Dr. James Coats and I are disaster team leaders for the Ozark Mountains Chapter of the American Red Cross in Harrison. Our job is to aid in small disasters. Usually, house fires, floods, and the like. When my pager goes off, it most commonly means there's been a house fire and the family needs assistance.

On Sunday, April 29, 2001, my pager went off approximately at 5:30 p.m. When I called the number it was the Sheriff's department from Newton County telling me a little six-year-old girl was lost. The rescue had been in progress for approximately six hours and the rescue workers were needing food. At this time there were approximately 40 individuals involved.

Dr. James, our 14-year-old son, and myself began making phone calls to acquire the requested items. Once we had them we made our trip to the mountain. The drive was an hour but it seemed an eternity. The entire way I was praying it would be a wasted trip, and we'd have 100 hamburgers and drinks that would not be needed. That was not the case.

We were stationed at the command post and stayed until midnight serving hamburgers, chips, and drinks before we headed home.

Haley's father was at the command post. He would not eat or drink. At one point he and his wife were sitting in their vehicle, and he began to sob. My heart hurt so badly all I could do was pray. And pray I did!

The next morning I called the law enforcement officer in charge to see if Haley had been found. She had not. That meant the rescue workers had been out all night.

At 6:00 a.m. Monday I began making phone calls asking for donations for breakfast for the rescue workers. (Our chapter of Red Cross did not have funds to handle this type of situation). I began to think of all the people I felt could and would help. Jerry Maland, owner of Harrison McDonalds, did not hesitate when I told him of the situation. He donated breakfast biscuits and coffee for 100 people.

The gratitude when I pulled up with coffee and food was heartwarming. At this point I asked the man in charge what they needed. I will never forget the look in his eyes when he said, "ma'am, we need everything."

Dr. James had his ham radio at the office monitoring in case I needed to contact him. When I told him of the situation, he called *KHOZ*, a local radio station in Harrison, and told them what was happening. They in turn sent the info out over the airwaves and asked for donations to be dropped by our office or the radio station and Dr. James would take them to the rescue site.

I have never seen anything like it in my entire life. It was as if the whole community donated. It began with food and coffee from McDonalds being served from the tailgate of our pickup to a vast layout under the shade trees ready to serve an army.

One man cleared an area under some trees so I could have shade then he brought tables and trash cans (with trash bags). I really think he was an angel. *(This was Doc Chester.)* This area became known as the staging area. Once the tables were in place, donations began pouring in. By the time Dr. James arrived with donations that had been dropped off at our office and the radio station, we had food to last for a long time. I prayed for porta potties and 45 minutes later three showed up. God is good!

When other ham operators heard our transmissions, they asked how they could help. Our signal was weak so they came out and made an antenna and boosted our power. They also stayed with us to relay messages so I could be freed up to coordinate the now full-blown operation of mass care. Their help made our operation run much more smoothly.

Other Red Cross chapters showed up to help along with hundreds of volunteers. Folks that were unable to go into the woods were sent to the Red Cross area. What a blessing. Ladies from all over the country came to help. A Red Cross worker from Indiana on vacation in Bella Vista heard we needed help. She came. Another couple on their honeymoon came to help.

One gentleman drove back and forth to Harrison to pick up the continued flow of donations. (Don't forget, it was a 60 minute drive on curvy highways each way.)

We began our efforts on Sunday evening. Beginning Monday we had Red Cross Volunteers at the scene around the clock. Francis and Vicki Fisher relieved me so I could go home for rest, shower, and clean clothes.

On Tuesday the Baptist Men's Association showed up to help cook hot meals and serve volunteers. This helped again because now my attention was needed in other areas. The law enforcement folks were asking for basic-necessity items such as razors, basins to wash, toothbrushes, toothpaste, tee shirts, underwear, and the list goes on. I had been home, but these men and women who were searching did not have that luxury. I felt it was my obligation to help. Once again, I told the ham radio operators our needs, they relayed the message to *KHOZ* and the word went out. We had every item requested except underwear and showers. I was determined to get both.

Working with the Fayetteville Red Cross we had the underwear gathered up and it would be transported by a sheriff from Washington County.

The next task, and a much more difficult one was the showers. The National Guard was on the scene so I assumed they could get them. If not, I would ask for RV owners to loan us their RVs. Seemed easy enough except we were in a National Forest. Protected from people like me. HA! I did not realize, you had to know where the gray water would go from the showers, where the fresh water supply would come from, and where the nearest streams were. I talked with the captain of the National Guard unit and realized this task would be a little more difficult. Once again though, God was on our side. I went in search for individuals who would know the answers and in 15 minutes all the questions necessary to get the showers were answered. The showers were on their way!

What happened next cancelled everything that I had focused on for the last three days.

A report came over the radio they thought Haley had been found. It was a difficult transmission to understand, so we waited for another transmission that would confirm what we thought we heard, and were hoping we had not just imagined it. Then it came again...

YES!!!!!! they found Haley!!

There were shouts and hugs and praises to God all over the place. Hugs and tears and laughter was all over the entire area. Grown men crying and hugging one another (these are real men in my opinion).

These emotions are not describable in words. If one was not a part of this effort, they cannot understand the tidal wave of emotion that hit the staging area when the call came in, "Haley's been found!"

It was with great pleasure that I called Fayetteville and stopped the underwear shipment! Haley has been found! I did not know the Red Cross volunteer was a personal friend of the Zega's. When I found out, I was pleased it was me who got to share the news of Haley's rescue.

For three days after Haley's rescue, I was still crying. I couldn't sleep without replaying over and over in my mind the events of the last few days and thanking God for taking care of Haley.

Never in my wildest imagination would I have felt capable of coordinating such a large group of volunteers to accomplish the feat of feeding and meeting needs of the rescue workers and family. I cannot take credit though because I can do nothing with out my Savior Jesus Christ. He's the one that did it all!!!

— Dr. Terri Coats (Coats Chiropractic Clinic in Harrison)

The following is from Fran Alexander, who is a regular contributor to the Northwest Arkansas Times. *Part of her story was published in the paper, but most of the following was left out.*

Fran Alexander

Jay and Joyce knew they would have to reach their daughter Kelly, Haley's mom. Joyce called Cathy Bass, wife of Clay Bass who was on the hike with them, and Cathy called me to go along on the unwelcome mission of telling Kelly that her child was lost. On our way to Newton County with Kelly, Cathy and I jabbered endlessly about the various heart-stopping exploits our own children had pulled during their raising as an effort to allay Kelly's fears, and our own. Kelly had begun shaking as she called her husband Steve at National Guard camp at Ft. Chaffee. Cathy and I were afraid we would be shaking too if we stopped talking long enough to think. We were driving into the middle of our friends' living hell, the horror of a missing child—a parent's worst nightmare.

The first staging area for the search centered around the Cave Mountain church house, unlocked by a nearby neighbor and quickly filled with arriving agency representatives. Sunday afternoon five or six dog teams entered the woods, and we felt certain they would find the six year old. The dog trainers carried pieces of her clothes, which we had brought with us from Fayetteville so the dogs would know her scent. It was all just like we had seen in the movies, except the part where we watched in disbelief when they returned without her. This was not going according to Hollywood plot lines.

Private trucks carrying cranky old generators arrived with fuel to refill empty helicopter tanks. Watching those bug-like flying contraptions landing in a tiny country cemetery beside a church began to make the whole scene uncomfortable to a rational mind, especially when the two fit themselves between the tombstones and the chainlink fencing. As night fell, the landing lights of the 'copters and their whoop-whoop-whoop, which blew the plastic decorations across the graveyard, gave me the bone chill of a close encounter with something unreal. When her mother murmured that Haley is afraid of the dark, several of us adults wandered off privately so our tears would not show. We were afraid of the dark too. We could not wrap our minds around what all was not adding up. And that was just Sunday, the first day.

By Monday, hundreds more volunteers had arrived and were fanning in grid precision, checking every crack, crevice, creek, tree top, cliff edge, rock cranny, and shelter, and all were calling Haley's name. Horseback riders checked out the places horses could go, and mule riders went to the rest.

The American Red Cross had been feeding us since the search began on Sunday, and food arrived from friends, from small country grocery stores, and from big town corporations and churches. Ambulances were lined up and waiting. Carroll Electric had erected a 40 ft. pole for better radio antenna reception and fed a higher electric service wire into the church area. Tri-County Telephone secured a line to the church by backfeeding from across the road. And by Monday night the National Guard was erecting a small city of tents, cots and showers. Smith's Two Way Radio volunteered their services and made a tremendous contribution to the effort. By Tuesday a military helicopter equipped with stronger and more precise sensing devices had left Oklahoma City and was headed for Newton County.

I had laughed when some shuttered to mention that bears, bobcats, coyotes, and snakes were out there to get her. We had not seen another living thing in the woods, including squirrels, after horses, mules, helicopters, hundreds of shouting people, and dozens of dogs had been loosed upon the terrain. Any wise, self-respecting wildlife had long since left for another county! The real fear in the woods, and especially to fear in the towns, is a fellow human, one of the warped kinds. This is hard to say after seeing the massive congregation of sleepless good people pouring their all into this rescue, but it only takes one bad human to cause a world of hurt. As remote as the possibility that some sicko was in the right place at the right time to nab a kid in the woods, what if...??? Since no trace of her had been found, that possibility and all its horror had to be considered.

All day and all night helicopters prowled the skies and searchers searched. Sheriffs and fellow National Guardsmen assured father Steve Zega she would be found, and we all put on our strongest armor of hope to believe that too.

Thankfully they were right. Everyone had worked so hard; and they had stubbornly refused to quit.

Fran goes on to talk about how stubborn everyone involved with the search was, including Haley. And how Lytle and William Jeff had stayed away from the official search parties and had struck out on their own, eventually finding Haley. At that point she concludes with:

So the two stubborn men on two stubborn mules set out with one stubborn child to join up with a mass of stubborn searchers to return her to her stubborn parents and grandparents who had absolutely refused to give up. Stubbornness can get you into messes and even kill you, or it can save you because any survival must be based in will-or-won't power. If the old adage, "That which does not kill us makes us stronger," is true, watch out world! Haley Zega is one tough cookie.

—Fran Alexander

Chapter 9

Dr. Arthur Evans

By early Monday morning the crowd of eager volunteers had swelled to over 200. There were many familiar faces, like Sierra Club friends, experienced backpackers with knowledge of the area and able to get around the woods with map and compass. More trained search and rescue units from other counties arrived, more police helicopters with heat-seeking detection equipment, more bloodhounds, more National Guard people and their equipment.

By noon the crowd of eager volunteers had reached critical mass; and, if the authorities didn't let them do something soon in an organized search, they were about to disperse into the woods and be running over each other, the dogs, and maybe the cliff as well. Finally they chose six local hunters and asked each one to lead a group of 20 volunteers strung out in single file, almost shoulder to shoulder, up and down the mountain in the most likely area. We quickly covered several square miles very thoroughly. All we found were briars, snakes, and wild azaleas, no little girls. Our friend Mike Faupel had searched a Forest Service clearcut which was overgrown with sawbriars. He was so cut up he looked like he had been sacking wildcats. The valley was now full of people, helicopters, and baying hounds. No one worried about bears or lions anymore. No doubt they had hightailed it out of there early on.

All day individual well-wishers, as well as groups, brought food and drinks to the Red Cross tents at the search staging area. The Tyson Company brought big chests of fried chicken and chains of fast food restaurants like Wendy's and Subway brought big chests of sandwiches to the volunteers. The groundswell of concern and generosity was amazing. People all over the U.S. heard about it on the usual media, but Tim Ernst kept the world updated on his *Cloudland Journal* web site, from his home where the Hale and Zega families waited for each bit of news. My wife, Crow Johnson, and I waited until dark and then rushed home to clean up and rest.

Back again on Tuesday morning, we covered old ground again and started to realize time in the open, even if she was not injured, must be taking a heavy toll on the child. It was obvious she was not in the area we had been searching. I had a nagging feeling that a tired little kid would rather go down hill than up hill. I asked several of the search organizers if the lower part of the Whitaker Creek hollow had been searched all the way down to the Buffalo River. They were emphatic that it had been. The hollow is about three miles long and very rough with no trail that a kid might find to make travel any easier. At the end, it opens into the slightly flatter Buffalo Valley, but it's still rough as a cob, requiring a lot of boulder hopping to walk down it.

Back up at the Cave Mountain Church headquarters, Captain Cantrell of the Washington County Sheriff's Office said that Carroll Electric had erected a big radio antenna, Tri County Telephone Company had installed a secure phone line for the search organizers, and Smith Two-Way Radio had loaned very valuable radio equipment to the effort.

Trent Morrison and a gentleman on horseback gave me identical reasons for joining the search. They both have little girls near Haley's age and couldn't bear the thought of losing any of them.

Sometimes technology saves the day, and sometimes it's intuition. This time it was intuition and the outdoor skills of two gentlemen from Mt. Sherman, William Jeff Villines and Lytle James, riding their mules, Big Momma and Copper, who saved the life of little Haley.

I was with the parents and grandfather at Tim's cabin when search officials rushed down to say that Haley had been found. The family ran to the truck while the rest of us laughed, cried, hollered, and hugged each other.

No one who has not endured the gut-wrenching fear and anguish of losing a child can truly understand the elation one feels when the lost lamb is found, but suddenly there was laughter, there was music and everyone felt they were part of something really, really worthwhile.

I don't have much patience with snipers who sit back and criticize, but blessed are those good Samaritans who not only talk the talk but also walk the walk of human compassion. I would hug every one of them if I could.

—Dr. Art Evans, (reprinted with permission from the *Gravette News Herald*)

Chapter 9

Tom McKinney

My wife and I have known Jay and Joyce Hale, Haley's grandparents and namesake, for well over 20 years and have watched Kelly, Haley's mother grow up since. When we heard Haley was missing we, like many friends of both families, immediately dropped everything and hurried over to help.

My wife, Victoria, and I played only small roles in the search effort, two among hundreds, but that did not diminish the relief we felt when we heard Haley had been found alive and safe.

The outpouring of volunteers for the search wasn't unexpected, because that is just what Arkansawyers do when one of us is in trouble. But the actual number of volunteers who showed up was a surprise.

Maybe it shouldn't have been, because despite all of our growth over the years, we are still a small state with such interconnected family, business and friendship relations that it takes little time for an impact upon one family to spread to dozens and then hundreds of people.

Such was the case with the search for Haley Zega.

The determination of people who put their lives on hold until the little girl was found was almost indescribable. I know of many who were not there the day Haley was found because they had to clear their calendars at work so they could go back out for the rest of the week, or for as long as it took.

The terrain we had to search was a combination of gently sloping and relatively flat benches above the bluff line, where the search began, to steeply sloping and treacherous hillsides leading down to Whitaker Creek in the bottom of the valley. The vegetation ranged from old growth open forests with large trees and little undergrowth to blowdowns where the vegetation was thick and gnarly. In some places the mayapples grew so dense and tall they could easily hide a small child laying on the ground.

Some of the searchers had to fight their way through old clearcuts outside wilderness area that were so thick and overgrown that even Forest Service personnel were cursing them.

But through all this, the volunteers trekked without complaining or without much concern for their own well-being. The Red Cross and various situation commanders who organized the search effort had to constantly remind people to look after themselves, stay hydrated, and avoid overexertion so they could drive home safely to their own families.

As for myself, I am one who never likes being too organized. I struck off with Tim Ernst, the well-known photographer whose nearby house was serving as a gathering place for the Zega family and friends, to explore for Haley outside the designated search area.

We dropped down to the bottom of the bluff line that runs under Hawksbill Crag and followed it for almost a mile and a half farther than we thought Haley would be able to travel in the time she was lost. We had incredibly mixed feelings of hope and dread as we searched. We hoped to find her alive, but we dreaded finding her at all because we were searching along the base of a tall bluff off of which she may have stumbled.

I gently yelled out Haley's name, telling her that her mother was worried about her, and strained to hear the faintest response, worried all of the time that I had walked within only a few feet of her without seeing her because of the dense ground cover.

I think it was the first time I had walked through one of the most beautiful areas in the Ozarks without appreciating it because I was so focused on the search. Even a close encounter with a timber rattler was merely an annoyance rather than an opportunity to observe.

Tim and I climbed up to the top of a bluff near a waterfall and proceeded to search an area back toward his house that had been gone over only once before. Still no sign of Haley.

I later went back down to the area where Haley was last seen and helped search all the nooks and crannies along the bluff line, accompanying numerous other volunteers who were climbing and repelling down to all of the intermittent ledges that dotted the area.

By Tuesday morning, I was feeling much more optimistic about finding Haley because it was obvious she had not fallen off the bluffs. She was alive and on the move, and that meant it was only a matter of time before we found her.

Maybe the situation commanders should have listened to my wife, who had been telling them all along to expand their search area because a determined six-year-old girl can cover a lot of ground if she puts her mind to it. She knew, because she used to be one.

And that turned out to be the situation when Lytle James and William Jeff Villines found Haley much farther down the Buffalo River than people thought she could have traveled.

This search had a happy ending for which we can all be grateful, and I know the people of Arkansas will be there to volunteer their time and talents again if and when they are needed.

—Tom McKinney (reprinted with permission from the *Arkansas Democrat-Gazette*)

Chapter 9

BROTHERS

I arrived at the staging area about 9:00 a.m. Monday. The morning search teams had already gone out and it was going to be several hours before I would be sent out to search. This gave me the time to wander around and watch the other people who had assembled for the search, and observe their actions and emotions. I got to meet several people who had various ties to Steve and Kelly. Some were friends from law school, some were friends of the family, some were acquaintances from civic & political organizations, and some knew Steve and Kelly from their childhood. The group that touched me the most was a group that I belonged to—Steve's College Fraternity Brothers. Fifteen years ago we lived together as members of Delta Upsilon fraternity on the University of Arkansas Campus, where two of our founding principles were the promotion of friendship and the development of character.

By all accounts, we were not even close to being one of the premier fraternities on campus. Our fraternity house was always in need of major repairs, and we never hosted any of the best parties. We faced numerous obstacles and problems from a lack of girlfriends, to a lack of academics, to parental problems, to budget shortfalls, to membership shortfalls, and then back to various problems with the girlfriends we did have. However, from those experiences came a group of men that have continued to believe that we were (at that particular time and place in history, and we still are to this very day) truly BROTHERS.

Several of us try to get together each summer and relive our long past glory years. Every year we play golf, go boating, and toast each other with drink, song, and the same stories of yesteryear. I have often heard my BROTHERS say that those years in the fraternity house were some of the best years of their lives. However, I have sometimes wondered if the friendships we established those many years ago would withstand the true test of time. We have all changed over the years, and I have wondered if we are truly friends today or just drinking buddies from our college years. Because of Ms. Haley Zega, I am pleased to report that we were BROTHERS then, and we still are BROTHERS today. In other words, I firmly believe that when the chips are down and one of us is in serious trouble, our BROTHERS will always be there to lend support and a helping hand.

As Monday morning turned into Monday afternoon and then into Tuesday, I was amazed at the number of fraternity BROTHERS who traveled great distances to lend their support to Steve and Kelly (his college girlfriend whom we all knew well and loved). Bankers, lawyers, computer programmers, executives, professors, and business owners were all in the woods calling Haley's name. They all put their lives, families and work on hold for one common goal; to help our BROTHER Steve find his most prized possession.

The BROTHERS came from every major city in Northwest Arkansas. They came from Little Rock and Hot Springs in Central Arkansas and as far away as Dumas in the Southeastern part of the state. They came from Springfield, Missouri and there was even a group driving in from St. Louis, Missouri when the news of Haley's recovery was announced on the radio.

There wasn't a single organized effort to gather everyone in Newton County. In fact, most of the BROTHERS heard the news of the disappearance in different ways. When each BROTHER learned that Haley was missing, they each knew what they had to do. Everywhere I turned, I found a BROTHER searching for Haley. There were some that I hadn't seen in so many years that I didn't even recognize them (like me, many had gained weight and lost hair). But they were there, ready to go to work, ready to search, and ready to find Haley Zega.

However, this gathering was different from the ones in the past. We were not trying to relive our glorious past, but we were focused on the task at hand. There were discussions of miracles and the power of prayer. There were words of support and comfort offered to Steve and Kelly. There were ideas and strategies debated. There were hugs and tears shared and always words of support. And late Tuesday afternoon, there were slaps on the back, high five's, prayers of thanksgiving, more than a few tears, several victory cheers, and a few beers (we were too tired to make that several beers).

After Haley was found, several of us got together and talked about our lives and the time we spend with our loved ones. We talked about our friendships then and now. A comment was made that today, in our busy lives, we all have several acquaintances, but our deepest friendships come from the brotherhood we shared as men of Delta Upsilon. We all made commitments to focus on the important things in life; our children, our wives, and our families. I can't help to think that we have all grown a little from Haley's misfortune. I believe that I have.

Several months have passed since Haley was found. The BROTHERS have had their annual summer get-together and played golf, gone boating, and shared drinks and stories. And yes, there were a few new stories created in the jungle of Newton County which will be retold over and over again. There was Chris who showed up in Newton County wearing this year's latest fashion design from the Polo Search and Rescue Collection; and even an unconfirmed rumor of Terry stealing glasses and towels from Tim Ernst's cabin, which he later gave away as souvenirs. In the end, the mood at the summer get-together was one of celebration and good cheer. However, under the surface, we all seemed to appreciate our BROTHERS and our friendship a little more.

—A proud brother of the Arkansas Chapter of Delta Upsilon

Chapter 9

Jodi Felkins *(Haley's kindergarten teacher)*

5:30 a.m. Monday morning. The phone at home rings and I answer to Kelly Zega apologizing for waking me up so early. She then tells me that she wants me to know that Haley is lost in the Buffalo National Forest. Kelly stated that she didn't want me alarmed by hearing it on the news when I awoke. She wanted me informed ahead of time so I would be prepared for myself as well as for my classroom.

I was horrified to think that little Haley had been in the forest all night alone. I told my husband, Paul, what was going on and then immediately went into the front room and prayed for a little while for God to put his hand of protection around Haley. I just seemed to pace around the house. I peeked into the bedrooms where my four children were sleeping soundly all cozy in their beds. My mind continually raced as to what Haley might be going through, have gone through, or where she might be. I didn't think Haley would be much of a trooper out in the forest alone. I imagined her sitting scared beside a tree and crying continuously. I prayed that God would somehow give her a peace and let her realize that He was there with her. I prayed that no harm would come to her from animals.

At 6:30 a.m. I was ready for school and made a few phone calls. I let Susan Shepperd, another kindergarten parent, know what was happening so she could talk with her daughter, Natalie before school. I also called our principal, Ashley Garcia, and another kindergarten teacher, Kelly Geiser. I felt so helpless. I went on to school Monday morning but was so bothered and upset that I could not hold my attention to the job I needed to do. I talked with the children about Haley being lost, and I asked each of them that if they were allowed to pray at home, to please pray for Haley to whomever they prayed to at home with their parents.

We heard at school that there were search teams out looking for Haley and that's when I knew I couldn't stay at school any longer to teach. My heart was elsewhere. I just kept thinking that maybe she was so scared that she wouldn't want to answer any of the voices of strangers out looking for her. I held on to the hope that she would recognize her teacher's voice and want to answer me when she heard a familiar voice.

My husband and I went up to help with the search and rescue. We were turned away because we didn't have any training in this area, and they were looking for experienced, trained people to help. We were told there were hundreds of people out there. I was overwhelmed when we drove up the dirt road and saw so many emergency vehicles, the press, the tents, just the vast amount of people out helping. I let the authorities know that I was Haley's kindergarten teacher and that I hoped maybe she would recognize my voice. I at least wanted to be able to be with the family. I was escorted down to the cabin where the Zega's were waiting for good news.

After talking with Steve and Kelly for a short time, I asked where Grandma and Grandpa were. We were pointed in the direction of Hawksbill Crag where Haley was last seen. We went down and talked with the many searchers down in the area and talked with Haley's Grandma and Grandpa. The place she was last seen had pink ribbons on the trees with flowers poked down in them. This was so hard to see because it just made everything just a little more real. I looked out among the vast wilderness and couldn't imagine being out there alone, nor could I imagine having one of my children lost out there. I felt like Haley was a part of me.

Paul and I began walking the terrain looking and looking. We were hoping to find a tired little girl that had crawled up next to a tree in a big 'ol leaf pile and was sleeping or else too scared to answer. I called, "Haley, Haley, this is Mrs. Felkins. Please answer me Haley-Bug" (something her Daddy always called her when he would leave her at school in the mornings). It was so strange to call her name out because I have a two year old named Hayley at home. It just brought a flood of emotions over me when I started yelling for her.

As we searched and searched, I kept telling Paul that I kept trying to put myself into a five-year-old child's mind and think what she would do. Since she was so close to the creek bed when she was lost, I just kept saying that I thought she would probably try to follow the creek bed down. I knew she was tired and hot, and I didn't think she would try to climb up because it would be so hard. I kept wanting to follow the creek down the mountain. We were told by many, and we could see for ourselves, that the search teams of people walking and the teams on horseback were covering all the area below.

There were many stories that evolved while we were there that day. Someone said they found her walking stick. Someone else said they were pretty sure they could tell where she had been playing beside the creek bed. These were all good things to hold on to. Everyone needed a little glimmer of hope.

One aspect that did not look too good was the fact that Grandma and Grandpa had seen four out-of-state hikers on the trail just right after Haley disappeared. If she stayed on the trail like they thought she would have, there was no way they wouldn't have seen her. Was foul play by these hikers being investigated? It was something no one wanted to think about but everyone had it in the back of their minds.

As the sun began setting, I was a little unnerved at how out of sorts I had become. Paul and I had gotten off the trail during our search, and I was very confused as to which way we needed to be going. I realized quickly how Haley could have gone any direction. Every direction looked liked the right way to me! Luckily, Paul knew right where to go. We went back up to the dirt road and gave a few hot, tired, search teams a ride back up to the main tent. They were all to be debriefed before they could officially end their search. We were amazed at how many people were willing to give of their time for a little girl they heard about on the news. God Bless the community we live in! The response was outstanding!!

Tuesday. I had determined on Monday that I needed a substitute teacher for today. I needed and wanted to be looking for Haley, or at least be with the family for support. It ended up that only professional searchers were being allowed up the mountain. They were turning people away down by the highway. I was able to get up to be with the family because I was Haley's teacher.

Gina Dillard, another teacher, and I spent most of the day at the Cloudland Cabin just being support for the family. Spirits around the cabin seemed to be on a fake high. As time passed, things just seemed so unreal and so much more frightening. Haley had already spent two nights alone in the forest and the thought of her spending a third was just unbearable to think about.

Kelly remained very together on the outside through the whole ordeal. She kept thinking of others and making sure we didn't want something to eat or drink. Steve kept watching the clouds and sky. Hoping the weather would hold up and not rain in the forest.

Gina and I left Cloudland right before Steve and Kelly made their public plea on television for any information somebody might have. Saying goodbye to them was very hard. I explained that I wouldn't be back on Wednesday because I felt the other 16 children in the classroom needed me back so they could have some stability in the classroom. I had a great substitute, but there's nothing like your own teacher.

Leaving was very hard! I felt as though part of me was abandoning Haley. But another part of me knew that my own family of four children needed me as well. (I couldn't stand the thought of worrying about them for the day and so I had them miss school for the day. I didn't need to be wondering where they were and if they were picked up on time and delivered home safely.)

Anyway, I came back to town in time for my son Jordan's baseball game. As we were entering the gate to the ball park, I received a call on our cell phone from my sister telling me the news had just been announced that Haley had been found alive and well. I was so elated that I didn't know what to do. I walked around telling everyone I saw and then had to just walk away from everyone and have a good cry. The emotions that had built up were unbelievable. Haley Jennifer Zega had been found! I couldn't wait to get back home and watch the news! I couldn't wait to go back to school with good news for her classmates! I couldn't wait to give her a hug! I couldn't wait to hug Steve and Kelly! I couldn't wait to have the whole ordeal behind us! Writing about this brings tears of joy to my eyes all over again.

The following two weeks after Haley was found were far from normal around our school and especially around our classroom. We were visited by the press on many different occasions. My class full of wonderful children were such troopers through all of this! I was so proud of them! They were able to stay focused for the most part, and they were so precious with their cards, thoughts, and actions towards Haley. We were very honored that Haley was looking forward to coming back to school to see us. What a glorious morning that was when she walked into our classroom. My emotions took over once again. I cried, laughed, smiled, and of course, I got my hugs in with Haley, Kelly, and Steve. I think Haley received 15 or 20 hugs. I kept asking her, "Have I hugged you yet? I don't think so. I think you're pretty special!"

Through all the publicity that Haley was receiving, I tried to make sure all the children in the class felt special. We were so glad when life got back to "normal" around our classroom. YIPPEE! What a happy ending! I serve an awesome God who answers prayers! Thank you, Jesus!!!

Other little things:

**When Haley came to school, the children were amazed at all the little scratches that covered her legs. Instead of bombarding Haley with lots of questions, we wrote our questions down on paper and sent them home with Haley. Kelly and Steve helped Haley answer all our questions.

**Ozark Guidance Center came in to the classroom and helped the other children with their emotions and thoughts. They were able to have a lot of questions answered.

**There were yellow ribbons tied on the trees outside around the school in hopes of her safe return. The entire kindergarten class was able to go out with Haley after her return to school and have a joyous time cutting them off and letting her take them home.

**Haley's mailbox at school was flooded with homemade cards and letters from all the students in the class.

**A new school year has now begun. I still smile big when I see Haley sitting in her first grade classroom. And I steal a hug now and then when I see her in the hall. Haley Jennifer Zega is a precious little girl that has a place in my heart forever.

—Jodi Felkins

The following is from the woman who spent many private moments with Kelly during the ordeal, and was whom I relied on for accurate information, and to be a rock herself.

Rebecca Wood

The weeks following Haley's trek through the woods, I found myself alarmingly numb to emotion. It seems the full intensity of those three days had either drained or simply overwhelmed my ability to feel emotion. Slowly, I returned and realized that I too had been on an extraordinary journey. I imagine that is just one of the many feelings experienced by all those close to Haley, Kelly, and Steve, as well as Joyce and Jay.

I used to say, "I cannot fathom what it would be like for my child to be missing." But now, I have a much clearer image of that horror. What I ask myself now is, "Could I handle it with the courage, composure, and faith that my friend Kelly displayed during those three days?"

The first night, I posted myself on the church steps surrounded by woods, that, without the single source of illumination rigged for the searchers, were the blackest of black, and God did it scare me. I sat there with the full expectancy that little Haley would be brought along just any moment by one of the search teams who was combing the crevices of the woods that night. I wanted to be a familiar face to our dear little Haley; I wanted to hand deliver her back to her mom and dad who were being given safe haven at Tim's—to be a part of that rapturous moment. Selfishly, I wanted my own terror to end. But, the dawn approached and the full seriousness of the situation settled in. Despite my intentions to be supportive, I felt like my soul had deserted me. All my training in crisis management, my ability to remain in control all left me as this was just too close to home.

By the early morning, I had summoned a ride to go face my friends, without Haley in my arms to return. It is here that I must admit that I could not be the rock of support that I wanted to be for them. It was Kelly. Ironically, she was the hero for all of us during those desperate hours. For without her determinedness and unwavering faith in Haley's resilient nature, we may all have fallen apart in rivers of tears that we were careful to let loose mostly in private. With Kelly in the lead, those of us there to support her and Steve were able to at least lend our energy and long, emotion-filled hugs.

It's not hard to say what the core group of friends was thinking. Repeatedly, I heard friends and family say this was all very surreal. We were all numb and at a loss as to what to say much of the time, as we knew our words weren't what were going to bring Haley out of those woods. We tried to make Steve and Kelly eat, we tried to keep up with where the search was headed, what had been covered, what the next step would be. The only way any of us could keep it together was to approach the situation with a matter-of-fact attitude and to find tasks to keep ourselves busy and feeling useful. But, of course, there were moments when one or the other of us would disappear to pray, to cry, to stare into the vastness of the terrain hoping for some sign from the heavens showing where Haley was.

At one point, again I feel selfishly trying to do something that would make me feel as if I were contributing to the search, I cornered my friend, and she sat with me, hand in hand while we sent positive thoughts to Haley in meditation. Once again, the friend whom I was there to support was instead the rock who supported me.

There were special moments when I would see Kelly and Steve huddled, face-to-face in companionship and love. The bond they had built together through the years, was not being tested, it was being strengthened. One of Kelly's favorite movies is "Steele Magnolias." A line from it seems rather appropriate to describe Steve and Kelly at this moment. "That which does not kill us, makes us stronger."

As the third day approached mid-afternoon, the cloak of friends had grown. Tim just continued to welcome all of us to his hideaway as if we were his best friends instead of complete strangers.

The quiet conversations had turned more desperate. Then came the whispered rumor that Haley had been found. Period, no more detail. Frantic I scrambled for the phone to call sources with the TV station that had made the report. But before I could reach it, I heard new silence. I rushed outside to the sweetest sounds that Haley was "looking for her mommy and daddy." That's all I heard as the hushed despair was literally shattered with shouts of undeniable euphoria.

Haley took us all on her journey in a very personal way for each of us. For me, it was a demonstration of certain philosophical beliefs that strengthened my love for life, family and friends. In a very real way, as Kelly and I discussed in the days after Haley was found, we were all literally with Haley. Our spirits were out there with her in the woods, our energy was flowing freely to her. Any time you have that many people with that much love being directed at one human being, there is a very real connection. Haley's journey brought hundreds of good people to a truly beautiful place. That place is inside each of us as a renewal in human spirit. It's a place where faith in happy endings begins.
—Rebecca Wood

Chapter 10
THE DEBRIEFING

News began to circulate that there would be a public debriefing about the search mission. I got the notice from several different folks in the SAR community; although as the time drew close, it became evident that it really was not supposed to be open to the public, but rather limited to the official groups that had taken part in the mission. The stated purpose was to "learn how to do better next time, and to promote an interagency spirit of cooperation and resource management."

The SAR folks had been taking some heat in the press, and it was widely reported that the two who found Haley were not part of the official search team (true) and had even been turned away by the SAR folks (not true).

My personal opinion going in to the debriefing was that while I could understand some of the frustrations on both sides of the issue, the SAR folks did an excellent job, and I thought it was a great idea to get together and figure out what could be done the next time to make things even better. I was also glad to have been invited, although I immediately felt a little out of place sitting there with all of those folks wearing guns and badges and uniforms.

At least 65 folks gathered at the Madison County Courthouse in Huntsville on May 14th, 2001. Guy Howe from the Benton County Sheriff's Department acted as the moderator (he did not participate directly in Haley's search, but he was en route to do so when she was found). Mark Clippinger, who was one of the Incident Commanders for Haley's search, would also be in front of the room and run the chalk board.

I sat next to other volunteers who were not associated with any group or agency—two of the Woods boys, Billy and Landon, and Duane and Judy Woltjen. The press was in the building, but they were not inside the debriefing room. From time to time members of the various SAR teams and other officials were called out of the room to give interviews.

And then Steve Zega showed up and quietly took a seat. A murmur swept through the crowd as many of the folks there recognized him, although there were at least as many who did not know him. During the proceedings Steve would stand up and make several comments. Each time that he did, he began and ended his remarks with "Thank you all for what you have done," and even noted that he would be saying that each time he spoke. It was obvious that he felt indebted to those in the room, and intended to let them know it every chance that he got. My high opinion of this guy continued to soar.

I was in awe of all the other folks gathered here as well. As the open discussion continued around the room, time after time, someone who stood up and spoke identified themselves as being from an agency or volunteer organization that I had no clue had been involved with Haley's rescue. There were many SAR groups present, along with various government agencies, law enforcement groups, and the Red Cross. Every single one of these folks and groups had participated in the search mission with one goal in mind— to find Haley Zega. Their dedication to this single goal was obvious. As far as I was concerned, they were all heroes. (As were the hundreds of unnamed volunteers who also helped.)

A general rundown of the mission was presented, including an estimate of costs. Not counting lost wages of volunteers and SAR folks, the actual out-of-pocket expenses was nearly $125,000. A lot of this expense was for the helicopters. That figure could easily have been much higher.

There was a wide range of topics discussed, but much of the focus centered on the fact that so many volunteers from the public at large had showed up unprepared and ill-equipped to head into the woods to help in the search. In fact, there was a great deal of animosity from some of the SAR folks at having to deal with the public in the first place. I kept hearing that people were showing up in "tank tops and flip-flops" and there was no way they would be able to help. It was obvious that many of the SAR folks were frustrated at the mass of humanity that they were forced to deal with at the staging area.

As the discussions continued, it was noted that having untrained volunteers may have not been the actual problem after all. Some of the folks who were complaining the loudest about the volunteers being there were also saying that they themselves had been overworked and really needed someone to help them with unofficial chores. Enlisting the help of a volunteer who had showed up in a halter top and shorts might have solved this particular problem.

It quickly became obvious that there was indeed a place for untrained volunteers. The key was for the SAR teams to have the management training necessary to handle all of the volunteers and to use them effectively (both of the incident commanders told me later that this would be a top priority in the future). It was noted that this type of training was available, and that all leaders should have that training whenever possible.

Then the discussion focused on communication problems. I had known about this from the very first night when Hasty One was unable to get a simple message over the radio to one of the nearby SAR teams. The biggest problem was different agencies and SAR groups used different frequencies for their radio communications. And while you would think it would be a simple matter to tune the radios to the same frequency, this was impossible. All of the radios did not have the same bands available to them.

(As it turns out, the simple FRS radios that you can buy everywhere often do as good a job as the really expensive ones—sometimes even better. The Wal-Mart Foundation is funding the purchase of a large number of these radios to be used by at least one of the SAR teams.)

The focus of the discussion was not entirely negative, and many of the positive points were stressed. This was, after all, a *successful* mission, and Haley was found alive. I think the sheer numbers of the SAR community who participated in the search for Haley made everyone at the meeting feel quite proud and quite deservedly so.

What an incredible opportunity there was for networking at this debriefing! There were several times when someone would stand up and talk about needing this or that, and someone else would raise their hand and give specific information about how to get exactly what they needed, such as training or equipment. I must stress that these SAR teams spend a great deal of time training—you would not believe all of the training that these people go through. Some of that training is extremely difficult, going through situations a lot tougher than anything they might face in a real search mission. And most of them are volunteers and do it at their own expense.

Once the debriefing was over, there was a reunion of sorts that went on for a long time. Many of these people never see each other except when in the middle of a crisis situation. What a terrific feeling it must have been for them to be able to converse and enjoy the moment. Steve got to personally thank a lot of the people who helped bring his daughter home alive.

Vixon James was there and showed me pictures that his dad had taken of Haley right after they first found her. To me these were incredibly historic photos. I had my digital camera with me and made quick copies of the pictures so that I could post them on my web page. Vixon later got me copies of the actual prints, which I used to find the exact location of where Haley had been found.

Once again, I would like to stress that while there may have been differences of opinion between the SAR folks and volunteers, everyone who took part in the search mission did a wonderful job and helped find Haley.

And while we all hope there is never another little girl lost in the wilderness, the fact is that there will be, and the experience gained from Haley's search will help everyone be better prepared. You can bet that every available SAR person will be on the scene and work tirelessly until the mission is a success. If you happen to know or meet a member of any SAR team, I suggest that you shake their hand, give them a pat on the back, and thank them for devoting themselves to helping others.

Later, Guy Howe gave me a few thoughts about the search mission. "The volunteer effort in Arkansas was shining at it's brightest, as one would expect for these kind of folks. On the other side of the coin, the turnout swamped the boat. The Incident Command System is the only system that can work on an event of that size. Unfortunately, there is a lack of understanding across the whole that can only be corrected with training. It is nearly an impossible task to get such a wide cross-section of people and agencies together for anything less than a full scale emergency. That type of multi-agency search management training and coordination does exist, and we will be giving it several times a year. I think some agencies that were involved will endeavor to increase their funding, and hopefully, start pre-planning for the next large SAR event."

If you would like to get involved with your local SAR team, contact your local Sheriff's Department, or go to the National Association of Search and Rescue's web page at www.NASAR.org.

Chapter 11
HALEY'S GRANDPARENTS MIMI & POP

J *ay and Joyce Hale are well educated, articulate, and have an undying love*
for the wilderness. They live in the Northwest Arkansas community of Pea
Ridge. It was their interest in sharing that love of wilderness with their
granddaughter that led to Haley's extra-long hike. No one felt worse about her
getting lost than these two. I asked Joyce if she would write about some of their
feelings during this terrible time, including a second description of those all-
important last few minutes of their hike before Haley disappeared.

Haley Zega is the only child of an only child. I know every child is special and unique, but this one is also rare. Our daughter, Kelly, honored the family by incorporating her maiden name, Hale, into her daughter's given name. It was an interesting way to compensate for having no male heir to carry on our branch of the family tree. Little did we know it would become a name uttered in thousands of prayers by family, friends, and people Haley would never meet.

Jay, Haley's "Pop," informed me when we learned we were to become grandparents that he couldn't imagine acting as silly about this role as other people did. However, it didn't take long after Haley arrived to show him how much fun it was to have her around. Grandchildren provide a wonderful opportunity to revisit all the "first" experiences, while having a link with the future.

Jay and I live on 25-acres of woodland with a creek; right on the edge of Pea Ridge, Arkansas. Our mechanical engineering business is there along with our home. Kelly lived here from 18 months of age until she left for college. She and Steve were married by the creek where Haley likes to wade. She is now following her mother's childhood steps, exploring for crawdads and collecting rocks and leaves in the woods. She is much more feminine than her mother at that age, hard to get out of dresses, and a Fayetteville "city girl," but she still enjoys the woods and critters.

Jay and I wanted to impress Haley on our first major outing together. I guess we can say we accomplished that mission! When we heard about a

Newton County wildflower hike on a Sunday afternoon, this sounded perfect. Friends of ours, Dennis and Michelle Boles, also planned to go and suggested we stop first to see the Hawksbill Crag. Another friend, Clay Bass, also came along. For some reason, Jay and I had never hiked here, even though we had been to Cave Mountain. In fact, Bat Cave on Cave Mountain was one of our favorite outings in our college dating days. Hawksbill Crag would be a new treat for us and hopefully wow Haley with its spectacular view. The walk in was short and easy to navigate with an interesting variety of things to point out to a child. Shooting stars and pink azaleas were at their height. Tree leaves had not gained their full summer size and allowed the mottled light to filter semi-brightness. Pale spring greens were transitioning into deeper summer hues. Temperatures were perfect.

Haley was given a drink of juice just before we started the walk. Since the time we planned to be gone was less than an hour, we took just one container of water. The day had warmed up nicely and extra clothes wouldn't be needed. We planned a quick return so that we could eat lunch at Robert "Doc" Chester's cabin. Haley already knew how to identify poison ivy. She made it very clear that edges of the bluff rim weren't fun for her. No reason to worry about the obvious dangers. What could go wrong… go wrong… go wrong? We still find it amazing to believe that in a few minutes, she was just plain gone.

We have learned what intense interest there is concerning a missing child. It must be a primal fear. Interviewers and reporters always have a key interest in "the moment" when panic or fear gripped Jay and me. When and what was it like exactly? I understand their need to capsulate and concentrate. The 15-second sound bite and sensational headlines come out of people's short attention spans. Bottom line summations are routine. However, at the risk of disappointing, I must say that the impact of Haley's disappearance didn't focus on a pivotal moment. Concern and worry slowly and steadily accumulated. The longer it went, the more involved and convoluted things became. The situation built from feeling that I would see her at any moment; to feeling she was bound to be with one of the rest of our party; to being sure that the first search with 15+ people would spot her; to knowing that she would surely be found by dogs; to hopeful that more people and helicopters and professionals would track her and and and…

I would love to be able to see an aerial view replay of the first ten minutes Haley was missing. My first thought was that she had found something interesting to look at along the trail as she lagged behind. For that reason, I didn't even call out to her right away. Looking back I wonder if that minute would have had her close enough to hear me. Instead of dawdling along, moving slowly, I suspect now that she was moving quickly on the wrong path trying to catch up. If she had taken one of the routes that split off from the lower trail and headed back, she could have been passing people below who didn't see her or know I was looking for her.

As I first moved back toward the falls, I walked quickly and called a few times. Then I had to start hurrying even more, to make up for the wrong choice. It was unsettling to head away from the main path that the others were on and go into places I had never been. The choices of paths and the inability to see very far ahead began to worry me. I wasn't so afraid of getting lost myself, I was worried about wasting time going in the wrong direction and putting even more distance between Haley and myself. How far was my voice carrying? As I strained to yell, I heard myself. Did I sound angry and would she resist answering if she thought she were in trouble? How long should I try to look for her on my own without getting back to the others? Were they in the opposite direction of where she was headed so that it would take even longer for them to find her? Was I being melodramatic? My head filled with questions, and I knew I needed to be making clear rational decisions.

I made it a point to start laying out a plan. I couldn't imagine Haley taking off bushwhacking her way into an unknown area. She was so cautious of poison ivy, and it was practically the dominant species. I figured she would look for the main path but might not have a sense of direction. I decided to hurry to the farthest likely extent of the trail going in the opposite direction of the others in the group. Precious minutes began slipping away. How far should I go before being satisfied that she wasn't just up around the next bend? I was very relieved to finally see hikers coming in from the public trailhead's direction where I was headed. They confirmed that they hadn't passed her. In addition, the three in their party would begin searching immediately. In fact, they would leave food and water there for her in case she happened on to it. Finally I was getting some organization together and had some assistance.

My pace quickened as I backtracked my earlier route. I was free to run down the upper path heading out of the woods. Now I was sure that I could overtake her. On and on I moved over new trail. When I came to a downed tree, I decided that she would have known that this wasn't there on the way in and hopefully would turn back. It was also a significant landmark to define how far I had gone in that direction. What seemed like an hour was probably 15 to 20 minutes in which I was separated from everyone else. I was surprised that they weren't looking for *me* by now!

The exertion, loud calling, and worry took a toll on my voice. I knew that it would give out all together if I wasn't careful. I started calling "Jay" since it was shorter than "Haley" and would get our friends' attention. Soon

Clay heard me. Other hikers spread the word to the rest of our party and a loosely organized search was underway. I felt an odd blend of being grateful to have so much help and guilt for diverting people from their plans.

When I met Tim Ernst with his dogs, I was very encouraged. Obviously the word was spreading fast. He knew this area so well and immediately checked below the bluff. I knew this had to be done as soon as possible just to rule it out, but I couldn't imagine that Haley would have gone near an edge. I felt we were eliminating the remote possibilities and extremities of the area and would soon come across her.

A couple at the Hawksbill Crag loaned me a cell phone to call 911. I could hear the sheriff's voice, but he couldn't hear me. By this time more than an hour had passed with no signs of Haley over a fairly broad area. I knew we needed outside help and headed with Michelle to borrow a phone at the Faddis Cabin. She and Dennis were the first to think about abduction. Michelle wished that Dennis had gotten the license numbers of cars at the trailhead parking area. Both are employed by the Fayetteville Schools and understand the importance of observing people. I had only been worrying about terrain. I was grateful that all possibilities were being considered, but abduction seemed even more remote than the chance Haley had taken risks at the bluff edge. I was glad that more people than I were thinking about the "what ifs."

Calling 911 is a serious move. I struggled with the possibility of overreacting versus waiting too long. Would the operator consider two hours too early to report? Would the call be taken seriously? I knew the calm voice of the dispatcher showed his training, but did he understand the need for quick action? I wanted some assurance that he understood the seriousness of the situation, and I wanted a list of people he would notify and the actions they would take. I urged that dogs be used as soon as possible. When told that they weren't readily available, I worried about when they would think it necessary to bring in some. I wished I could see his face to get a better sense of his concern. I told him point blank that I was depending on him and would leave it in his hands. I left the conversation knowing that the world outside was now informed, but unsure about how long it would take to see help. I needn't have been concerned. The system worked promptly.

After I made the call, I went with Michelle to see if Dennis had found Haley on the road. I also talked to Pam Ernst, who had left the cabin and was checking the roads. I wanted to be able to cancel the 911 call if possible. My good frugal, German genes were kicking in. It bothered me that I was asking for more than volunteers' time; I was requesting action which would require public expense. I hoped to cancel this next level of involvement as soon as possible.

Time continued to slip away. I had to admit that we were really in trouble. Now it was unavoidable to let Haley's parents know what was going on. While the realization that Haley was really missing came on slowly for Jay and me, I knew it was going to hit Kelly and Steve between the eyes. I had postponed telling them as long as possible; any further delay would make matters worse. They were going to have to digest the entire event in one gulp. Jay and I had been taking it on bit by bit. There was no way to soften the reality that a search had already been underway for hours with no success and that now we had to step up the effort with search dogs and helicopters! The only positive thing I could think of was that they would be there when she was found. I knew they would be the only ones who could comfort Haley.

This time Michelle took me to Doc Chester's cabin to use the phone. We needed an information base where we could be contacted and stay for a while. Fortunately I knew just where Kelly was. I was relieved that she hadn't gone shopping or visiting with an unknown friend. She was at the Fayetteville Film Festival. I could have called her to the phone, but I wanted someone to be there with her so that she wouldn't have to drive. I tried reaching one of her best friends, but she wasn't home. Then I thought that an older person might be better to give her reassurance.

Clay's wife, Cathy, had chosen not to come with us on the hike and was easy to reach. She was given the task of getting Kelly and bringing clothing items with Haley's scent. I knew I could rely on Cathy to remain cool headed. She was a special friend that I could entrust to handle such an ordeal. She contacted Fran Alexander, another friend in Fayetteville, who knew the area and could direct her. Together they worked hard to minimize the seriousness of the situation for Kelly, but at the same time packed clothes for an unknown stay.

At this point the search took on a life of its own. People began gathering at the Cave Mountain Church. Authorities were now on the scene. I emptied my billfold of current Haley pictures, described everything I could think of, gave pet and proper names, and Haley's extra garments for dog teams to scent. I couldn't believe that *two* helicopters were landing in the small cemetery. One of the pilots explained the sophisticated heat sensing equipment that was to be used, and I thanked him for his help. Next food and water began arriving. Even at this early stage with only a few dozen people involved, I felt swept along and amazed at the consequences of my actions.

Kelly arrived at the church and every measure of worry was written on her face. I had seen her through many emotions but nothing to compare with this. She was controlled, but fragile. There was nothing for me to say except try to detail what had happened. I had no consolation to offer. All I could hope for was a quick resolution to the questions we all were asking.

Finally I saw Jay for the first time in many hours. We had spoken only briefly at the beginning of our search and wondered aloud, "What in the world are we going to do?" He had been hiking and searching constantly for hours. Soon Steve arrived. He was attired in his National Guard uniform since he had come from camp in Fort Chaffee. He was sober and focused. The canine team from his hometown, Lincoln, was on its way and he wanted to go in with them. The number of people increased. A flurry of activity followed in order to take advantage of the waning light. I tried to stay on the fringe at this point and just be with Kelly. We waited at the edge of the woods as Jay, Dennis, Clay, and Steve worked with dog teams. After Jay had shown the necessary places to his team, he came back for Kelly and me, and we went back to the falls. Kelly took everything in with quiet observation. We came out after darkness had filled the forest and returned to the church. It had become the command center with more and more familiar faces arriving. Kelly and Steve's friends were first to arrive. Her calls to people before arriving at Cave Mountain started an alert that grew over the next 12 hours. Little did we know that it was only the first wave of support that would carry us through the next two days.

The evening proceeded with fresh tears to greet each friend. We told and retold the sequence of events for officials and friends. Everyone hugged and held one another, still finding the situation unbelievable. The National Guard chaplain, who had come from Steve's unit, gathered the family together for prayer. We were informed that Colleen Nick of the Morgan Nick Foundation was on her way to be with the family. This added drama and thoughts of loss that none of us could accept. Eventually the evening slipped away, and we gratefully accepted the offers to stay at Doc's and Tim's cabins.

I had already spent some time at Doc's and had given his telephone number as a way to reach me. It was the smaller of the two places offered and would be handy for Jay and me. I had only met Doc less than 12 hours before, but already he had become a good friend. His traditional mountain cabin was the perfect refuge. Kelly and Steve accepted Tim's offer and went to his home. I hoped that we would have a better chance to rest if we separated at night. We all needed to find some quiet and the chance to reflect without creating a facade for each other's benefit.

When Jay and I reached Doc's cabin, we found it full of children. The Woods brothers' families had come out in force, and the adults were all searching through the night. Parts of this area had been in their family for generations, and they knew it intimately. The children waited patiently for their parents. Doc displayed his usual good host nature and tried to find food that was acceptable to this unexpected crowd. I was glad to help with the dishes as a gesture to do something constructive.

My mind continued to race considering the options. I was open to any theory or any possible help. The idea that a psychic might offer information was acceptable to me at this point. Hope was the only thing we had going for us. If a positive statement from someone with spiritual experience could be offered, I wanted Kelly and Steve to hear it. I called a friend that I thought might have an idea about finding someone in the area, possibly Eureka Springs. I gave her Tim's number where Kelly could be reached. We were at a point where no one could imagine how Haley eluded so many people. While searching, Jay had discovered that it was fairly easy to go down the bluff from the little falls. We managed to convince ourselves that this must have been what she did. If a psychic could reinforce any theory at all, we needed it.

Well after midnight, Doc rousted some of the Woods' children, who were sleeping in the guest beds, to give Jay and me the bedroom. They joined their older brothers and sisters on the deck and continued the vigil for their parents. Jay and I lay down but proceeded to relive the day over again. I could see Haley coming down the path through the foliage, her walking stick appearing before she did. Had my eyes been playing tricks on me? Had I really seen her before moving on? Had we been separated earlier than I thought? As I pulled a light blanket over me, I wondered how cold she was. Was she injured and unable to make anyone hear her? Was she so traumatized that she would need therapy? Would Kelly and Steve ever let us keep Haley again? Would she ever want to stay with us? Did she really think we would abandon her?

Much later, the Woods family returned for their children, and the helicopters began serious heat sensing maneuvers. The rotors were a disturbing yet reassuring sound. Jay and I would occasionally speak knowing that the other wasn't asleep. Our only comfort was the knowledge that every possible human and spiritual resource was focused on this rescue. He was optimistic that she would be okay. I fulfilled my customary pessimist's role and continued to consider the worst.

In reflecting back on that moment, I think Jay and I have demonstrated that personality profile most of the time. Jay is a mechanical engineer. He is a problem solver. Years of experience have taught him to carefully think through the options before acting. Problems are the "norm" when building machines. He analyzes, adjusts, and keeps working through the complications. I am quicker to act without thought to the consequences. I become discouraged more easily. It's my job to worry on Jay's behalf, and I was working overtime!

Before daylight Jay and I quietly left the cabin to learn what the officials at the staging area were organizing. More friends began to arrive. The family was free to be involved if they wanted, but those in command preferred that we leave the search to others whose emotions weren't running so high. We went to Tim and Pam Ernst's home, Cloudland, for the first time, to be with the rest of the family. Steve's family arrived during the night and Colleen Nick, of the Morgan Nick Foundation, came to help.

If the Hales and Zegas were cast for the roles in this drama by some Greater Power, I applaud the Director for choosing Cloudland as the perfect location for Kelly and Steve's refuge. Tim Ernst's home met every need: communications center with telephones; fax; computer; plus it was large enough for 100 drop-in visitors and visually close to the search yet isolated from the press. In addition it was owned by a gracious host, who quietly stepped aside and let the activity envelop him as he chronicled events to the world through the Internet.

A telescope was set up on a back deck to observe the helicopters' maneuvers. One of Hale Engineering's primary projects involves designing equipment suspended from helicopters. Jay and I are aware of the risks pilots take when they hover. Their slow movement in and out of the bluff edges worried us. The thought that someone could be injured while trying to help was another burden. The same concern for the safety of other searchers was also in our thoughts.

By early afternoon dozens of our best friends had assembled. Many of them were Sierra Club members who loved the Buffalo River Country in a very special way. It was as though an unscheduled club outing had developed. More familiar faces joined us as we hiked in toward the falls. Everywhere were signs that the woods had been thoroughly walked. People were scattered in all directions. Even Haley's teacher was on the trail. On our way back out, one friend requested our group stop to discuss an idea. It was clear to him that Haley was not in that area. He felt abduction had to be considered. He proposed creating a reward fund and made the pledge for the first contribution. Quickly others offered support. This display of friendship was very touching. Everyone headed back to confer with Kelly and Steve. They were already discussing the same idea with their friends.

Offering a reward had pluses and minuses. The intent was to loosen a person's lips if he or she knew about abduction. The money had to be a serious enough amount to make a person turn in a friend or acquaintance. We were out to buy information. It was obvious that the hundreds of volunteers were already physically pushing themselves to the limits. A reward would not make them work any harder! More volunteers weren't needed; in fact, the roads were now being blocked to turn people away. Those in charge knew that an announcement of a large reward could complicate their jobs, but they understood the need and were willing to work with us.

This was a good project for Kelly to oversee. She could stay busy and know that she was doing something constructive. Her organizational skills put her at the top of her game. Jay and I were extremely proud of her capability and composure. It was an impressive team that quickly developed. By coincidence, or by design, certain friends that were together at that moment had professional experience in event planning, fund raising, media, and crisis management. Each drew on a particular expertise and experience. What would have taken most people several days to accomplish was organized in a few hours.

Jay and I had an unusual hosting responsibility. Various unrelated groups of friends gathered at different locations. We wanted to see and thank them all. Pea Ridge friends were meeting at Doc Chester's cabin, so we left to be with them. I also needed to start making some phone calls. A big question that really worried me was how much of the calendar to clear. I was scheduled to go to Concordia, Kansas in a couple of weeks to make a friend's wedding cake. It was impossible to know what our family situation would be in two weeks when I didn't even know what the next day would bring. I needed to cancel everything in order to focus on what was happening. I was very sad about this. After making dozens of cakes for over 44 years, it was the first time I had to let a bride down.

The flurry of activity and visits during the day soon gave way to an unwelcome second night. We were physically drained; and hoped that after losing one night's sleep, we could finally get some rest. Temperatures seemed a bit cooler than the night before. Jay tried to convince me that we still had time to find Haley and that the weather was on our side. But he had to admit he was getting scared too. All along he and everyone had tried to reassure me that it wasn't my fault. I knew what they were trying to say. It was the same thing I would have said to someone in the same situation. But it wasn't a matter of fault. It was a matter of who had responsibility. I had assumed that duty by being the last adult to watch for her. No words could change that reality.

If I slept at all, it was between active mental pictures of walking through Kelly and Steve's house. Every room had a significant reminder of Haley. Her bedroom was so lovingly decorated to please her every whim. I couldn't bear the thought of their return to that house without her. Again, all the dark questions dominated my thoughts. How could the family ever be put back together? How long could we search before we would have to leave? If Haley weren't found, would I lose my good relationship with my daughter? Was Haley suffering? Would we find her in time? My fears were overtaking hope. As I listened to a helicopter on its mission, my sadness became physical. Tears often bring relief. This time an ache just built that left me feeling drained.

Two friends came the next morning to find me at my lowest point. They had arrived at Cave Mountain the night before and tried to find me. When they could not find me, they stayed and volunteered where food was being served to the searchers. Extreme situations leave their marks on friendships. The mutual sharing of exceptional moments creates a bond. By coincidence one of these friends was with me during the single worst and single best moments of the entire ordeal.

Slowly my friends got me up to prepare for another day. I needed to do a lot of things. A shower did wonders, and I dressed to leave for Pea Ridge. They would take me home so that I could transfer reward money and get Jay's medicine along with some fresh clothes. One friend would return in the afternoon to bring me back to the search. Coming out that morning was my first realization of just how enormous the operation had grown. That was reassuring. I felt sure that Haley would be found, but would it be in time? We stopped to get gas, and I saw the first newspaper story and picture of Haley. The clerk told me that 75% of the traffic that morning had been connected to the search. We saw trucks with supplies and equipment all along the route, particularly bottled water.

It felt as though I hadn't been home for a week instead of just three days. I quickly packed up the clothes and medicine and went to the office. There were so many people I needed to contact. E-mail was a big help. In a short time I let dozens of friends and family know what was happening and how they could help with the reward fund. By the time I had completed my correspondence and financial transactions, my friend returned to take me back to the search.

The Springdale traffic was coagulated in its usual 5:00 p.m. rush. I had been completely out of touch with events for 6 hours. Suddenly my friend's cell phone rang. Her secretary had stayed in touch with the command post, ready to alert us if there was news. Word was in that Haley had been found! That was all. What did it mean? I held my breath. The suspense built. I felt absolutely numb and didn't know which emotion would come next. Then we learned that she was okay with only minor scratches and was headed to the hospital in Harrison. The relief was enormous. Many have told me of their sudden tears when learning that she was found. For some reason I stayed dry eyed at that moment, but I breathed more deeply and smiled wider than I ever expect to again in my life.

Now the trip took an entirely new focus. Instead of returning to Cave Mountain we went directly to the hospital. Topics of conversation broadened. I could look past my own situation. I learned that these same dark days for me had been very difficult for my friend for other reasons. My emergency had been a diversion from her personal problems. Now sharing mutual consolation had a certain irony.

We arrived at the hospital before the press, but not before Steve's stepfather. He had experienced a kidney stone attack after participating in one of the searches and was admitted to the hospital the day before. We were ushered into the emergency room to find him in a wheel chair talking softly to Haley. Kelly was radiant. I remembered the last time I had been in a hospital with Kelly and Haley was the day Haley was born. This was almost like a second birth. The nurses were administering an IV to rehydrate her. She cooperated with the same bravery that had carried her through the previous days. Sleepy and finally warm, she rested while the room cleared with just my friend and me left to watch her. Kelly and Steve went out to share the good news with the press in time for the 10:00 o'clock news.

The hospital lobby was full of hugs and smiles. Dennis and Michelle Boles came and were anxious to actually see Haley with their own eyes. Gratitude is such an inadequate word, but I was most grateful that I could now feel good about going home and that Kelly and Steve would soon return to their house with Haley. My friend took me home shortly after Jay had arrived. He had chosen to stay on the mountain rather than come to the hospital. As the search was wrapped up, he was the only family representative left to express thanks and say good-byes. Brief celebrations broke out; but for the most part, it was time to change focus and think about the things that had been set aside to make room for this event. I'm sure the long drives home were used to reflect on what they had just experienced. Some resolutions were made. Some realignment of values took place. Some friendships were strengthened. All would remember for a long time that they had been a part of something very good. But life would slowly return to normal.

Jay and I talked on into the night. It was as though a debriefing was necessary before we could finally rest. I wished that I could have been with the crowd when she was found. I could only imagine the euphoria. Finally we talked ourselves out and got the first rest in many days. May 1st will forever be a Hale/Zega family holiday... joyous and full of love and friendship.

Just as it took a while for the reality to sink in that Haley was a missing child, it has taken me several months to digest what went wrong as well as the scope of the search, issues, and people involved. Jay and I have tried to pick apart the events and circumstances to define the problem exactly. What made things go sour? Hopefully people will learn from some of our conclusions and remember the appropriate times.

First, the trip was primarily for Haley's benefit. She slowly warmed to the setting, but just when her curiosity and interest kicked in, we allowed a self-imposed schedule to alter the trip's objective. Haley had finally become inspired by a place, she wanted to see more, but we had to move on. Building an interest in Nature was what this trip was all about! If we had taken an extra five minutes to accomplish what we had set out to do, the next three days would have been very different for hundreds of people.

High on my regret list is that we made false threats saying we were leaving her. It is such a common tactic to use with children. Comments are made in such an off-hand manner. It haunted me to think how she possibly could have thought we would really leave her there! Haley told one of her classmates that she felt "sad" while lost. In its simplest terms that is a perfect description of what Jay and I felt. A huge, black, heavy, smothering sadness that seemed to grow heavier by the moment. Was it possible she felt this by believing she had been abandoned? I truly hope not. In the future, I know I will be more careful to say what I really mean.

The real danger that we should have prepared Haley for was never even considered. What should she do if we got separated? Of course, that wasn't likely to happen! Five adults and one child seemed like a pretty safe ratio. But separation was the whole problem. This is the danger to think about first. Whether in an airport, mall, camping spot or hiking trail, plans should be discussed about what to do if separated. We should have told Haley to stay in one place if she couldn't find us. We forgot to review this most basic of rules that all children should know when lost.

—Joyce Hale

Kelly, Haley, Mimi & Pop

Chapter 12
COLLEEN NICK

*C*olleen Nick's daughter, Morgan, was abducted in June of 1995 and has not been seen or heard from since. As a result of her experiences, Colleen formed The Morgan Nick Foundation, an organization dedicated to finding lost kids, working with the parents and officials to find them, and helping to see that kids of all ages (and their parents) are educated so as to keep them from getting lost or abducted in the first place. Colleen showed up at our cabin in the middle of the night soon after the search for Haley began. She would become an important figure in the search and rescue mission, working tirelessly throughout the entire ordeal. I asked Colleen to write down a few thoughts about it all.

It was a Sunday night, a little after 10 p.m., the house was quiet and my children had been tucked into bed for an hour. As I sat down to watch the news, the phone began to ring. When I answered, it was George Stowe-Rains from Devil's Den State Park. I knew George previously from working with a search and rescue team he was part of. My heart began to chill as George informed me that a six-year-old girl, Haley Zega, was lost in the wilderness area of Newton County. He asked if I could come and talk to the family. Without hesitating I agreed to come.

After quickly giving me directions, George and I discussed several options, one of which included activating the Morgan Nick Alert. Although the rescue teams felt that Haley was most likely lost in the woods, they wanted to cover all their bases, just in case she had not walked off the wooded path, but into the path of a predator.

I immediately called my assistant Chip Hurst, who works at the Morgan Nick Foundation (MNF) as a case manager. (She was christened "Chip" by her big brother Mike when she came home from the hospital—when trying to say "sister" it came out "Chipper," was shortened to Chip and the name stuck.) Chip's primary job at MNF is to serve families of missing children by taking phone calls and gathering information from parents, law enforcement, media, etc. She is an initial resource person for families, as well as assists in follow-up for ongoing cases. Chip grew up in the northern part of Arkansas, and I knew she would be familiar with that region. I briefed her and she agreed to go with me to the search.

My second call was to the Arkansas State Police to ask if they were going to use the Morgan Nick Alert in Haley's case. The Morgan Nick Alert was developed to ensure that when a child is missing every available resource would be utilized to find them. When a child is missing, and the Morgan Nick Alert has been activated, over 350 media outlets are notified of that child's disappearance, along with more than 300 police and sheriff departments.

The Morgan Nick Alert was established with very strict criteria, one which states that a child must be confirmed as being abducted. The other criteria state that a child must be at risk of losing their life or the child must be in extreme physical danger. Any or all of the criteria must be met before the Alert can be activated, and I certainly believed that Haley fit the last two criteria and possibly the first one. Thus, it was my recommendation that the Alert be issued; however that was a decision that could only be made by the State Police.

Next I called Kelly Zega, Haley's mother, at the phone number I had been given. We talked for several minutes about what she was feeling and thinking. The number one thing I always tell parents is to have Hope. Giving up Hope is not an option when your child is missing. Hope is not a choice. A parent must believe they will find their child and believe it strongly enough for everyone else involved in the search. A parent's Hope for their missing child is what fuels the searchers when they are just too tired to move even one more step. It would be this attitude that I would encourage time and again with Haley's parents. And this would be their focus, from which they never veered during the endless hours that had become their personal nightmare. Before we hung up we prayed together for God's protection on Haley, His peace for the Zega family and wisdom for the searchers.

I pulled my sleeping children from their beds and drove them to their dad's house. My son Logan, age nine, was still awake when the phone rang about Haley. He was very worried and hurried to help me pack belongings for himself and his sister. Taryn who is only seven, did not wake up enough to even realize that she had changed houses during the night—she woke up in a bit of a shock the next morning.

On the long, three-hour drive to Newton County, I reflected on all that my family had been through for the last five years. My stomach had a knot in it as I realized that the Morgan Nick Alert was to be issued for the very first time for a six year old girl. When the Alert had first become a reality, I spoke with great certainty that although it had not been there to help Morgan, it would, indeed, be there to help another child. And here we were, full circle. Because of one missing six-year-old girl, another six-year-old girl was being given every possible and available resource.

On the drive to Newton County, Chip and I felt certain that with the dedicated search and rescue workers at the scene, we would not be needed. We felt that we would arrive to find that Haley was safe and had been returned to her parents. We were wrong.

It was after one o'clock in the morning when we reached the general area where the search was under way. We got lost as we drove towards the area where Tim Ernst's cabin was located. Thankfully we met up with some State Police officers. These officers were in the process of transferring Haley's photograph onto a disk so that it could be sent out via the Morgan Nick Alert to every television station, radio station and law enforcement agency in our state, just in case Haley was more than lost. Just in case the unthinkable had once again become a reality in our state. These dedicated officers showed us the way to the command center where we were briefed. We then were driven to Tim's cabin where the Zegas were staying.

Often I do not know what to say to parents of missing children. What I can do is offer to lend them my strength. I can remind them not to give up Hope. I can reassure them that their child is waiting for someone to come and rescue them and that it is the parents' job to make sure everyone is doing just that. So when people want to know what it is that I say to a parent, it's really not so much about what is actually said. It is more about sitting there, face to face, looking someone in the eye who has already walked this nightmare that you have suddenly been thrown into. It is the reality of seeing them breathing and functioning, even while everything inside of you is dying.

When you look into the eyes of the other parent there is a painful realization that you will survive. Even though you don't want to. Even though you don't think you can. Even though you cannot think of eating or sleeping or living. But you have to. You are the parent of this child and it is your job to find them. It is in that realization you begin to find encouragement. This is the sharing of strength. This is the gift of Hope. This is a gift that was given to me by Mary Ann Witt after her daughter Melissa Witt was abducted from Ft. Smith, Arkansas and murdered. Even though Mary Ann already knew that Melissa would never return home, she was able to come sit with me after Morgan was abducted. She quietly looked me in the eye and said, "You cannot give up Hope." And then she sat there and gently lent me the gift of her strength. This is the gift that I am able to share with other parents when their child is missing.

We met Steve and Kelly Zega and their families when we arrived at Tim Ernst's cabin where they had been given refuge. It is never our intention to intrude into someone's pain, but rather to simply be there should they need any resources that we can provide. It is always my hope that we have already paved the way for any family with a missing child by enhancing access to any and all means of finding their little one. The Zega family greeted us warmly and we were able to take time over the next several hours to talk to each of them about the different emotions they were experiencing.

There is no feeling on earth to equal the one that overwhelms you when you realize that you do not know where your child is, and you are completely powerless to help them. Your entire world is changed in less than an instant. And in that one instant you suddenly realize there is not much in your life that is truly significant. As the hours pass and the reality grows stronger, a decision is made to fight or to give up. Not everyone is strong enough to fight, but I must say I was struck by the determination in Kelly, as a mom, to fight for, and find, her daughter. It was a determination that never wavered. The dismay and horror that would fill the hours to come would test the Zegas to their very limits, but they never once considered any option but that Haley would return safely.

Many friends and family began to come and go. Wonderful, warm, encouraging friends who put their lives on hold to help Haley. We talked with Steve and Kelly often while trying to be unobtrusive so that they could draw strength from their friends. We were there to do whatever the Zegas felt they needed from us. It was their wish that Chip and I stay in direct contact with the command center and relay any information from the center that we could share with them. Even at this early point they understood that they might not need to know everything about the search. They understood that knowing every minor detail might not be the best way to retain their sanity. My respect for them grew immeasurably as they trusted us to keep them informed and educated as the long hours crawled by.

Most of our time was spent traveling back and forth between the command post and Tim's cabin, Cloudland. Unless you have ever been to Cloudland, you cannot understand what traveling "back and forth" entailed. You could not simply walk back and forth nor jump into the nearest vehicle to traverse this wild country. This is remote wilderness, as in can't use your cell phone—no street signs—forget the grocery store—remote wilderness! We found ourselves using every available means of travel, including a Humvee at one point. The Zegas were trusting us to be the voice for Haley with the searchers at the command post, and that meant a great deal of going "back and forth" was necessary.

I must say that I had the greatest respect for the incredible work done by the teams at the command center and out in the field. These men and women worked tirelessly night and day to coordinate the search. When they would change shifts, instead of heading for a bed and a shower, they would simply curl up in a blanket on the nearest available piece of ground and grab what precious sleep they could. No one went home. No one gave up.

I have had the opportunity to work in partnership with the search and rescue community in the past and have the greatest respect for the work they do. In turn, they have been more than willing to listen to the thoughts and ideas from the people who work at MNF. During Haley's search we continually pushed and questioned the search and rescue managers, asking them to explain to us what was happening and why. And we tried to share with them the thoughts and fears and feelings of Kelly and Steve.

The search for Haley was an amazing process as search teams were coordinated and sent out into the woods. Exhausted searchers would come into the command post completely disheartened. Just when we were sure they would stop and rest, they requested another assignment.

The men and women at the command post were exceptional in their dedication as they were called upon to make split second decisions. These people carried the complete weight of the search on their shoulders, knowing that their determinations would be the guiding force of the entire search. To carry that weight, to know that a child's life rests in your hands, is an unbelievable burden. They stood resolutely under the weight, staying focused on finding Haley alive and returning her to her parents. It was an emotionally challenging time for each searcher as well, as their thoughts centered not only on finding Haley, but on their own children at home as well. The total commitment of the searchers to a little girl that they had never met was absolutely incredible.

We met several times with Kelly and Steve and the Search and Rescue Incident Commander to update the family on any changes. The command post asked us to be present during each of these briefings as they trusted our judgment about how and when to talk to the family. Their respect for my personal feeling, as well as knowing that we were indeed familiar with the emotions the family was experiencing, was a tremendous help. My deepest fear was that there would be bad news and we would be asked to be with Steve and Kelly when they were told. A knot lived in my stomach over the unthinkable.

Late in the day on Monday I was at the command post and I saw Kelly's mom, Joyce Hale, just standing there with tears running down her cheeks. I immediately went to her and asked her what was wrong. As she began to sob, she poured out the anguish and sorrow in her heart. With tears washing her face, she told me how this was all her fault. If only she had not turned her back thinking Haley was following her, then Haley would not be lost now. And then she said, "I have lost the only child, of my only child." I began to cry with her; it was impossible not to do so. I have struggled with this same pain for years, the "If only" guilt. If only I had not let Morgan play. If only I had gone with her. If only I had heard or seen something. If only I had stopped it. If only...

We stood there together, bound by common pain, our tears running without restraint. As I looked around I could see several law enforcement officers trying to discreetly wipe their eyes. I hugged Joyce as tightly as I could and told her that she had to understand and believe that she had not done anything wrong, that Haley's being lost was not her fault. I told her that I had heard so many stories about Haley's zest for life and about how she liked to do things her way, and how independent and headstrong she could be. I reminded this dear lady that Haley's determination was the one quality that would see her through this situation.

I also acknowledged to Joyce that head and heart knowledge were two completely different things. No matter how many times someone tells you it is not your fault, and even when your head believes it, your heart is another matter. Joyce's heart was broken and aching. She believed she was responsible for losing her only grandchild and the unbearable guilt was tearing her apart. Her grief and regret were beyond human comprehension; her pain, all consuming. More than any other person, I feared for this special grandmother, should this little granddaughter not come home.

Action often is the best antidote to the horror of reality, so late Monday night we assisted Haley's family in making contact with all the necessary agencies you need help from when your child is missing. The National Center for Missing & Exploited Children and the Arkansas Missing Children's Clearinghouse began to immediately process Haley's information via computer. (God bless Tim Ernst for having technology so far out there in the wilderness!)

Friends and family of Haley wanted to begin setting up a reward fund, just in case. We walked them step by step through the process. What amazing people these folks were! Every bit of energy or resources each one had access to, they gave to the Zega family. By Tuesday morning the reward fund was a reality, and Haley's information had been distributed across the United States. Just in case.

Early on Tuesday morning we began to work with the command post and the Zega family to facilitate a press conference. Steve and Kelly wanted to make a plea for their daughter in case someone had seen her and had information as to her whereabouts. Whether someone had passed Haley in the woods and not realized that she was in trouble, or worse, whether someone had stolen their precious child, the Zegas needed to let the world know that they would not give up the search until Haley was found.

Up to this point Steve and Kelly had remained secluded at Tim's cabin, letting the press talk to everyone else but them. Facing your deepest fears in front of the press was something the Zegas had not wanted to do, but now it became necessary. Chip and I helped set the parameters for the press conference so the media would have a chance to meet the Zegas without intensifying their pain.

Before the press conference I had a private meeting with Steve and Kelly. We were standing outside Tim's cabin at the edge of the woods. It was the strangest sensation, to look out over such natural, unequaled beauty, and to have it leave such a vile feeling in your stomach. I asked Steve and Kelly what they were feeling, what they most wanted people to know.

Steve looked me in the eye, and with great clarity shared that he and Kelly refused to believe that Haley might not have survived out in the woods. They were both realistic enough to know that after so many hours had passed this might be a possibility. But they rejected it outright. If their daughter could not be found in the woods, then they would not accept that she had died and was beyond their reach. Instead they would forcefully fight back and work with the theory that somehow, beyond anyone's comprehension, Haley had been taken out of the woods. They were determined that they would find her, no matter what it took. This was a conscious decision for them, and I had the greatest admiration for these parents.

Steve and Kelly were looking at what was beginning to appear to them as fact: that Haley was lost to them forever; that the wilderness had claimed a new victim. But they refused to accept it. Pride and tears filled my heart as we exchanged hugs and vowed that together we would do whatever it took to bring Haley home. You must understand that a parent not giving up on a child is the single most important thing that happens during the search for a missing child. Steve and Kelly were outstanding, and never gave up.

We had set the interview up at a remote cabin so that it could be controlled and not mobbed with onlookers. The problem was that the cabin was definitely remote and we could not even find it! A gentleman who uses it as a summer place had provided it to us, but the directions and wild roads were incredibly confusing. Truly this was a frustrating and yet amusing moment as we found ourselves retracing our path several times while we searched for the cabin. The entire time we had an ever-growing trail of media vehicles following us. Occasionally they would pass us going in the opposite direction and find a place to turn around and join the caravan. They all thought that we knew where we were going! Of course, there was no good place to turn around, but turn we did every time we didn't find the cabin. And everyone turned behind us. What a catastrophe! Everyone was so tired by the time we finally did find the cabin, we did not know if we should laugh or cry. (I was so relieved later on to hear that our wonderful host, Tim Ernst, confessed that he could not find the cabin either—he lives in that neighborhood!) Consequently, the press conference, scheduled to begin at 2:00 p.m., started late.

The only time that was completely overwhelming for me happened during the last moments before the press conference took place. I had slept only a couple of hours in a borrowed sleeping bag at the command post since we had arrived and was certainly exhausted at this point. I had just spoken to my children on the phone while we were waiting for the press conference to begin. When I hung up it suddenly hit me just how badly this could all turn out. I could not imagine looking into the eyes of Steve and Kelly and knowing that they would feel as I have for five years. A huge pain filled my chest as I was overcome with missing my own daughter, Morgan.

The reality of it all was so terribly painful—to think that I was standing here in the middle of the woods wanting so badly to help Haley's family, knowing that the only reason I was here was because my own bubbly, sweet, blonde-headed, blue-eyed little girl was missing. All of the terror, the panic and the deepest emotions that I had kept locked away inside came rushing to the surface. The pain in my chest was so great, I felt that my heart would surely explode.

I know what it means to have a broken heart. It is an acute pain that physically tears through your chest. My heart was pounding and huge sobs began to build deep inside me. Chip and Chaplain Wes Hilliard, whom we had spent a great deal of time with and who was a friend of the Zegas, both came to my rescue and walked with me away from the crowd. One of the hardest times of the entire search came for me at this moment.

I needed to shut off the thoughts, the pain and the emotion from Morgan and return my focus to Haley and her family. But I did not want to focus on Haley at that moment. I wanted only to go home to my other children and hug them and then go out and somehow find Morgan. I did not want to be the parent of a missing child. I wanted my own child home. Now! I had to ask God for the strength to walk back to that cabin and face the press and fight for Haley. And, as always, He met me in my need and somehow gave me peace.

When Steve and Kelly arrived, I was able to focus on them and what needed to be done. Yet again, I thought my heart would break as they looked into the cameras and begged for Haley's life. No parent on earth should ever have to live through that horror.

What we did not know at that moment, what we would have given anything to know, is that while Haley's parents were pouring their hearts out to the world, their wonderful, determined, strong willed little girl had just been rescued.

After the press conference we returned to the command post while Tim took Steve and Kelly back to his cabin. As much as we wanted to stay with the search, we faced the fact that we needed clean clothes and supplies and would have to leave the mountain. Chip and I met one more time with the Command Post as they coordinated the search teams for the early evening. We made sure that someone was assigned as a liaison to relay information to the Zegas in our absence. We went back to talk to Kelly and Steve before we left and let them know we would be returning as quickly as possible.

At 5:15 p.m., with our hearts heavy, we started our dusty decent down the mountain. Once we reached civilization (qualified by where you can actually pick up service on your cell phone!), my cell phone rang. It was the command post. They wanted to inform us that Haley had been found alive and well and was being brought into the command post as we were speaking!!! Chip was driving and she almost wrecked the car. We were crying and laughing and crying again!

Chip's daughter also called to give us the account that our local news station was broadcasting about Haley's return. We stopped the car and gave thanks to God for keeping her safe. We were exuberant and talked about going back to the search site, but were sane enough even in our overwhelming joy to know that they did not need us now. Our work was done. As we drove home we just kept saying over and over, "She's okay!" I can't believe we missed it. We only missed being there for Haley's safe return by 15 minutes!

The amazing joy that followed me home and stayed with me for days was incredible. One television station asked me later, "How does it make you feel to see Haley home when Morgan is not?" The answer is simple. I am envious. How could I not be? But I am not jealous. Every single child who is lost deserves to come home. One child is not better or more important than the rest. We must fight for every child the way we fought for Haley and the way we continue to fight for Morgan. I am also completely *thrilled!* Why wouldn't I be? A lost child is home, and that is the ultimate goal that we at the Morgan Nick Foundation fight for every single day.

The Zega family had enough of a nightmare to last them a lifetime. And incredibly, they had also just been handed the gift of a lifetime to share with their child. The best part of this successful rescue is that everyone who helped search for Haley will now get to watch her grow up. This wonderful little girl who beat the odds with the determination and spirit of a world changer has touched all of us and made us better for it. And I feel blessed to have been part of this family's life long enough to witness the miraculous.

Hope—A belief in something you cannot see. (dictionary)
Hope—Love always hopes. (I Cor. 13:7)

We will never give up *Hope* for any missing child. We will continue to fight for them all and to rejoice with overwhelming joy when they make it home.

—Colleen Nick

Chapter 13
THE PARENTS

*S*teve Zega is an attorney, a Justice of the Peace with the Washington County Quorum Court, and a Captain in the Arkansas Army National Guard. His wife Kelly is the Director of Development for the North Arkansas Symphony. They live in Fayetteville, Arkansas because they love the area and its people. They were not with their only child Haley when she got lost in the wilderness. Neither of them was quite prepared for the horror they experienced when she disappeared, nor for the incredible outpouring of love and support from friends and total strangers that followed. I spent a lot of time around Steve and Kelly at our cabin during the ordeal, but I really could not tell what was going on inside their heads, or in their hearts. I waited until the very last minute to ask if they would write it all down to be included in this book. I had asked so much of them already in preparation for this project— there seemed to be no end to their generosity and eagerness to help. Once again, they both gladly accepted the chore. So here are their thoughts, in two parts. First, from Steve.*

My story really begins about two weeks before Haley was lost. I was in Ft. Smith on business and was on my way back to my office in Lincoln by way of Van Buren. For some reason I had to stop at Wal-Mart. There on the wall in the entrance to Wal-Mart were the many pictures of missing children. The one my eye was immediately drawn to was Morgan Nick. I was a brand-new parent when Morgan went missing in June of 1995. My heart ached for her parents then, and I followed the story for the next six years with probably the same interest as an average parent—I was sad and sorry for Morgan's whole family but especially for her parents. Like most people, I never really did anything to prevent children from becoming missing in the first place or to recover the ones who did become missing. This particular picture of Morgan had two images on it: one real photo taken at the age she was last seen, 6; and one computer-enhanced photo to show her aged as of the time of the poster, 12. It sent a chill down my spine, and I had one very selfish thought, "Wow. I feel sorry for her parents. Thank God it's them and not me. I don't know how I'd act if I lost Haley."

About two weeks later, I found out how I would act.

I was on my way to National Guard Annual Training (AT) at Ft. Chaffee on April 26, 2001. I was leaving two days early to make up for a weekend drill I had missed. The night before I left, Kelly, Haley and I had dinner at my favorite restaurant, Asahi. I got to pick because I was going away for two weeks. We had a nice dinner at the sushi bar. We vaguely discussed everybody's plans for the next two weeks. Haley was going to hike with Kelly's parents that weekend, and Kelly was going to go to the Fayetteville film festival. I was going to come home to sleep as often as I could, which meant Friday and Sunday that first week. I decided not to come home Saturday night because Kelly had a concert that was going to run late into Saturday night, and Haley was going to be with her.

AT was going very smoothly. My boss, Major Ron Brazzell, asked me to help brief Major General Don Morrow, the top military official in the state, on Monday morning. As my unit's personnel officer, I was also tasked with making arrangements for the General's informal dining out Sunday night. I was occupied Sunday morning and afternoon with writing, editing, and rehearsing my part of the General's briefing. I thought I just about had it down cold when my cellular phone rang at 3:00 in the afternoon. There was no number on my caller ID. I answered and heard my wife's voice on the other end.

"Zega, we have an emergency. Haley is lost in the woods in Newton County."

Kelly holds a bachelor's degree in broadcast journalism, and she is an accomplished public speaker. I knew immediately from the tone in her voice that Haley was in serious trouble. I managed to ask her how long Haley had been lost, and Kelly told me since about 11:00 a.m. Four hours. My heart instantly sank. That was all we managed to say to each other before the tin-roofed building I was in at Ft. Chaffee killed my phone's signal. I went outside and waited for what seemed an eternity for Kelly to call me back because I had no number to redial. When Kelly did call me, she managed to get me a phone number for somebody named Doc Chester in Newton County. I told her I would be on my way as soon as I got directions. I called Doc's number and spoke alternately with Doc, Michelle Boles, and my mother-in-law. Between the three of them, I got directions I could follow to the Upper Buffalo River Wilderness from Ft. Smith. I went in to tell Major Brazzell that I was leaving to look for my daughter and that I would be back when I was back. He said, "OK." At 3:15 p.m. I left Ft. Chaffee for Boxley Valley.

Naturally, my truck was out of gas, so I had to fill up on my way. In the meantime, my mind was racing. I had not been to the Buffalo River since the year before Haley was born, and what I remembered was not good for a barely-six-year-old girl, who had lived no farther than 50 feet from pavement her whole life. Newton County in general, and the Buffalo in particular, is the least populated, most densely wooded area in our still-rural state. I might have been imagining things, but I remembered a very large water moccasin outpacing our canoe when we last floated the Buffalo. I tried to put all of this out of my mind and drove as fast as I could east on Interstate 40. Unfortunately, most of I-40 was reduced to one lane each way with construction, and for the most part I could not exceed 50 miles per hour.

I made two phone calls that I remember. The first was to my friend, Gerald Goss. Gerald owns the police dog school in Lincoln where I instruct. I asked Gerald to gather up as many dogs and handlers as he could get his hands on and meet me in Boxley. I gave him as adequate directions as a person who has never been someplace can possibly give. The second call was back to the Chester cabin. I talked to Joyce (Kelly's mom) in an attempt to ease my worried mind. It didn't work, despite Joyce's confidence that Haley was very near the area where the hiking party had last seen her. I kept waiting for my phone to ring and someone to tell me that Haley was found, tired, thirsty, hungry, and scared, but just fine. The call never came. I was, in fact, a bit relieved when I lost cell phone coverage about 10 miles north of Clarksville on State Highway 21, thinking that for the remainder of the trip that someone had indeed called me, and I just wasn't in coverage range to receive the call.

I vacillated between a prayer and a hope for the entire drive. The prayer was simple: "God, please bring my daughter back safely to me." The hope was equally simple. I kept thinking Haley would be found by the time I got to the Buffalo. An hour after I turned north from Clarksville, my hopes were dashed. As I came down the long hill into the Buffalo Valley, I knew which road to turn on because I ran into a woman pounding a sign that said "RESCUE" on it into the ground. The effort to find my daughter was not only still underway, but was also obviously escalating to the point where strangers needed to be shown the way to the rescue area.

Two things immediately impressed me about Cave Mountain Road. One was the steep hill it was carved into; the other was its narrowness. As I drove on the road, I also became impressed with how far removed Cave Mountain Church (search headquarters) was from the paved road. I drove for at least 20 minutes to cover 6 miles on this dirt road. I was beginning to believe I was lost when I finally happened on the Church.

Good news—the helicopters are here. The authorities are sparing no resource to find my child. Bad news—the helicopters are here. Haley is really, truly, deeply lost. My legs went numb.

It was 5:00 p.m. There was still plenty of daylight in late April, but even plenty is finite. At the church I saw no one I recognized and began to inquire after my wife. Someone told me she was at the trailhead, about a mile farther down the road. I debated momentarily on leaving my truck at the church and walking, but I decided I had no time to waste with walking. When I got to the trailhead there were only two or three vehicles and no Kelly, Jay or Joyce. I saw a uniformed National Park Service officer who was patiently briefing a searcher on the hood of the Park Service truck. When the officer finished briefing the searcher he asked if there was anything he could do for me.

"Yeah. Find my daughter."

The officer read the name tag on my Army uniform and apologized. He started to explain the search effort to me when I finally saw someone I knew. Tom Triplett was a friend of mine from the days I officiated basketball. He was still in the coaching business; I had since quit refereeing. Tom was one of the coaches for whom it was a genuine pleasure to work, and his face was a comfort. Soon after I shook hands with him I finally saw Kelly and Jay. I hugged Kelly for what seemed like an hour. She was remarkably composed, explaining where she had been, filling me in on details of Haley's disappearance that I hadn't known before, and trying to comfort me. I told Kelly that I had called Gerald, and that he expected three teams of dogs and handlers to be on the scene at any minute. Tony Lee, a Lincoln Police Officer, arrived with Gerald and a dog at about 5:20 p.m. Gerald and I immediately took one of the Haley's scent items, a favorite dress-up outfit, from Kelly and got a map orientation from the National Park officer. This lasted for about five minutes when I impatiently said, "We're burning daylight. Let's go look."

Despite the fact that I was dressed in the Army's Battle Dress Uniform—woodland camouflage fatigues—I was very poorly equipped to search for Haley. I was wearing my favorite pair of Corcoran jump boots, not my jungle boots. The jump boots take a shine very well, but I have had them for ten years and never resoled them. They are about as slick on the bottom as old penny loafers and just not very good for tromping through the Ozark woods. We had no map, so we committed to memory the terrain from the trail. Downhill led to a bluff overlooking a tributary creek to the Buffalo. Uphill was the county road.

Coach Triplett, who had hiked in the area many times, and Jay and Joyce led Gerald and me at a pace just slower than a sprint down the trail for perhaps a half mile (a very hard, rocky, steep half mile) to what would later become known as Haley Falls—the place where Haley had last been seen. Daylight was still good, but definitely fading now. Gerald put his dog's nose on Haley's dress and instructed Coach Triplett and me to search the double-tiered bluff for Haley while his dog followed whatever scent it could. We went in three different directions.

For the first time I felt something near panic as I looked for real over the bluffs to the creek bed at least eighty feet below. Dear God, if Haley took one wrong step . . . Well, my mind, searching for anything to pin hope upon remembered that the Park Ranger told me that the creek bed had already been searched on foot twice from one end of the bluffs to the other, and no one had found Haley's body. Thank God. Still, I had to suppress more than one fit of panic-driven tears as I walked about two miles up and down the length of both shelves of the bluff. No Haley. I called her name out the whole time, "Haley, honey, it's your Daddy. Holler if you can hear me." No Haley.

Daylight was leaking fast from the sky. I met Tom at Haley Falls again, and he reported the same thing. We decided to look individually back away from the bluff, uphill. For what remained of the daylight that first day, I made larger and larger concentric circles with Haley Falls as the center point. At some point I began to sing without realizing it. I was singing the theme to Haley's favorite cartoon:

> "Fighting crime
> Trying to save the world
> Getting there just in time
> The Power Puff Girls."

I was by now exhausted, a bit lost myself (although I knew if I kept going uphill eventually I would find the road), and it was dusk. I ran into a line of searchers from Madison County who, upon finding out who I was, told me I would do best back at the Church. They pointed me to the road and told me to turn left once I got there. I followed the road and turned down several offered rides—the last thing I wanted to do now was to talk to anybody except Kelly. I got back to the church at probably 8:15 p.m., and there were easily three times as many volunteers, park rangers, police officers and search and rescue team members as there had been at 5:00 p.m. I asked about Kelly. One of the cops told me she had been with a dog team for about two hours. I then began for the first time what I would do for a good deal of the next 60 or so hours. I waited passively. It drove me nuts. I noticed about 15 minutes into my waiting that Tony Lee (the Lincoln cop) was never more than ten steps behind me.

"Whatcha doin', Tony?"

"Oh, just watching you, Steve."

"Why are you watching me?"

"They asked me to."

I chuckled at this internally, wondering if I had been put on suicide watch. I told Tony I was fine, he could put himself to more productive work, and that I was going to the bathroom and preferred him not to follow me for that. I also asked Tony to get in touch with my friend, Lincoln Police Chief Jim Acker, to go personally to my Mom's house in Lincoln and knock on her door to tell her what was happening. I did not want her to hear it on the news or get it from anybody but me over the phone.

Shortly thereafter a very nice gentleman introduced himself to me. He said his name was Lytle James and that his son, Vixen, and I were in the Guard together. Just at that point I put it together that Vixen was indeed from Newton County and had graduated from Jasper High School. Lytle, typical of the folks in and from Newton County, told me if there was anything at all he could do, to holler at him. I assured him I would.

Kelly finally got back from her trip with the dog team. She told me that the dog had obviously alerted on a scent and took them straight up from the falls area to the county road, where the trail dropped off completely. We talked in the relative privacy of my truck for a while, reflecting on how lucky we were as parents, marveling at the size of the rescue effort, and holding each other. Our friends began to arrive. Mike and Michelle McCarver and Phil and Kelly Carter, parents of Haley and Elizabeth, respectively, Haley Zega's two closest friends, were the first of our friends to arrive. I completed a Lost Person Survey on Haley. The prayer became a mental mantra, "God, please bring my daughter back safely to me."

At some point around ten o'clock, I wept. The three hours of darkness, the dropping temperature, the helicopters taking off, our friends coming over, the fact that I knew Haley was by now scared, cold, hungry, thirsty, lonely, and exhausted all hit me like a fast ball in the head. I cried like I do not ever remember crying in my whole life, as an adult or a child. I cried for my little girl who was lonely and lost. I cried for myself—my failure, as the one person she looked to more than anyone else in this world for her physical safety, to find her. I cried for Kelly. We decided not to have any other children after Haley, and we took medical steps to make sure Haley would be our only child. I felt suddenly and profoundly guilty for that decision. I cried for Jay and Joyce, who, although they did not show it most of the time, felt enormous guilt. I cried out of fear for Haley's six-year old friends who might never see her again. How do you really explain to one six-year old that another one is dead? I think at that age most children have at least a passing acquaintance with death, but it is usually from losing a grandparent or a pet. No child expects another his or her age to be gone forever. My body shook from the sobs. Kelly cradled me in her arms for at least 30 minutes, and I just wailed. Kelly and I thus began roles we would have throughout the whole ordeal: she was strong—an emotional rock, and I was a complete emotional basket case, given to falling apart at almost any time.

It was nearing 10:30 p.m., and two things happened. First, the Information Officer from the Arkansas Game and Fish Commission found Kelly and me and told us that Colleen Nick, Morgan's mother, wanted to come to the rescue site. Instantly I felt a rock in my stomach as I remembered my trip to the Van Buren Wal-Mart only a few weeks earlier. I kept that tidbit to myself. Then, Fran Alexander (a woman I knew mostly from reading her wonderful columns in the Northwest Arkansas Times and her activism before the Fayetteville City Council on the subject of tree preservation) came up to Kelly and me and suggested that we should go rest for the night in a nearby cabin. We both resisted at first, but Fran used gentle, forceful persuasion to convince us that we would do better with this whole thing showered and rested (although neither of us had any clothes to change into) and that the press would soon be at the Church, and we probably needed to be removed from that situation. We agreed, and by 11:15 p.m. or so someone had taken us to the "cabin" I learned later was called Cloudland.

Tim Ernst's home on the Buffalo River is a "cabin" in only one sense in my mind: it is made out of logs. It is huge, with two complete stories and a "loft" bigger than many houses. It has all the modern amenities: phone; computer with Internet; etc. About 150 yards from the cabin is Tim's office, which had a fax machine. That item proved to be an enormous help to us over the next two days. Cloudland's one limitation is its scarce water supply, which I assume works fine for the daily needs of Tim, his wife, and daughter, but was not ready to handle the demands of scores of people over the next two days.

Tim was waiting for us when we got to his house, which is probably only three miles from the Cave Mountain Church as the crow flies, but a 20-minute drive away down the narrow dirt road at night. The fact that he was willing to lend us his home was evidence enough of his generosity. We could not have asked for a more gracious host. He led us to his daughter's room on the first floor, and immediately started to apologize for all the Barbies and other little girl's things there. I didn't want to hear an apology from a man who had opened his home to us, especially for the non-sin of having a child's things in a child's room. He let it go, and we got along famously.

He let us know that whatever we needed we could have. Kelly first took advantage of that offer by calling a psychic. I was frankly skeptical, even though I believe in psychic powers, because I have a healthy disinterest in people who advertise those kinds of services. After all, if someone were really psychic, wouldn't she know you needed her services and call you? The psychic told Kelly that Haley was alive, tired, and cold, and that she was near a body of water. That made sense since we were so close to the Buffalo. The psychic also said that a dog team would find Haley, just fine, before noon the next day. That actually gave me something sort of real to hope for.

I began to think as afterthoughts about needing to call my friends. I called James Graves, my best friend. He already knew. He said he, his wife Angie, and two of my other closest friends, Ray Dunwoodie and Dave Dubriske, were on their way. I asked him not to come that night, because frankly I didn't see what use they could be in the dark. He agreed. I was also paying attention to the temperature. Tim had the sliding glass back door of his cabin thrown open to the beautiful Arkansas spring night air. It was getting downright chilly already, and there were still 6 hours to go before real daylight. We thanked Tim and shortly thereafter turned in to bed.

Neither Kelly nor I slept that night. While daylight seemed to run out of the sky, hours of darkness were downright slug-like. There was also a parade of family and friends. I'm not sure who came first. I think sometime around 2:00 a.m. Vixen James and Wes Hilliard arrived. They were both still in uniform. Thirteen hours earlier, Vixen and I had been preparing for the same briefing to General Morrow. Wes is our unit's chaplain and was, at the time, a minister at Central United Methodist Church in Fayetteville. They let me know that the Guard was prepared to assist in any way they could. Vixen assured me that the people of Newton County would stop everything they were doing to look for Haley, and from what I had seen so far, he was right. Then we all prayed briefly together. Wes thanked God in advance for keeping Haley safe and delivering her back to us.

Colleen Nick arrived next, and asked to talk to Kelly alone. Maybe it was exhaustion, but I didn't understand what she could possibly say to Kelly that she couldn't say in front of me. I know now. She and Kelly had something in common only mothers can share. They talked for perhaps thirty minutes. Then together my Mom and her husband, Al, showed up at the cabin with Ray, Dave, Angie, and my disobedient best friend, James. They were followed by my Dad, my brother Joel, and his wife Karen. I cannot remember what we talked about or for how long. I have no idea where everybody camped for the night. Several of them, I'm sure, stayed at Cloudland. There were plenty of big soft couches, chairs and unoccupied beds.

Sometime around 3:30 a.m., Kelly and I went back into Amber's room alone. Again we laid down, but we did not sleep. We talked about what a wonderful child Haley is. We talked about how far she had progressed this year in kindergarten. We talked about how much she had improved over the spring at softball. We talked about how smart and sweet and caring and loving she is. We talked about how everyone, without exception, who knows her, loves her. At the risk of sounding and being immodest, my daughter is an exceptional little girl. We are blessed completely as parents.

We resolved two things that night. One, we would stay together, no matter what the outcome of the search was. The divorce rate, nearly fifty percent amongst married couples in general, goes up astronomically, to something like 95% when parents lose a child. We promised we would be better than that to each other. Two, we swore we would not harbor anger or resentment at God if He did not return Haley to us. I know that sounds easy to say now that she is home with us. Maybe we would have made that promise and maybe we would not have. I know this. I was grateful to God every day from March 24, 1995 until April 29, 2001 for the privilege of being Haley's daddy. I have been even more grateful every day since May 1, 2001 for the same thing. How could I be mad at God for giving me this gift, this angel in my house, even if it was only for six years?

We laid there for three or so more hours. Sometimes we talked, sometimes we didn't. Nighttime was moving painfully, slowly. Kelly cried for one of only two times. I cried off and on a lot. Just like it always does, the sun rose.

Kelly stirred first on Monday morning. That was just like normal. I don't know how long she had been up and about when I got out of bed. The first thing I remember doing was listening as Kelly called Jodi Felkins, Haley's kindergarten teacher. Kelly told Jodi that she didn't want Jodi to hear about it on the news and to please reassure Haley's classmates. The people I noticed in the house were Colleen, her assistant, Chip, Tim, and Angie Graves. Kelly and Colleen began a dialogue about the resources available for parents of missing and exploited children. Sometimes I was part of this conversation; sometimes I was not. Colleen and Kelly began a process of bonding, mother-to-mother, in which I could not participate.

A good deal of that first morning I spent on the couch in Tim's living room, feeling no small amount of relief as the room got lighter and warmer. I was sort of vaguely aware that as soon it was light, Tim took his dog and went looking for Haley. Ray, Dave, and Jim all stopped by Cloudland before they went out to look for Haley. John Goodwin, another friend and fraternity brother, came in. He was the first friend of mine who stayed around Cloudland for any length of time. Helicopters, active all night, became noticeably louder as, I assume, more of them came up and aggressively searched the bluff corner upon which Cloudland sits, and each bluff line, north-south and east-west.

No description of that fist sunrise would be complete without describing the view out of Tim's back door that first morning. Even in my exhausted, emotionally confused state, I was arrested by the spectacular beauty of Tim's back porch view. Wow! I know why he picked this location to build. The view was, of course, invisible to us when we arrived at night. Now we could see as light shone over the Buffalo Valley and the mountains surrounding it. This late in April all trees were already in full foliage, and it was sort of idyllic. No power lines, no road cuts, in fact no buildings other than Cloudland are visible. You don't realize how much visual pollution there is in your everyday world until you get to a place like the Upper Buffalo Wilderness. The only work visible is that of God's. With my admiration of the raw natural beauty of my surroundings came a creeping dread: Haley could not have picked a more remote place within 500 miles to become lost. "Please, God. Keep her safe. Bring her back to us."

10:00 a.m., the time the psychic said Haley would be found, came and went. I anticipated the time on a digital clock on Tim's wall. When it passed, I thought, "well, it will take time for them to get the word to us." When 10:30 a.m. came and went, John suggested we take a walk. I agreed, and told Kelly that I was getting stir crazy and needed some air. That much was true. I also told her we would be back in a half hour. That was not quite so true. John and I walked up the driveway leading into Cloudland down to the trailhead coming out near Doc Chester's cabin. This is where Haley had gone into the woods perhaps 24 hours before. We started down the trail, taking note of the fences and other landmarks. We ran into a group of perhaps 10 men, a group of brothers, fathers and sons—Newton County farmers all, who with smiles on their faces, had given up their farm work to look for Haley. They knew these woods well from hunting and hiking in them all their lives. Upon learning who I was, they assured me, like everyone else did, that we would find Haley alive and that they were happy to help.

John and I continued down the trail, opposite the way I had come in the day before. I began to see how easily Haley could have lost the trail. The trail generally followed an east-west direction, but took several forks around big boulders and trees, crossed several fallen logs, and most important, was covered up entirely for 50 feet at a time with overgrowth and dead leaves. While I could see the other end walking at 5'9", I squatted to Haley's height and lost the trail. John and I took different parts of the trail when it forked. We came back together shortly before a part of the trail I had walked to previously from the other end, Haley Falls. There, encircled in fluorescent orange engineer tape, was Haley's point last seen. Not five feet away, a bouquet of pink wildflowers was bound to the trunk of an enormous hickory tree in silent tribute to Haley. Together they reminded me of a crime scene and a funeral, and it was more than I could bear. I didn't tell John why, but I told him I wanted to go back to Tim's cabin right away.

Kelly was less than pleased with me when we got back. After all, I had been gone for nearly two hours when I had promised her that I would be back in thirty minutes. She was perfectly understanding when I explained to her why I had been gone and what I had been doing. She also told me she had enough to worry about with Haley being gone, and asked me, please, not to leave her again. I told her I wouldn't. After my hike I was genuinely hungry for the first time in 36 hours or so, and I ate a McDonald's hamburger, which I understood had been imported from Harrison. All of corporate Northwest Arkansas gave generously to us in ways I am still not wholly cognizant. I know Wal-Mart donated case after case of bottled water to the volunteers. Tyson's kitchens gave hundreds of pounds prepared, cooked chicken tenders. Pizza Pro in Jasper kept us in pizza. All of these corporations and more gave generously, and Kelly, Haley, and I thank them.

—Steve Zega

September, 2001. In an ironic twist of fate, Steve's part of this chapter—in the book and in real life—began with the National Guard, and had to end with them as well. He was called away to Guard duty in the aftermath of the World Trade Center tragedy before he could finish his thoughts.

I would imagine that the greatest fear for any parent is the loss of your child. It has to be worse for the mother, because, well, mothers are like that. They give us life, and so the pain cuts deep when it is taken away. Like several of us have already stated, Kelly was a rock throughout this entire ordeal, the glue that held the rest of us together. Here is her story.

I never thought an experience so intense and emotion-producing could ever become a memory I could calmly take out and rationally look at from every angle. Yet, that's exactly what I still do every day. My never-ending analysis of those three days without Haley, and the weeks and months that followed, comes from the impact it made on the lives of my family, friends, and strangers—an impact that remains a part of every day as we go about our lives. Even as "normal" routines have taken hold again, the uniqueness of our experience makes my family anything but "normal." We have somehow come to openly symbolize a range of things to people: how something life-changing can happen to *anyone* in an instant; how we must keep hope in the toughest of times; how a little child can exceed all possible odds with a strong spirit and common sense; how prayer *works*; how we should all take stock of the little blessings that come every day and hold closely those people we love; how truly good and pure the intentions of strangers can be in this world; and how we should all take deeper breaths, celebrate life, and say the things that need to be said while we openly and honestly feel the things we should feel.

It is interesting how many people feel cautious about asking questions about what our family went through—how Haley's doing, how we handled it all, what Haley told us after she was found. And it's funny to me how people occasionally will ask us questions in a tone barely above a whisper when Haley is within earshot, as if she wouldn't remember what she went through or that she might somehow be more traumatized by hearing someone else speak of her time in the woods. I'm pretty certain that Haley has recovered so well because we have talked about every detail and asked her so many questions, but we've always tried to keep the element of fear out of our discussions. Haley isn't scarred by her experience because we've insisted from the moment she was back in our arms that no one ever imply that being lost in the woods should be terror-filled. The world is full of things we can use to implant fear into our children, but I believe that fear (quite different from caution) is one of the greatest things to paralyze us from being able to solve our own problems and achieve our goals. My job as a mother is to try to make sure that Haley never is held captive by her fears or the fear of others; as a result, her mind and heart can be clear enough to work together and accomplish her dreams.

It all began with one of those perfect weekend days—busy with friends and family early in the day and a rare afternoon full of time for myself. With Zega gone for military duty and a big load off of my mind from having survived the end of the North Arkansas Symphony season and a post-concert reception the night before, I enjoyed having my parents spend the night with plans to rise early to take Haley hiking. That Sunday morning I pulled together a bag full of snacks for Haley to take on her day trip—lots of her favorites to nibble on. I got her dressed in her favorite t-shirt, a souvenir from the Kennedy Space Center, shorts and tennis shoes. She was chilly before loading up in the truck with her Mimi and Pop, so I got her a big red sweatshirt that she could take off as the day warmed up. Most importantly, we all made sure she didn't pull out of the driveway without one of her flannel security blankets. In this case, she took one of her favorites, "Stripey Blankie." Haley and my parents, along with family friend Clay Bass, headed out in perfect spring weather with everything they could possibly need to meet two other friends, Dennis and Michelle Boles for a special day in the Ozark National Forest near the Buffalo River.

I went on with my obligations, ultimately going to the Fayetteville Film Festival early in the afternoon to enjoy a range of short films at the Continuing Education Center. I had hoped a friend of mine would join me there, but I ended up going on my own. I watched a few films, one of which was disturbing enough to leave me feeling a little sick. Soon after the fourth film began, the concerned voice of my friend, James Alford, came over the auditorium loud speaker, asking me to come to the lobby. I was already a bit out of sorts from the movie I had seen, but the announcement made my heart pound wildly. I knew immediately that something was wrong, and my first impulse was to think that Zega had been injured in a training exercise at Fort Chaffee. Once I reached the doors of the auditorium, James led me to two people I certainly didn't expect to see—Cathy Bass (Clay's wife) and Fran Alexander, another family friend. Before I could get thoroughly confused, Cathy calmly told me that Haley "had wandered off" and that everyone was looking for her.

Visions of the Buffalo River went through my mind—I had to know if Haley had been hiking in that area of the forest. The two of them assured me that the trail she was on was a long distance from the river, but that it did run close to a bluff line. They kept repeating to me that everything was under control, the Newton County Sheriff's Office had been called in, and that it would just be a matter of time before Haley would be found safe. I grabbed the nearest phone and called Zega on his cellular phone. All I could get out before being cut off was that we had an emergency, and Haley was lost in the woods. I was trying so hard to be calm, but I could barely speak. Matters were made worse when I got him back on the line and started trying to give driving directions to a place I didn't even know how to find. My hand was shaking so hard, I couldn't legibly write down the directions Fran was giving me to tell him. Eventually I handed the phone to her, and she tried to describe how to get to Boxley, Arkansas, from Fort Smith. She gave him another number to call in Newton County that would put him in touch with my parents or their friends so he could get updates.

Within minutes, Cathy and Fran were driving me home to pick up some extra clothes and a few items of Haley's to give to scent dogs, in case she wasn't located right away. I changed out of the dress I was wearing into jeans and a jacket, grabbed a pillow and my glasses (in case it got late and I decided to ditch my contacts), and then ran through my room and Haley's trying to think what would have the greatest concentration of her sweet little girl smell. The first thing I found was her nightgown, from when she slept with me in "the big bed" the night before. Next, I hunted down her favorite purple dress-up dress, an item I knew wasn't washed all the time and something she wore almost daily. Cathy knew not to touch any of the items and had me stuff them into a plastic bag in her trunk. I locked up the house, and we raced off to Newton County.

On the first leg of the trip—before we lost cellular service—I tried to call one of my best friends, Kelly Carter. Her husband, Phil, answered. I doubt I made much sense at the time, but he immediately knew the severity of the situation. This one phone call triggered the first wave of phone calls to all of our friends—a chain reaction of our close friends getting the word out to each other. Thankfully, the process worked well; within minutes, I lost all phone service.

A few miles down the road, I felt completely dehydrated. That feeling didn't go away until four days later. Fran and Cathy did everything in their power to keep the conversation light, alluding to things their own children had done to worry them sick...all of which came out perfectly well in the end. We tried to laugh about Cathy's Lexus, a car with a real history regarding Haley. When Haley was a couple of months old, a number of family friends threw us a wonderful baby shower, during which a massive hail (hail...Haley...) storm blew in. We watched helplessly (before a dozen of us hid in the bathroom in case a tornado came) as baseball-sized hail smashed into all of the cars in the driveway, one of which was the very same Lexus we were using to try to reach Haley now, over rough, steep dirt roads. We tried to see the humor in the fact that Haley obviously had it out for that poor innocent car.

The whole time we were driving, I focused on two things beyond my fevered prayers that Haley be safe and sound: finding the words to assure my parents that I didn't blame them, because I knew the guilt they would be feeling had to be overwhelming; and praying for my own strength and calm. I knew that if I fell apart, even for a little while, it would only serve as a distraction to impede the progress of others. From the very beginning I made the conscious decision that my role in this whole nightmare would be to answer questions, take care of details, be a source of comfort if necessary, and to have my act firmly together so that *when* she was found, whatever her condition might be, I would be able to respond to her in whatever way she needed me. While those things may seem a bit detached, these processes and actions kept my mind active and didn't allow me to wallow in dangerous levels of sick worry.

Another more basic thing that kept my mind distracted was an unbelievable and interminable need to pee! I didn't know at the time that high levels of stress can cause great thirst and constant urination. I did know that I tend to yawn non-stop when experiencing a case of nerves, but the full-to-the-brim bladder was a new wrinkle. Between yawns, I asked Cathy to pull over on the rough and narrow Cave Mountain Road. I jumped out, and per Fran's advice, leaned against the back bumper to relieve myself. I probably could have stayed in that position for a good five minutes and still not been done, but I was more concerned about getting up the road as fast as possible. We headed on, with every bump feeling more and more uncomfortable. I scolded myself for letting the call of nature slow me down. (That wouldn't be the only time I and others would be similarly inconvenienced—finding a rock or tree to hide behind when hundreds of people and dogs are combing the woods is a unique challenge.)

We finally arrived at the church that had been described to us as the place to meet up with my parents and some of the early law enforcement folks. As I had expected, my mom was beside herself. She asked me if I could ever forgive her, and I remember telling her that there was nothing to forgive. I knew there was no blame to be attached in a situation like this—Haley has her own mind (thankfully a very bright one), and I was certain there was no irresponsibility on the part of my parents. After all, I had been raised by these two people and knew that they were anything but inattentive to a child—especially one they had centered the whole day around. Instead of hearing regret, what I wanted to hear was details. I wanted to know when she was lost, what she was doing, if she had eaten or drunk anything, and how she was acting when they last saw her.

Soon after getting the basic facts, we moved down the road a short distance to a clearing near the trailhead. By that time, a number of local search and rescue volunteers were arriving. I'll never forget the faces of the women who were there waiting for their instructions or to support their husbands—every expression quietly told how badly they wanted everything to work out and how much they sympathized with how I felt. No one spoke much, beyond the questions and briefings from the search and rescue people. As much as I tried to be calm, I didn't feel like I could maintain my composure for much longer while I waited for Zega to make the drive from Fort Chaffee. I worried that he might be so upset that his driving wouldn't be safe—and then I worried more when we realized that he'd been given driving directions as if he were coming from farther south than he actually was.

I sat for what seemed like an eternity on the tailgate of a pick-up truck, wishing I could do more to help but knowing I had to stay put. Finally, I saw Zega drive up and park along the side of the road. I jumped down to run up to him and managed to snag a giant hole in the back of my jeans from the tailgate, scraping my leg. Normally I would have cared, but I barely felt a thing. We hugged tightly, passing strength to each other, and then went to find out the details Zega needed to know. His first impulse was to head straight into the woods, but he was discouraged from doing so right away. The search team was concerned about disturbing the trail or harming the potential for the dogs to get the best possible scent. I knew he wouldn't be able to stand not being able to go into the woods for long (even though all I wanted him to do was to stay with me), so I backed off and let him do what he needed to do. The search and rescue leaders agreed to let him go in.

About the same time, two dog teams were ready to head out onto the trail from the end where Haley started her hike. They asked me to come along, at which point I began learning more than I ever wanted to know about scent dogs. I actually had a role at this point, because the dogs needed to have an opportunity to eliminate my personal scent from Haley's clothing near where she was lost so they could focus on just her smell. It was one of the only times throughout the whole ordeal that I actually felt useful.

Once we got into the woods, and I got near the point where Haley was last seen, I suddenly lost all of my energy. I felt drained, unbelievably thirsty, and began to get concerned about a low blood pressure problem I've been troubled with in the past. I kept telling myself to get over it— mind over matter—that Haley needed me to think for her and to hear my voice. I called and called until I felt dizzy. Darkness was closing in fast, and our group only had a couple of flashlights. I tried to rest on the rocks along the bluff line, but couldn't get over the distraction of how far down the drop was. We finally headed back up to the road, digesting the news that the dogs had trailed a scent right up to the road...where it stopped cold. That didn't make sense—how could she just disappear into thin air—unless someone had stolen her? My better judgment told me that abduction was very unlikely, but the possibility of it lurked in my mind more than I cared to admit.

The next couple of hours were a blur. Returning to what was now the official command center illustrated how large the search was becoming. That knowledge was horrible and calming all at the same time. I was thankfully able to relieve my mind regarding my blood pressure when an incredibly nice deputy sheriff left the scene and drove into town to get me some prescription medicine from an off-duty pharmacist. Meanwhile, our friends had begun to arrive. Seeing the faces of the other people who knew Haley so well—who would do anything for her and whose children are her own dearest friends—was wonderful. We didn't have much to say to each other; I was thankful because I was certain that if I had to do much talking, I would lose it. While I watched my fabulous, competent friend Rebecca Wood take charge of what would eventually become a crush of press, I knew my family was in the best possible hands.

I stepped away from my friends to find Zega. We hunkered down in his Jeep, where I did everything in my power to comfort him. He was consumed with grief, remorse, and helplessness. I have never witnessed such raw pain in someone I love, and I never want to again. Strangely enough, though, his ability to express his wretchedness helped galvanize my own strength. Even though I couldn't be with Haley, I could do my best to help the other person I love most. I kept praying for strength—for Haley, Zega, my parents, and myself. After a while, I stepped out for some fresh air. I was approached by one of the deputies who pressed a slip of paper into my hand and led me toward the one squad car equipped with a working mobile phone.

He told me that Colleen Nick, mother of missing child Morgan Nick and activist for missing children and their families, wanted to speak with me. My gut reaction was irritation that quickly turned to dread. It couldn't be that serious yet, could it? Why would she think that it was that bad yet? I didn't want to call her. It would force me to admit that things were really as bad as they seemed. Yet, I decided it would be rude if I didn't call her back, so I went ahead and called. I was left alone in the car to make the call, and when it went through, I could barely hear Colleen due to the static on the line. Her voice was gentle but firm, and she asked if she could say a prayer with me. She prayed calmly, only part of which I could understand, but I felt better afterward. She then told me that she would like to come be with my family if we didn't mind. I knew instinctively that she needed to be there—that she would know what steps to take next. Colleen then began her journey to (and with) our family that has changed how I look at everything. She left her own children safely behind so she could be with us—total strangers—and made our next two days infinitely more bearable.

Soon after getting off of the phone with Colleen and returning to the frenzy of activity around the old church that had become the stopping point for many vehicles, Zega and I finally admitted that we needed to step away to some peace and quiet to calm down. We had so many of the locals willing to do anything to help, offering their homes and beds—but the option that kept coming up was to drive down to Tim Ernst's cabin. While I'd never had the opportunity to meet Tim before this day, I certainly knew of him from photographer friends who spoke glowingly—almost with reverence—of his work. I had enjoyed his books and large prints depicting the Ozarks, but never thought much about the person behind the camera. I guess that somewhere deep in my mind, despite the horror we'd been witnessing over the past hours, I still had a real curiosity about this artist.

I don't even remember who led us in to Tim's cabin, but I was stunned at its beauty once we arrived. I hated that we were obviously keeping him up at a very late hour, but he seemed to be content to putter around on his computer. (Much later we figured out that he was spending time telling the world through his on-line journal about the noisy drama that had unfolded in the forest and was now invading his home.) While Tim apologized profusely for the toys and things in his daughter's room—thinking they'd upset us—I was actually comforted by those little reminders of a sweet little girl. Nothing about seeing Amber's things or her pictures was upsetting to me, and I wanted to know more about her.

After a few minutes I worked up the courage to ask Tim if I could use his phone to call long distance. I hated to admit why, but I had it in my mind that if I could talk to a psychic (or intuitive), I might get some news that could help me visualize Haley's situation. I just wanted someone else—a stranger—who was completely detached from the whole scene to tell me something soothing. My logical mind had been working overtime while we talked to the search and rescue commanders and other law enforcement; I was ready to let my emotional side take over for a while. After a quick hunt through the yellow pages, I located a name. I woke the poor woman up, but she was so kind. She told me that she could feel Haley shaking from the cold and possibly some fear, but that she was very alive. Just hearing that made me breathe a little deeper, even though I had no clue as to the legitimacy of this person. My need to keep hoping was fed by any possibility of happy resolution, and this woman gave me strength.

Now that I was calmer, I realized that I hadn't eaten for more than twelve hours. I asked Tim if I could have some crackers—I felt so sick to my stomach. I tried to remember what I could stand to eat when I was pregnant with Haley—I now felt that same feeling. Crackers were about the only thing that came to mind, and the last thing I wanted Tim to do in the middle of the night was to have to dig out a bunch of food. I sat down at the kitchen bar and asked him about a million questions about Amber, told him a little about Haley, and then made the statement that when we finally got her back home again, things were going to have to slow down for us. I began feeling twinges of guilt that I hadn't cleared my busy life enough for the one person who depends most on me, and that she deserved better. I had convinced myself over time that my being involved with so many community projects was good for her and would teach her that we have a responsibility to think beyond ourselves. At that moment, I started questioning whether or not I had thought enough about my beautiful, gentle child. Had her six years of life been too full of meetings and running from one place to the next?

The next few hours were sleepless and brought family and friends to Tim's cabin. I don't remember much about any of those middle of the night conversations, but I do remember getting up out of bed repeatedly and wandering into the bathroom. I would just stand there with the window wide open, thinking that I didn't deserve a warm bed with a soft pillow and a loving husband to hold me tight. I wanted to feel exactly what Haley was feeling at that moment—I wanted to be as cold as she was, hear the same sounds she was hearing, feel the same wind. I felt that if I could gauge how all of that affected me, I could understand her mental state better. I became obsessed with the fact that she didn't have her "Stripey Blankie" with her. I was convinced that the only thing worse for Haley than being cold and hungry would be her trying to cope with the darkness and strange noises without her security blanket. I worried more for her emotional state than her physical safety, fearing that she might just give up or be so distraught that she would fall and hurt herself. After a while, I would start to shake and feel weak, so I would crawl back into bed with Zega.

After essentially no sleep and horrific mental images, morning came. The first thing I made myself do was to get up at about 5:00 a.m. and call Haley's kindergarten teacher, Jodi Felkins. I couldn't stand the thought of her and the children in Haley's class hearing about the situation through impersonal newspaper or television coverage. We didn't know how much news had already broken overnight, and I hoped that I could alleviate some of the shock by delivering the story in person. Thankfully, Jodi hadn't heard yet and was willing to immediately get on the phone to call Washington Elementary's principal, Ashley Garcia. News of the situation spread rapidly, and by the time school started that Monday morning, the faculty and staff were ready to handle questions and requests from children, parents, media, and the community at large.

With the rising sun, my ability to smile came back. More and more friends were arriving and Colleen Nick had established a method of communication between the cabin and the command center. With daylight, I renewed my vow to keep a strong face and remain absolutely hopeful in front of the people who love Haley. I knew with every new face that arrived, people were expecting to find us in pieces, but I felt that if I gave in to my grief and fear, it would be a domino effect to pull down everyone around us. I wanted the atmosphere to remain positive and full of faith in Haley's intelligence and strength, faith in the hundreds who were continuing to arrive to find her, and faith that God would watch over her, giving her what she would need to survive.

The one thing that made Tim's cabin perfect for our family and friends was also the thing that made it the most difficult. Even though Colleen and her colleague, Chip, had worked out a way to act as an information liaison between the search effort command center and the cabin, the time between phoned or personal updates often spanned hours. We had excellent communication with the outside world—phone, fax, and e-mail—and yet, it seemed as if we barely knew how things were proceeding at "ground zero" and out in the woods. The seclusion of the cabin had a huge impact on keeping us all as upbeat as possible, but we also longed to see first-hand what efforts were taking place on Haley's behalf. We knew instinctively, however, that getting into the middle of the search and rescue scene would only cause commotion for the volunteers, extra work for the commanders, and a certain media frenzy. And, I personally knew that if I wandered into the mix and saw for myself the magnitude of it all, my resolve would break.

As the morning wore on, dozens of our friends began arriving at the cabin. Some of them had already been searching for hours. I'll never forget how miserable Haley's "Uncles" Ray Dunwoodie and David Dubriske looked when they came in for a rest. In addition to their own grief surrounding Haley's disappearance, the two of them were suffering from extreme allergies from all of the pollen that covered the woods. Ray, with eyes nearly swollen closed, showed me the caked-on pollen that covered his socks; I've never seen anything like it and could easily imagine what effect that must be having on searchers. They, and others equally devoted to covering every square inch of that forest, would flop down for a quick rest and a drink, then would return to the command center to receive another search assignment. James Graves, another close friend of the family, told us later that he kept pushing himself to look more, hike farther and ignore his own exhaustion and pain because he continuously reminded himself that Haley didn't have the benefit of resting in a comfortable cabin to refuel.

The flow of people in and out of Tim's cabin was constant, and with almost everyone came this expression of uncertainty as to whether or not they should be "bothering" us. Frankly, the sheer numbers of people coming and going was a welcome distraction; seeing the faces of those we love and trust was completely therapeutic. I don't claim to have had any real prior knowledge about grief or dealing with a life-changing crisis, but I do know that in our situation, seeing our friends and family was the best thing for us. It was almost as if the horror of the situation could be disbursed somewhat if we all shared it.

As we sat and waited, one of the healthiest things we did was to laugh and share stories about Haley's exploits. While on one hand I feared that it would seem that I wasn't taking her situation seriously enough. Yet I was convinced that laughter and positive energy would go much further toward her recovery than falling into deeper sadness. Haley is such a happy little girl, often displaying a silly and irreverent sense of humor. I knew she deserved for us to channel our thoughts in that direction; I refused to think fatalistically during those daylight hours, and I didn't want to see that from anyone else.

Thankfully, everyone tried to maintain a similar attitude. But as hard as we all tried to keep our chins up, the pressure would occasionally get to each of us. Zega was clearly miserable. He would gaze into space, sometimes crumpling into tears and sobs. He eventually took a walk with friend John Goodwin to clear his head. Zega told me that he was going to get some fresh air for a few minutes, a short time that turned into a couple of hours, as he and John returned to the trail area where Haley was last seen.

While he was gone, I observed a few of my dearest friends. Angie Graves sat in the living room nearly the entire time, keeping a firmly positive expression on her face. I knew she had to be worn out—I think she and James slept in their vehicle the night before—but she maintained an almost stoic calm. She didn't have to say much; just being a steady presence, almost always in my line of sight, was a blessing that lifted my spirits. Rebecca Wood used every bit of her strength to stay up-beat. I remember her pulling me aside at one point, during a quiet moment, taking both of my hands in hers while we sat facing each other. She told me to visualize Haley, and together we would send her good, hopeful thoughts to signal to her that we were looking for her and that help was on its way. But then, the pressure would be too much at times, and Rebecca would step away to the back porch to look out over the river valley and collect her thoughts. Peggy Sue Osing was also around all the time, ready at a moment to give warm hugs and pray hard.

Peggy Sue's little Adam, Haley's "betrothed" since age three, and Rebecca's three-year-old Maggie Jane, the original president of the "Haley Zega Fan Club," were in my thoughts constantly—as were Haley's best friends, Elizabeth Carter, Haley McCarver, Laura Lee and Mary Elizabeth Goodwin, and classmate Natalie Shepperd. Everyone seemed reluctant to talk about their children, as if discussing them would be painful for me. I was actually surprised myself by the fact that the thought of other little ones safe at home or in school was not hard for me. Quite the contrary—I wanted to envision those other sweet, familiar faces and gain strength from knowing that they were secure. Thinking of those children going on with their lives made it so much easier for me to see Haley doing the same thing. I actually longed to have a child nearby—to hear irresistible giggles. The next best thing was Aspen, Tim's own friendly, dedicated Superdog. I'm surprised we didn't wear his fur off with all the attention and affection we gave him.

Throughout the day, the secondary mission of my friends and family seemed to be to get me to eat. Despite my attempts at a brave exterior, my stomach wasn't fooling anyone. Everything I tried tasted like cardboard and took every ounce of my effort to swallow. I nibbled here and there, just to satisfy everyone, but I was constantly afraid that the next bite would bounce back. Donated food began coming in—pizza, chips, meat trays, and bags and bags of fast food breakfast sandwiches. Everything I looked at made me nauseous. Water was the only thing that sounded good.

Other necessity items started to arrive, namely, toothbrushes and underwear. Everyone in the house had discovered that a person can continue living fairly comfortably with unwashed hair and clothes, but un-brushed teeth and dirty undergarments might be asking too much. The office manager and paralegal for Zega's office, Barbara Lane, was a saint, bringing us bags full of toothbrushes, men's boxers, and white cotton briefs. Men and women alike delved into the supply, and a lively discussion amongst the females donning new men's briefs revealed a resounding approval for their comfort.

Though we all sought those moments of levity, the mood invariably would return to worry, concern, and fierce concentration on the positive thoughts and prayers that would bring Haley back. We prayed not just for Haley and our hope that she wasn't suffering or terrified, but also for the hundreds and hundreds of people who had ventured into the forest to find her. I began to think about the fact that time had taken on a whole new meaning. Every minute felt like an excruciating hour, yet time was passing too quickly toward darkness. As we headed into the evening hours of that second day, our hearts felt sick.

I couldn't stand the thought of Haley being cold for another night, but worse, I couldn't imagine her state of mind. As time wore on, the determined efforts to keep the mood positive became more and more difficult. Scores of our friends came and went from the cabin, all with grim expressions that spoke of how hard they were trying to keep a brave face for my family's benefit.

I, however, had a major task at hand to keep my mind busy. In the late afternoon or early evening, my mom asked me if we would consider the idea of offering a reward for Haley's safe return. We had all begun to further explore the notion that Haley might have been abducted; after all, the woods had been combed to such a degree, it was hard to imagine that she wouldn't have been found yet. Friends of my parents had rallied around them—not just with emotional and physical support, but with financial commitment, as well. In a matter of moments, they had tens of thousands of dollars pledged on Haley's behalf, ready to offer to whomever would be willing to return her to our family. We decided together, as a family, that a reward for Haley was the proper next step. I threw myself into the details.

For several hours that second night, I made phone calls back to Fayetteville. I worked to find a bank to handle the establishment of an account for transfers of funds for Haley. I then called Clay and Sandy Edwards, leaders in the University of Arkansas' fund-raising efforts, to see if we could have the University's development office handle incoming calls regarding the reward fund, and help us track where gifts would be coming from so that we could properly acknowledge them. I kept thinking how lucky I was to know competent, professional people firsthand who could help so immediately and make crucial decisions that might impact Haley's return, that is, if someone who could be influenced by money possibly had her. I spent what seemed like forever e-mailing friends to tell them about the reward fund, asking them to forward the information to anyone they could.

Meanwhile, Rebecca was busily working with Colleen to craft exactly the right news release to announce our fund-raising effort. The process of publicizing the reward was tricky and involved a number of decisions that we wouldn't have been equipped to handle correctly without Colleen's guidance. The expertise and connections she and Rebecca pooled together resulted in a very strong message distributed to the media in a matter of moments. The next morning saw phones at the University of Arkansas' development office and at the Bank of Fayetteville ringing off the hook with transfers of funds to Haley's rescue account. Since that time, people have told me of the consolation that fund gave them—the fact that it offered a way for them to physically do *something* in the midst of their overwhelming feelings of helplessness. It was a major blessing to have the talent, brains, and resources right there at our fingertips. I've marveled before and since at the caliber of our friends and family—they're not just people with phenomenal character, but also individuals with incredible skills. I'd hold the combined group of us up against *any* team of problem solvers *any*where.

The hours ticked on, and I kept looking for ways to keep myself sane. Over the previous day and a half, I had amassed a major pile of paper scraps with names, numbers, and e-mail addresses for everyone from friends and relatives to volunteers and psychics/intuitives. I decided to compile everything into one huge, single list so that we weren't all constantly digging and hunting for information. This job kept me focused and proved to be one of the smartest things we did. It was a small illustration of the far-reaching and mind boggling impact of the whole scenario.

Many of the dozens of friends who had come to the cabin to rest up that evening began heading back home to their own children and other pressing responsibilities. Most were returning so that they could make longer-term arrangements to be back in Newton County by morning, and stay for as long as was needed. Two friends, Karen Boston and Karen Gartside, offered to stay at our house in Fayetteville overnight and through the next day, as well as find other volunteers to do the same. I couldn't believe how they were clearing out their schedules to be there to answer our phone and keep the house secure. I was so happy to think that our friends would be there to take calls—just in case Haley somehow called the one phone number she knew. In a very short time, Karen had arranged for a number of women to do a shift, several of which were members of the Northwest Arkansas Junior League with me. I couldn't get over the fact that the very organization I had joined to offer my own efforts for community service was coming to my family's assistance. I was honored.

Yet, those late Monday night and early Tuesday morning hours of darkness were horrific. Sometime well before dawn, I got up to wander the cabin, and just broke down. I had asked Zega how long a person could survive without water, and his answer tore at my soul. I couldn't imagine how Haley might be suffering and was terrified that she was thinking that no one was searching for her, that she'd been abandoned. That blankie and thumb of hers kept running through my head, and how once she'd told me that she had wanted so badly to suck her thumb at some point and couldn't because she didn't have her blankie to wrap around her fingers and rub against her chin. How in the world could she comfort herself now? I cried in a way that I never have before, feeling a physical pain in my heart that was so real, I didn't know if I would ever again take a deep breath. Zega did everything he could to comfort me as I tried to be quieter in expressing my grief. I didn't want everyone else in the cabin to hear me, but it was impossible to cover up those ripping sobs. I told him that if we didn't leave with Haley, I was never going back to our home again. I could not envision stepping into my cozy Fayetteville house and walking through rooms filled with Haley's art and photographs—seeing her toys scattered about—hearing her kitties calling for her—looking at the mass of pink dresses hanging in her closet. I couldn't do it. If my life had to continue without Haley, the only future I could fathom was one sterilely rebuilt from scratch.

Somehow, daylight came again. Along with that came the necessity to face some facts. We were going to have to speak to the media, and even worse, we were going to need to meet with the search and rescue commanders to find out the level at which the search could continue. Colleen arranged for the commanders to come to the cabin to meet with us privately and speak heart to heart. We all went into the downstairs area of Tim's home to hear the news. Honestly, what I feared would be said did not come to pass. I was terrified that we would be told that resources were running out and that there was little chance that Haley would still be out there alive. I had a rush of thoughts as I prepared for our meeting. How would I keep the search going if they weren't willing to continue? Where would I go to start looking on my own? And how could I possibly manage to do what hundreds and hundreds of able-bodied individuals hadn't? Yet, what we were told was quite different. We were briefed on what had already taken place, then told that no one was giving up. However, we learned that the scale and method of the search could not continue as it had up to that point. The command team had made the decision to eliminate all untrained volunteer searchers by later that night, and they would begin using only specifically trained search and rescue individuals. Furthermore, if individuals not cleared to search were found after a specified hour, they would run the risk of being arrested. The news struck me as good and bad. I had to face the notion that this could not go on forever, but I was temporarily renewed by the obvious continuation of hope on the part of those men.

Once we were briefed, Colleen sat down with us to make arrangements for the inevitable news conference. She stressed to us the importance of speaking publicly to get the word out about the reward fund for Haley, as well as to appeal to any individual who might have her. Colleen helped us create our roles: Zega would be the one to thank the innumerable volunteers, as well as the employers and businesses that gave resources and people to help; my job was to make the emotional appeal. Colleen knew from her own personal struggles with handling media when Morgan was missing that mommas have a way of saying what needs to be said to best pull misguided hearts in life-saving directions. She told me that she and everyone else knew that I had tried to be tough and brave up to this point; but for the conference, it all needed to go out the window. Colleen promised that it was all right—even preferable—for me to cry, and that I should try to speak of things that described Haley's importance to us in very personal ways. I knew she was right and was almost thankful for permission to mourn Haley's disappearance openly.

We sat around for a bit more, and then Tim loaded us up to deliver us to the hunting cabin that would house the news conference. It was a somber ride as we passed scores of volunteer searchers on our way. We got a bit turned around a couple of times, but finally made it. As we got out of the truck, I made note of how unbelievably quiet it was. Colleen was there to meet us, greeted us with hugs, and then held our hands in solidarity as we walked several yards to the cabin. Camera operators ran in front of us, photographing every step. The only sound I remember was that of clicking shutters; no one spoke. We entered the tiny front room, winding our way to a couch as we stepped around video cameras, reporters, and the sparse furniture. I tried to look at each person in the eye to somehow convey to everyone how thankful we were for the courtesy they had shown by giving us privacy up to that point. Zega and I took deep breaths and then began our statements.

He thanked those who needed to be thanked beautifully and eloquently. As he neared the end of his statement, he began to falter and shake with tears. I took over, saying words that needed no rehearsal. I started out pretty strong, but as I began to describe Haley—her sweetness and tenderness— how much she means to us—I began to cry. My wish was to hold my face in my hands, but I forced myself to keep my head up and continue talking in what I hoped wouldn't be unintelligible words. I showed everyone her blankie and tried to describe how much she needed it. Then I told the world that Zega and I would give up everything we had to have her back in our arms, that she was the single most important thing in our lives; and that it didn't matter why someone might have her or how we had to get her back. I pleaded for my baby's life in hopes that someone would hear me and know that her only place was with us. Zega buried his face in my shoulder, and thousands of Arkansans watched us painfully express how much we loved our child.

179

Haley Zega Falls

As soon as the news conference began, it ended, and we were being escorted back to Tim's truck. No questions were asked, and I was stunned to see tears on nearly every seasoned reporter's face. I knew we had done the right thing, no matter how hard it was.

As we drove back to the cabin, I felt like a weight had come off of my shoulders. We had finally taken an active role in Haley's recovery, and I felt good about it. Tim, Zega, and I made small talk about the area, some of the local volunteers, and then Tim told us something amazing. He said that he'd made a decision that no matter what happened, he was going to officially name the waterfall near where Haley was lost "Haley Zega Falls." I began smiling through happy tears and was momentarily speechless. I couldn't believe that this man, who had already given us every aid and comfort, was going to honor our child—a little girl he'd never met—by naming a beautiful, symbolic place for her. Though I still sensed that Haley was still out there, knowing that such testament would keep her name alive forever was an incredible and comforting feeling. Zega and I both thanked him, looking at each other as we wondered how in the world this amazing man had entered our lives.

We returned to Tim's cabin, still full to the brim with our friends. Since we had been gone, more food and supplies had arrived. I wanted us to get things better organized so that maybe the cabin would not be in such disarray. We all puttered around, answering phones, putting things away and trying to maintain that grim determination we had all become so familiar with.

The phone rang, and while I usually rushed to grab it on the first or second ring, Tim was nearest and picked it up. I could immediately tell that he was hearing something important. Tim motioned for me to come out onto the front porch. I held my breath. He didn't look upset, but he didn't look particularly happy, either. I stepped outside and time stood still as he told me that someone (who I found out later was Kelly Carter) had just called to say that it had been reported on the local TV news that Haley had been found alive, and wanted to ask if it were true! Tim quickly said that we couldn't be sure what to think yet, but that we had better check it out. I drew in a long, ragged breath and then asked how we could get in touch with the command center. We had been told that the number we had been using wasn't good anymore. My mind raced, while my body felt like it was moving in slow motion. As we began discussing what to do next—and how we didn't need to jump to conclusions—we could see a truck coming down the hill to the cabin.

We watched quietly as Washington County Sheriff Steve Whitmill and Zega's National Guard Chaplain Wes Hilliard climbed out of the truck. They began walking toward us with serious, but not sad faces. Sheriff Whitmill calmly told the gathering crowd that they had found a little girl who was looking for her mommy and daddy. A huge, joyous sound went up from the dozens of people standing outside—a sound of immediate and intense celebration, and the best sound I've ever heard next to the voice of my recovered child. Zega and I ran and nearly tackled the Sheriff. I knocked my cheekbone into his elbow, something I didn't remember until the next day when a mysterious bruise appeared. He laughed, telling Zega that he had promised they would find her. We couldn't have been happier with who got to tell us that news.

We immediately jumped into the truck, when suddenly I realized I was missing something. Everyone looked at me like I'd finally come unhinged when I sprinted back into the cabin and began running everywhere. I knew I had to find Haley's Stripey Blankie and deliver it to her hands as soon as I got my first hug. Because we had been picking things up, I couldn't figure out where it had gone. I started getting frustrated as I was thinking that all those screaming people should be helping me look! Finally I spotted it, grabbed it and ran back to the truck. We roared off, screaming out the windows to searchers along the road that Haley had been found! I found myself laughing out loud and breathing huge, gulping breaths. I was about to see my heart and soul!

With a huge cloud of dust behind us, we jumped from the truck as soon as we reached the waiting ambulance. We still didn't know Haley's condition and prayed that she wasn't too injured or unresponsive. I saw countless more friends in the immediate area, but didn't take any time to greet them. In seconds we rushed to the back of the ambulance, where an EMT quickly helped me up to Haley's stretcher. What I found surpassed every prayer and hope I had for her after all she had been through. I saw my beautiful, brave daughter curled up, safe and sound. Her face was thinner than what I knew it should be, and her bright blue eyes seemed bigger than usual despite their obvious exhaustion. She was covered in minor scratches, bug bites, and had a bump on her forehead, but had no broken bones or anything else that appeared serious. Haley was very quiet, but as I climbed nearly on top of her, she told me she was OK. As I hovered over her and put her blankie into her hands, my impulse was to crush her to me—to somehow pull her back into my own body so that she could never be lost again without me. I knew, though, that she had to be sore, so I forced myself to be gentle. Zega thanked the people around the ambulance, including rescuers Lytle James and William Jeff Villines. Then after the two of us loaded up, the ambulance began its trip to the North Arkansas Medical Center in Harrison, and we began repeating our mantra of "I love you" to a sleepy Haley. The pain was finally over, and our time to give prayers of thanks had just begun.

There's still not a day that we forget to offer up those same prayers— words spoken to praise Haley's safe return, for the thousands of people who prayed for us, for the volunteers who searched beyond exhaustion, for our friends and family, for the kindness of strangers, and for an event in our lives that gave new meaning to the power of love and hope. And, we give thanks for the fact that Haley gets up every day still with the mind and heart of a happy, innocent child—a normal, healthy little girl unscathed by trauma. Perhaps that's the biggest blessing of all.

—Kelly Zega

Steve, Haley, & Kelly

Chapter 14
THE MEDIA

The media coverage of this event was simply incredible, from the very first reports that started to air on Monday morning, to live coverage throughout the entire ordeal, to the follow-up articles and TV coverage that continued long after Haley was rescued. The Morgan Nick Alert that went out was carried by every media outlet immediately. There were many TV stations from around the region on-site, most of them giving live reports during each newscast; newspaper reporters and photographers sending off digital images from the scene; and radio broadcasts talking about the story all day—one station even reading the *Cloudland Journal* live on the air with my reports of the mood of the family. Everyone in the region knew about Haley Zega by Monday evening. The media not only gave updates, but helped spread the word of the need for volunteers and supplies—and for untrained folks to stay away once the woods were filled to capacity. The media no doubt had a hand in finding Haley alive and well.

I tried to obtain and read every single newspaper article and watch tape of all television reports from area stations when doing the research for this book. I must say that I had to wipe tears away many times while doing this. The plight of this little girl and her family and friends and volunteers, the outpouring of support from the community, and the remarkable search efforts that went on to find her, were all well documented. Huddled at my cabin most of the time with Steve and Kelly (out of ear and eye shot of the news media), I had no idea that the eyes of the world were focused on our little wilderness backyard.

SAR officials appointed Press Information Officers (PIO) early on to give regular updates and keep the media informed. Kevin Thomas from the Arkansas Game and Fish Commission and Randall Dias from Arkansas State Police briefed the media and took them on field trips into the search area.

The first newspaper article came out in *The Morning News* on Monday morning. It was a front page story that set the scene, complete with a photo from the command center. (Most other Monday papers had already been printed Sunday night before the news broke.) Radio stations and television stations reported the news during the morning and noontime programs. The 5 o'clock television broadcasts began to air extensive reports. By this time several satellite TV trucks had gathered in Boxley Valley, and reports were going out live to concerned residents across the six-state region.

The steep and rough Cave Mountain Road from Boxley Valley up to the command center kept the television satellite trucks down in the valley. It was a bit awkward because the reporters and photographers had to gather their information up on the mountain, then drive 30 minutes down to their trucks in order to file the story. Only one satellite truck ever made it up to the search area, but not until Tuesday afternoon.

Those reports on Monday included Haley's picture and description along with a phone number for anyone to call with information. It was also aired that anyone hiking, camping, or canoeing in the area over the weekend who had seen Haley, contact the State Police. Calls for food and water for the volunteers went out. Fayetteville television station *KFAA 51* even collected a ton of supplies and sent them to the staging area.

One thing I noticed from the television tapes that I watched was that the reporters in the field and the anchors on the air were thanking the volunteers, officials, and the community at large over and over again. This sentiment was universal. Even though they were professionals, it was obvious that this story was touching them deep inside—there was more than one long face looking into the TV cameras.

By the 10 o'clock news on Monday night, it was being reported that the area was being overrun with well-meaning volunteers, and that they no longer needed or wanted untrained folks to come to the search area. "We don't want to end up rescuing the rescuers or searching for the searchers" was the mantra from the command center.

Tuesday morning brought more grim faces on the air, pleas for untrained volunteers to stay away, and more detailed newspaper stories with maps and photographs of the search efforts. Most of the media outlets used the same photo of Haley. That snapshot—actually a wallet photo pulled from Kelly's purse—would become the image of Haley that everyone connected with.

From the very beginning, the SAR folks kept the media away from Steve and Kelly and from our cabin. Most everyone honored this request, although there were two reporters who tried to sneak into the cabin. They were quickly turned back by our crack security staff (consisting of whomever happened to be standing at the front door). Other than those two, I thought the media handled themselves with a great deal of class. In fact, the only other media folks I saw (other than at the press conference) were friends of the Zegas plus one photographer who appeared at my office looking for a power outlet to recharge his camera batteries.

The only report that ever made it out to the press from the family headquarters (other than my *Cloudland Journal* updates) was the telephone interview that I did with Kelly Kemp on her noon show on *KFSM TV5* from Fayetteville.

On Tuesday afternoon Steve and Kelly had decided that they wanted to make a statement to the press, and so that was set up in a remote and tiny hunting cabin located several miles from our cabin. I must re-state how incredible the press was during that most difficult time for Steve and Kelly. I don't know how in the world the reporters and photographers kept from breaking down while listening to Steve and Kelly's statements, or shouting out questions to them like the media has been known to do. The media conducted themselves with a great deal of dignity and class, and I know the Zegas were extremely thankful for that.

One of the television reporters who was on the scene the entire time talked a little bit about the emotional part of it all from her perspective:

As a journalist, we know to remain impartial while covering stories. There is simply no possible way any journalist with a heart could not get involved in the search for Haley Zega.

When I came to work and found that my assignment was in Newton County and that a six-year-old Fayetteville girl turned up missing after hiking with her grandparents, my heart immediately went out to the parents. In fact, on the drive over, the first phone call I made was to my church, Christian Life Cathedral. I asked the office crew to spread the word that this family needed our prayers. Then I started calling sheriff's departments and getting any possible information on my assignment.

After our six mile trek up the mountain to the command post, I was amazed at all the searchers who had already heard the news and were on the scene to do whatever they could. During the two days that we were stationed on the search story in Newton County, we got one hour of sleep. We were working the rest of the time. We wrapped up our first night at 2 a.m. I sympathized with my sleep-deprived photographer, but all I wanted to do was go search the wilderness in the darkness for Haley. Pure adrenaline was driving me.

The next afternoon, the Zegas held their press conference. All of the media on the scene went into this tiny cabin. We set up our cameras and waited for Steve and Kelly to arrive. When they did, no one said a word. Haley's parents sat on a sofa; Kelly was clutching her daughter's favorite blanket. When the couple started speaking to us about their lost daughter, tears began to roll. As I looked around the room at my colleagues, there was not a dry eye in the house. I had a lump in my throat as I listened to these parents with desperation in their voices. It was one word from Kelly Zega that stood out most for me. At one point in the interview, I heard her say, "Our daughter was precious." That is when tears started streaming down my face. I thought, "Oh my God, she used the word *was*." They've given up hope and they don't even realize it.

I've done several stories that have stayed with me emotionally, but none will ever touch my heart the way the search for Haley Zega did. It's not often that we as journalists get a story with an ending like this one!

—Rhonda Justice, *KFAA Arkansas' NBC* (Fayetteville)

It was shortly after that press conference that Haley was found and delivered to the command center. The one television station that had managed to get their satellite truck up to the staging area was *KY3* from Springfield, Missouri. Like everyone else, they had been doing their live reports from Boxley Valley, but their 5 o'clock broadcast was live and direct from the staging area, with helicopters landing and taking off in the background.

The *KY3* reporter was Dennis Graves, whom I have known for a long time. He is an avid hiker and outdoorsman, and was the perfect personality to be reporting on this event. He had hiked the trails in the area many times, often with television camera in hand. In fact, when he hiked the entire length of the Buffalo River Trail one fall he did three live reports from the trail each day! Little did I know it at the time, but my wife Pam first heard the good news about Haley from Dennis—she had just returned from work to her home near Springfield and turned on the TV—she knew about Haley's rescue before I did. Dennis had heard the screams of joy from the command center, got the sketchy details that Haley had been found alive, and broke back into his station's broadcast to tell everyone the good news—he was still standing in front of the helicopters.

Journalists deal with so much ugliness, so much tragedy, day in and day out. It piles up. Thirty-five years of bad news had scarred my spirit. Like the hundreds of volunteers searching for Haley, I had prepared myself emotionally for more bad news. What a wonderful ending to a potentially tragic story. Boy, my soul sure needed a victory!

—Dennis Graves, *KY3 TV*, Springfield

Other television stations called in the report and were able to get the good news on the air before ending their own 5 o'clock broadcasts. It was one of these reports that prompted the call to me at the cabin with the good news, which I passed on to Kelly and to a cabin filled with stunned and grateful family, friends, and volunteers.

There were many tears shed in front of television cameras on Tuesday night, both with that tiny bit of news at 5:25 p.m., and again at 6 o'clock, when a more thorough report could be aired. In fact, it seemed that some of the veteran broadcasters were the most emotional—how could they not be!

The SAR folks did a great job of securing a buffer zone around the ambulance for Haley's return at the command center, but did leave enough room for television coverage of her being carried and placed into the ambulance, and of her anxious parents running to grab her—that little bit of video opened the flood gates of emotion for all who watched.

There were lengthy television reports at 10 p.m. (including interviews with Lytle and William Jeff plus Steve and Kelly). The coverage continued with the early morning news on Wednesday, the noon news, the 5 o'clock, 6 o'clock, 10 o'clock news—Haley was the lead story over and over again.

Steve and Kelly sent word out through the media that folks wishing to contribute gifts or cash should direct them to The Morgan Nick Foundation, and that info was given out on the air. (Haley would be showered with gifts from well wishers.)

The national media got involved early Wednesday, as the Zegas appeared on *The Today Show* and *CBS's This Morning* from the hospital in Harrison. This would be just the beginning of the onslaught of media requests—the world wanted to see this precious miracle child and the heroes who found her.

The television cameras were there for Haley's departure from the hospital in Harrison, at their home in Fayetteville when they arrived, and at her school when Steve and Kelly walked her back to school for the first time. This turned out to be one of the best news stories that had ever been told, and no one wanted to let it go.

When I awoke on Wednesday morning and turned on the radio for the first time since the saga began, I heard one of the most popular, veteran radio personalities talking about Haley (the "Rotund One" from *Magic 107.9* in Fayetteville). He talked about how the community had come together for her, and how it was such a great story for him to have had the privilege to report. I asked him to write down a few thoughts for this book:

I've been a broadcaster for almost 27 years...in a number of towns and cities across this great land. And, candidly speaking, I have a tendency to be a little jaded. Day after day while I've hosted morning radio shows, I've had to hear and endure sundry tales of death from car accidents, shootings, and such. Don't get me wrong, I love my job. But when you work for a radio station like *Magic 107.9 KEZA* in Fayetteville, whose broadcast signal is so large and with such a large cross section of listeners from every walk of life, I know that every one of these horrific stories is going to somehow touch the life of at least one of our listeners. Most times, they hear the news and go on about their morning routine. But sometimes, they'll call, as if to confirm tragic news they can't fathom and need me to confirm their worst fears. That's when I hate my job.

So it was when Haley Zega disappeared. Friends and neighbors calling to question, "who are her parents?" "My son goes to school with her." It is then I know I can say nothing to quell their fears. I leave the dispensation of information up to the professionals in our news department. I don't dare speculate. I won't give false hope. There is no need for me to discuss her disappearance. Her story is on the mind of everyone in our community. I feel, in times like these, it is my role to make sure we get on with the everyday things with which we need to deal, to stay focused on getting through the day. You already have your private thoughts, theories, and fears. You don't need to be burdened with mine.

I was sitting in my recliner in my living room in Fayetteville with my four-year-old son Zyggy napping in his mom's chair when I heard the news that Haley had been found, safe and relatively well considering her ordeal. I felt like an anvil had been lifted from my chest. I felt the collective sigh of relief from everyone in Northwest Arkansas. And this longtime, jaded broadcaster shed tears of joy that Haley was safe with her family...and that my son was safe with me. And I'm grateful I've had an opportunity to spend so much time in a community that, in times of crisis, looks out for each other. I'm thankful I would be on the end of another kind of telephone call the next morning when we'd have the opportunity to spread some wonderful news for a change.

—Chip Arledge, "The Rotund One", *Magic 107.9 KEZA*

I later learned that Al "Papa Rap" Lopez, an announcer for Spanish radio station *La Bonita, 1590 KZRA*, had followed the search on the air from the moment Haley was reported missing. "We were talking about it on the radio, trying to educate Lationos to be careful out there with their children," Lopez said. "If it happened to a person who has always lived here, imagine what could happen for those who just moved here."

The Zegas got a flood of requests from all corners of the country and all types of media. They patiently honored most of them that were within reason, including a segment on *Inside Edition*, and articles for *Women's World* and the *National Guard* magazine.

A call from *Dateline NBC* producer Carol Gable began a lengthy relationship that would culminate with a major national network program to air in the fall of 2001 (they were also approached by *20/20*, but opted for *Dateline* instead). Because of the sheer length of the *Dateline* broadcast, and the fact that the crew spent a week in Arkansas filming (and no telling how many weeks doing research), this one show would prove to be the most complete story of all that would air on television.

A couple of days after Haley went home, Tony Owens from *KFAA* television in Fayetteville came out to our cabin to do a story on, well, *the cabin*, and what role it played in the event. Later Shannon James and John Young from *KTHV 11* television in Little Rock drove up and spent an entire day with me in the woods. I took them into Dug Hollow and to the Buffalo River, and we explored several possible cave locations where Haley might have spent her second night. I was surprised that these two city folks not only survived the trip themselves (carrying a great deal of heavy camera equipment), but actually did quite well on the trip. It turned out to be a great story.

There were a dozen newspaper reporters that did telephone interviews with me in the days following Haley's rescue. Most of them just wanted to know what it was like being at ground zero during the ordeal and how I felt now that all the crowds were gone.

I have heard a bit of criticism about the accuracy of media reports and stories that aired during the search for Haley. It is true that there was a great deal of misinformation given out, but it seemed to be simply a matter of the media picking up bits and pieces of information from folks coming out of the woods, which was repeated and broadcast. Heck, even the official spokesmen were giving out incorrect information some of the time (they were merely passing on information that they thought was correct). In the final analysis, few folks ever knew if the information was precise or not, nor really cared.

It is interesting how some of this information got skewed though, and not too difficult to figure out. Take the name of the trail for example. It was widely reported that Haley was lost on the "Double Falls Trail." Well, there is no such trail. She was actually on the Hawksbill Crag Trail. Early on it was noted that the group had been on the "trail to that double falls." The waterfall near where Haley had last been seen did not have a name (now it is called Haley Falls, of course). Many folks referred to it as a "double" falls because it has two different drops—the upper drop that Haley had wanted to see up close and the lower drop. Soon the world was hearing of this "new" hiking trail in the Ozarks, which was a bit confusing to those who knew the area so well.

When Lytle and William Jeff emerged from the wilderness with Haley in hand, they came out onto Cave Mountain Road near Bat Cave. This is where they turned her over to friends who then drove her up to the command center and the waiting ambulance. When they encountered Roger Atkinson from the Forest Service along the way, he radioed back to the command center that Haley had been found. He also gave them his position, which was on the road near Bat Cave. This radio transmission was being monitored by the media. The first reports that went out over the air were that Haley had been found alive and unhurt—absolutely true—but that she had been found "walking down the road near Bat Cave by a forest ranger." One TV report showed an elated official in uniform at the command center confirming this on the air. Had someone not convinced Lytle and William Jeff to go to the command center themselves with the real story, it would have been quite a while before the truth was known.

Knowing how things can get twisted, especially when emotions are soaring, I was hesitant to tell Steve and Kelly about the initial TV reports that were being aired about Haley being found alive. That is why I prepped Kelly with, "this is an *unconfirmed* report," when I told her the good news after it had been reported on TV. Thank goodness that confirmation was only two minutes away, or we all would have gone nuts.

My bottom line thoughts about the media and their coverage of this event are as follows. First off, it was obvious that they pulled out all the stops to send reporters and television crews out into the wilderness—often at great expense—and they committed whatever time or space was necessary to tell the story. Secondly, the reporters not only were there to cover the event and report the facts, but also aided the search efforts a great deal by passing on critical information about the description of Haley along with the need for supplies for the searchers. Some members of the media even took off work and joined the search. And finally, it was clear to me that they went out of their way not only to be respectful of the family, but also to thank the community and volunteers for all of their efforts, both during the search and after the ordeal ended. The media reports spread the word and told the story that captivated the region for a week and brought everyone a little bit closer together. It would indeed have been a much different story, perhaps with a tragic ending, had the media not been involved. Our media people deserve a tremendous pat on the back for their dedicated, professional service.

Chapter 15
CLOUDLAND
JOURNAL

I really just wanted to see if I could write. Little did I know that thousands of folks from all corners would follow Haley's drama and be moved to tears from the *Cloudland Journal*. Several years ago I began writing a daily journal of life out here at the Cloudland Cabin. It started out as a notebook with blank paper for guests to register and leave comments. It quickly outgrew the hard copy and soon was being posted on my www.Cloudland.net web page. OK, I thought, I would write the journal for a year, then publish a book of the contents. When I tried to end the journal after that first year, a flood of e-mails from regular readers around the country convinced me to continue writing and posting.

It was never meant to be a literary work of art, in fact, the writing is rather raw, simple, and not edited before being posted online. Every now and then the words are spelled correctly! You can read about all sorts of things—from wilderness prose like how to identify bear scat (complete with close-up pictures), to stories of my broken heart when my date to my own New Year's Eve party stood me up. You can also see the changing of the colors in the fall, dogwoods blooming in springtime, unknown waterfalls all year long. And now you can follow along as my new daughter grows up and as I realize my dream of finding the perfect lifemate.

When Bob Chester first called to alert me to Haley's disappearance, I was at the computer writing the last entry in the third year of the Journal. I have not been able to stop writing it, nor have I had the time to publish the book that I started out to do—yet.

After helping out with the search efforts on the first day when Haley got lost, I returned to the computer late that Sunday night to file my report online. Steve and Kelly had arrived at the cabin, and we were all in sort of a daze, not knowing quite what to do. I managed to type for a few minutes and posted the following to the journal, which would turn out to be the first notice to many people that Haley had been lost:

4/29/01 Today began as a wonderful day with blue skies and birds singing and my wife and I on a hike, holding hands. The day has now turned to horror, and a potential tragedy. Shortly before noon, a six-year old girl who was hiking at Hawksbill Crag with her grandmother and friends got lost—it is now midnight, and she has not been seen since. As I sit here and type this there are nearly 100 brave and caring volunteers out in the woods continuing the search that has gone on since noon. I have never seen such an incredible display of caring in my entire life—there are four different sheriff departments, the state police, search and rescue teams from several counties, forest service & park service officials, game and fish commission officers, fire departments, as many as six teams of K-9 units, plus literally dozens and dozens and dozens of other volunteers all out here looking for this little girl. There have been two helicopters criss-crossing the area—they even flew for several hours after dark, and may take off and continue at any minute.

The little girl's parents are here at my cabin now, trying to cope with it all, and it is just so sad. Their daughter quite literally just disappeared, and the search began within minutes, but no trace has been found.

This precious child needs a prayer from you right now. I know she is out there somewhere, wrapped around a tree and scared to death and shivering, and counting the seconds until first light. It is not too chilly tonight, and if she is not seriously injured she has a good chance of making it through the night and being found alive and OK. But she needs your help. And while you are at it, please add a bit in there for all of the volunteers who are giving so much of themselves for someone they have never met—their very lives are in danger out there in the dark. Thank you!

We had asked that the press be kept away from the cabin to give the family some privacy (and to reduce the traffic coming down our narrow gravel driveway). The only way for information to get out about what was going on at the cabin would come from the *Journal.* However, I wanted to protect the privacy of the Zega family too, so I kept my reports short and tried not to relate the many private things that were taking place. The computer and both phone lines were kept pretty busy anyway, and I really didn't want to interfere with what was going on. I also didn't take many pictures—who wants a camera pointed at you as tears are streaming down your face? No, there would be no pictures of the horror that the Zegas were experiencing.

I was able to sit down for a few minutes on Monday and post the following:

4/30/01 It was a very long, or actually short, night for everyone involved. The traffic to and from the cabin was heavy, and not much sleep. We got a report that four of the search dogs all headed over the same spot in the bluffline on a hot trail—one of them quite literally over the bluff (he landed on a ledge below and is OK). The teams sent guys over the edge with ropes, and they worked the bluff all night. At first light the helicopters took to the air again, and ground teams were sent out. Other teams that had been working throughout the night returned without any good news. Steve and Kelly (the parents of the little girl) and close friends and family are back here at the cabin trying to keep away from the sea of concerned people up on the main road. It is a very difficult time for everyone.

At one point this morning one of the helicopters was working the bluffline right below the cabin. Most everyone at the cabin stood or sat on the back decks in silence with their attention glued to the plane. It was a very surreal experience to say the least.

So far no news at all this morning, but hopes are still high that Haley (the little girl) will appear with tears streaming down her face, a few scratches, and a cry for ice cream.

And later in the day I made another post:

4/30/01 Update. The long day continues. Hopes soar, then fall back again. No news. No news. No news. The last update that we got here at the cabin was that there were 120 searchers in the woods right now (probably more like 300), three helicopters, several dog teams. The search area has been expanded three times during the day. The national guard has been called out. The number of family and close friends of the family here at the cabin continues to rise, along with the support they are getting. The phone rings constantly, and we have been running back up to the office to scan photos of Haley, fax maps, etc. There has been a great deal of traffic to the cabin, although most has been stopped by the authorities. Several search teams have come by on their way into or out of the woods. Pizza just arrived from Jasper. Volunteers are working overtime. Law enforcement has been working overtime. I have heard there are satellite trucks lined up along the road in Boxley, and a great deal of press on the scene (they are being kept away from the cabin area). Lots of tears here, but still a great deal of hope for the young angel out there fighting for her life. At one point today we heard that a walking stick that Haley was using was found at a point that had already been searched yesterday—no new update on that.

The weather has been warm and windy. Those brave young men in their flying machines have been doing some incredible feats—much of it right before our very eyes out there in the wilderness. Searchers come out of the woods exhausted and sweat soaked and their clothes and skin all torn up, with long faces, yet full of hope that the next sweep will find a smiling little face.

There have been so many volunteers that there is an official sign-in sheet and waiting list for anyone who wants to help—there is a long line. We have heard that by tomorrow morning many of the volunteers will have had to return to town, so they will need a fresh supply. I still have not been to the command post, in fact have not been out of this immediate area except on foot.

Right now as I am typing this eight horses w/riders just emerged from the forest and are crossing Fox meadow, there are two four-wheelers in the driveway, and at least a dozen folks on foot are sweeping through within sight—and this is just one of many search teams on the ground right now. It is one monumental operation being conducted by the most wonderful people in the world. I am going to try to post a picture of Haley for those of you who have not seen one, and will post again when I get the time, and have something to say. Until then, keep those fingers crossed and prayers coming.

A radio station from Ft. Smith—*KISR*—found the *Journal* online and began to read it on the air. Fred Baker, the station manager and morning show host, read the posts word for word. A number of his listeners later wrote to tell me about it:

...I had no idea this wonderful land existed until the horrifying ordeal with young Haley. I heard about your web page from Fred Baker on KISR radio here in Ft. Smith. He was reading the journal of events surrounding the lost girl, and I was absolutely glued to my radio. I was on my way to work early in the morning and stayed out in my car (rather than going in) to listen to him. I was late for work, but went in with a new found happiness that rarely finds me so early in the day...

...I was just listening to KISR radio and Fred Baker read your journal on the air. Fred read it as he does so well. Tingles went up my spine as I heard about Haley. My wife and I said a prayer for her and her family. My daughter is her age, and I felt heartsick about the little girl lost. I am glad you are there to lend a hand!...

...BLESSINGS TO EVERYONE THERE! I have been listening to the local radio station KISR 93.7 out of Ft. Smith and would like to send my heartfelt prayers to everyone there who is helping in the search for Haley...and to the family and friends who are so concerned with her return.
MAY HER GUARDIAN ANGEL PROTECT AND KEEP HER SAFE!...

...Thank you for your journal and your updates about little Haley. KISR Radio Station here in Ft. Smith read your journal on the air for us. As a result many prayers went out...

By Tuesday morning there was a flood of e-mails coming in from concerned folks all over the place. The *Arkansas Democrat-Gazette* had listed the *Cloudland Journal* web site address in their main article about Haley, and a local television station that was using the *Journal* as a source gave out the web address—thousands of browsers dialed it up. Many of the e-mails offered support and prayers for the family—many times I passed e-mails around for all to see. Several of them brought us to tears. Here is the post from late morning on Tuesday:

5/1/01 My alarm this morning at first light was a helicopter right outside the bedroom window. The cabin was much quieter during the night than the night before, and I think some of the family members managed a couple hours of much-needed sleep, or at least rest.

Nothing new today. Still hundreds of volunteers and law enforcement and search and rescue people on the ground and in the air. I had to make a quick trip up to the command center at Cave Mountain Church and could not believe all of the activity there, and the hoards of folks. While I was there a helicopter took off shuttling a new search team down in to the canyon in front of the cabin—this team will begin there and sweep up Whitaker Creek all the way to the Hawksbill Crag Trailhead. One of dozens of sweep teams that will work today. There are quite a few mules and horses and four-wheelers at the camp that has been set up next to the mailboxes on the main road, plus food and porta potties and water—enough supplies to support a small city, which is what it has become up there.

Speaking of water, all of the activity at the cabin had drained the well (can't believe it lasted that long). But the national guard came to our rescue, and we were up there at the well location in the late night darkness filling the well with fresh water from one of their tankers. You just can't imagine how wonderful it is to be able to flush the toilet!

There continues to be dozens of folks at the cabin, plus many hoards more coming and going. At one point yesterday there were more than 100 people here at the same time. No end to the wonderful folks who have been asking "what can we do for you?" I keep telling them "truckloads of gravel to fix the road"—but so far, nothing. All of the traffic has really made my driveway a rough trip!

Media pleas for volunteer help and supplies have had quite an impact on everything, and in fact right now there are many more volunteers available than they need. (I just heard that they even put up roadblocks on the main road to keep excess folks out).

The family is holding up quite well, especially considering the terrible situation right now. They are moved and uplifted by the incredible amount of support out there by the searchers and the public at large, plus all of their friends and family who have been able to get through and down here to the cabin. It is obvious that Steve and Kelly Zega are made of some pretty tough material, and their attitude has been infectious to all. No doubt their precious daughter Haley is made of the same stuff, and is still out there holding on.

I might add that I have been flooded with e-mails from Cloudland Journal readers, and your thoughts and prayers for Haley and her family have brought warm feelings to them and smiles all around.

That's about it for now. I will make another post later today. The computer and internet access here has become a great tool for the family, and I am trying to keep out of their way and let them use whatever they need.

Before I made another post, Haley was rescued. In the pandemonium that followed, I was torn between wanting to be a part of the reunion at the command post and staying behind at the cabin to tell the world that she had been found. I choose the latter and put a simple post (in bold, flashing red letters) in the Journal and on the main Journal web page—**HALEY ZEGA IS FOUND ALIVE!** That was the only post I made until later in the evening—there was just so much to do, including saying goodbye to the many people with whom I had shared this ordeal. The phone lines were jammed for a while, but when things got quiet, I sat down and added a few details. The next day I made a brief post in the morning, but it wasn't until later in the day that I would write a lengthy report, which is included in the first five chapters of this book.

5/1/01 Update at 10 p.m.—Haley Zega is found alive! Wow, what a past couple of days we have had here at Cloudland. I will try to lay out a few of the details as I know them of the final hours of the search mission, and what happened here at the cabin. Later, I will make a more-detailed post.

This will be a two-part story. First off, let me tell you what happened at the cabin. It was just before 5:30 p.m., and the cabin was filled with folks as it had been all day. There were also a number of searchers outside milling around, all having just completed sweeps. The phone rang and I answered it. The person on the other end said that *TV 40/29* had just announced that Haley had been found alive. "What?" "WHAT!?" After quizzing the caller a bit more, I hung up the phone. I went to find Kelly (Haley's mom), and pulled her outside and away from the crowd. It was just the two of us out on the front porch. "Do you *know* anything?" She looked at me very puzzled. "No." "OK" I said, "now please know that this is strictly rumor, but it was just announced on TV that Haley has been found alive." Kelly gasped.

The next couple of minutes were a frantic attempt to find some way to communicate with the command center—their cell phone was not working, and no one around had a radio to contact anyone. We were all collectively holding our breaths and frustrated at the same time. Could this be true? Then a police vehicle pulled up. Kelly and Steve (Haley's dad) were together on the front porch, along with a growing crowd around them. The two officers got out and walked towards the cabin, both with frowns. "We've got a little girl up there who is looking for her mommy and daddy!"

The place erupted into an incredible blast of shouts—the loudest sound that I have ever heard here at the cabin. The officers talked with Kelly and Steve for a few moments and they all quickly loaded up in the vehicle and sped away towards the command center where Haley was. None of us at the cabin were told anything other than she had been found and was alive. I have been a part of many celebrations and moments of elation in my life before, but *nothing* to match the feeling of pure joy, relief, and utter euphoria as this.

I spoke with those who went with Haley to the hospital in Harrison and they told me that she was in fine shape.

It is getting late at the cabin now, and all of the volunteers and family have left. I may try to write about some of the last two days here later, but for now I would like to put things away and get some sleep. A few minutes ago I looked around the empty cabin—there was an emptiness in my heart since all of my new friends had gone home—most of whom I had never met before—but my spirits are soaring because of the life that continues to shine through little Haley.

This cabin is empty now, yet is filled with the sound of a child's laughter...

5/2/01 Some details of the past three days. There is a giant red ball hanging in a hazy sky in the east this morning—no helicopters for the first time in what seems like an eternity. The river far below is singing—or should I say whistling—and the tune is a happy one. This mighty wilderness swallowed up this precious child whole, then took care of her until she was ready to return to civilization. The radio just reported that Haley will be released from the hospital today after being treated for dehydration (she said that she did not drink any water during her ordeal). Otherwise, only a few scratches.

Chapter 15

It is hard not to dwell on the events of these past few days—they keep racing back and forth through my empty head. There were many things that went on here but were not written down—incredible feats of bravery and heroism by ordinary people (I mean *extraordinary* people!). Tender moments between husband and wife who at times were being held together only with scotch tape. Times of intense sorrow and crying. Very high frustration levels. And a great deal of hope—there was *always* a great deal of *hope*.

Here are a few more exerts from the over 500 e-mails that I received during the week of Haley's search:

...Thanks for the wonderful coverage of the "human side" of a concentrated search effort. I have been involved as the coordinator at a national level on some similar searches, and it would have been great in those times to have had contact with some of the emotions that go on during the waiting and watching. So many times you deal with the cold reality of the searchers, and only seldom did we get the emotions of the family and friends...

...There was much rejoicing and high fives around our house after we received the good news from your web site last night about Haley. God does indeed answer prayer...

...Please know that we checked your journal many, many times for updates on Haley's rescue. The updates you wrote, and the account that you wrote after she was found, was written with such feeling and compassion, no one could read them without crying...

...Thanks so much for keeping us informed on the search for Haley. I tried to find news on the radio, but all I found was annoying songs, comedians, and commercials. The newspaper only had old news, but least they published the address of your web site...

...Thank you so much for keeping this journal about Haley. I am a good friend of Kelly's in St. Louis, and your journal was my (and other's) only connection...

…We wanted to thank you for the wonderful journal that you kept of Haley Zega's ordeal. My husband just happened to see the address for your web site in the Arkansas Democrat/Gazette *and decided to check it out. It really helped us to feel like we had inside information. We wanted so badly to do something to help. At least, reading your journal helped us to gage how much to worry, and, at most, we realized that the best way for us to help was to let the people who knew what they were doing do their jobs…*

Chapter 16
THE ZEGAS
SAY THANKS

The Zegas felt they owed a huge debt of gratitude to the people of the state of Arkansas and surrounding areas, indeed to everyone who had anything to do with the search and rescue mission, from near or far. Saying "thank you" many thousands of times simply would not do it for them. From the very beginning, they found unique ways to thank the community of volunteers who saved their daughter's life.

On day three of the search, before they learned that Haley was found alive, Steve and Kelly called the media together. They not only wanted to plead for Haley's life in case someone had taken her, but they also wanted to let the community know how much they appreciated all of the efforts on their behalf.

Their statements on camera were filled with emotion for the genuine gratitude they felt for all who were helping out. They began and ended their statements with "thank you." This would become a recurring theme from them for a long time to come.

Later, at the hospital in Harrison, when asked what they had to say to the public after Haley had been rescued, Steve and Kelly summed it up quite well: "We are overwhelmed with your generosity. That is what everyone needs to see" (Steve, pointing to Haley, who had just been put into their car for the ride home). Kelly added, "Thank you from the bottom of our hearts for putting your lives on hold and for making ours whole again."

Even before the Zegas arrived back home, they began planning a thank you party for the community. A group of close friends of the family helped out and formed The Caterpillar Campaign Committee (named after White Spot, the caterpillar that Haley befriended on her hike), and they organized a large gathering at Gully Park in Fayetteville, open to all. (The group plans to continue the efforts to educate the public about missing children.)

The announcement for the party in newspapers read "Thank You. For Caring, Praying, And Searching!" Mayor Dan Coody of Fayetteville, who himself took time out of his busy schedule to come to the woods and help search for Haley, declared it a "Day of Thanks to the Haley Zega Search and Rescue Volunteers."

Arkansas Governor Mike Huckabee sent the following letter:

> To: All who assisted in the safe return of Haley Zega
>
> It's a pleasure to join the people of Fayetteville and Northwest Arkansas in recognizing those who volunteered their time to ensure Haley's safe return.
>
> People across our state ceased their daily activities to come to the rescue of a child. I'm reminded of the story of the Good Shepherd who left the 99 to rescue the one. It was an opportunity to test our spirit of brotherly love. Once more, we saw why Arkansas is such a great place to call home. All who participated in the search are heroes. So are the thousands who said prayers on Haley's behalf.
>
> It's a blessing to live in a place where people come to your assistance in a time of need. In this case, a life was saved and a child was returned to the arms of her loving parents.
>
> God bless you all.
>
> —Mike Huckabee, Governor

It was a bright sunny afternoon on May 26th, 2001, and folks gathered to remember, to tell stories, to hug. There was lots of food, soft drinks, and great music (Jed Clampit, Al "Papa Rap" Lopez, and the North Arkansas Youth Symphony entertained the crowd). But there was work to be done too, as this was not just a thank you party, but also a fund-raising event for the Morgan Nick Foundation. Colleen Nick was on hand and gave an emotional account of the day that her own daughter disappeared years ago. The Foundation also gave out valuable information, including DNA kits for all kids.

Local law enforcement agencies were there too, photographing and finger printing kids, giving this data to the parents for quick identification in case their own child becomes lost. SAR teams set up booths, passed out information, and did a "Lost in the Woods" skit to help teach kids what to do when lost.

Haley was there, of course, and many of the volunteers who spent hours in the woods looking for her met her for the very first time. She was just like any other child there, running around and playing and enjoying the bright spring day. Her parents got up on stage and continued their mantra of thanking everyone for the incredible job that was done and how honored they were to belong to the community of Arkansas. It was a remarkable moment to see this family together and smiling.

The Zegas also went on a personal campaign to try to reach as many people as possible to say thanks, using ads and letters in newspapers. One ad showed a smiling Haley held in the arms of her parents, with the following:

Thank you for being there for Haley Zega and her rescue! The good people of Arkansas stood tall to help us in our hour of need. We sincerely appreciate the individuals, businesses, organizations, and agencies that worked hard, donated much, and prayed for a child in need.

—Kelly and Steve Zega, Parents

—Joyce and Jay Hale, Grandparents

And then the following letter of thanks was published by newspapers in the region—it is one of the most eloquent and heartfelt messages ever written.

How do you ever find the way to say enough thanks for having your child returned safely to your arms?

Perhaps the only way our immediate and extended family, as well as our dearest friends, can ever begin to repay the unbelievable outpouring of support we've witnessed—shown through physical searching, providing of food and supplies to volunteers, working past the point of exhaustion in a multitude of ways, and, perhaps most of all, through an amazing display of faith, prayer and positive energy—is to ensure that we continue to carry the torch of hope for children who are still lost, and to be a voice of comfort to families struggling to keep it together when everything around them threatens to tear them apart. We've been handed a mission, and we gladly accept.

We have always been proud to be Arkansans, but never have we seen a single instance so strongly prove the existence of the cumulative heart, soul, and spirituality of the people of this beautiful state. It is truly overwhelming to have had our only child, Haley, be the recipient of such unwavering energy. We continue to gaze at her healthy, happy, lovely little face and are filled with wonder at what divine plan will be revealed in her as she grows into a confident, self-sufficient adult.

Many times before this life-changing couple of weeks, we have told Haley how lucky she is to be able to call herself a native of Arkansas and Fayetteville. We certainly never expected to have that so perfectly illustrated through her own life, but now we know how right we've been to instill that pride in her Arkansas heritage at a very young age. She's still such a little girl—as remarkable as she is—but, in some way, we feel she understands.

Though we can never fully express our gratitude, we would like to offer thanks to every individual who struggled to know how to respond, for every "mother or father bear" instinct that took hold on Haley's behalf, for the churches and prayer groups around the world that focused their voices on Haley's behalf, for every employer who supported the multitude of employees who left their jobs or tied up office phones to call in help or allowed them time to reflect or pray, for every person in uniform or with a badge who focused their training and hearts on Haley's safety, for the children whose prayers we've always known to have a direct line to God, for each volunteer—trained or untrained—who tromped through poison ivy, swallowed dust and pollen until they choked and never gave up hope—thank you.

And to the best friends and family three people could ask to have—a strikingly large collection of remarkable people who bless our lives every day—thank you for being there to get us through, for holding our hands, giving us your hearts, and for always loving Haley as if she were your own, thank you.

We are wealthy because of the relationships we have, and we weathered this test because of you.

And, a special thank you to Colleen Nick and the Morgan Nick Foundation, for holding us close and making some extremely tough decisions bearable.

Tim Ernst, thank you for giving us your home, your technology and your compassion—and your sweet "bloodhound" Aspen!

We are better for knowing these remarkable individuals.

Finally, thank you for the mountain of cards, letters, gifts, and phone calls from friends, family and perfect strangers. The steady stream of communications we've received has shown just how this has touched our lives—and how a few days of agony can potentially flower into a lifetime of renewed vision, faith, and appreciation for our relationships on every level.

Cherish the simplicity or complexity of every day—and rejoice in our collective human experience.

We love you.

—Steve, Kelly and Haley Zega

What a beautiful statement this was. And they meant every word of it. In fact, they have taken on lost children as their mission in life and will continue to be involved on many levels for a long time to come. Within a week after Haley's rescue for instance, the Zegas were on hand in Little Rock to help dedicate the "Arbor of Hope" in McArthur Park, a monument to honor missing children.

Steve returned to his National Guard unit to thank them personally:

"The first people I saw when I arrived at the search location were members of the Guard...my Guard brothers. I've said 'thank you' a lot the last week, but it doesn't seem to be enough. I've spent 15 years in this uniform, and I always thought I was there to serve, not the one who would need serving."

"Being part of this family," Steve said, touching his uniform, "helped me find *this* family," he added, hugging Kelly and Haley.

Every time that I see Steve, he comes up to me with an outstretched hand saying, "Have I ever told you how grateful we are for all of your help?" "Yes, Steve," I tell him, "at least a thousand times." This family will spend the rest of their lives thanking others in many ways, but really, all you have to do is look at Haley, with her bright eyes and broad smile, and that is enough thanks for anyone.

Chapter 17
DATELINE COMES TO CLOUDLAND

The Zegas were contacted by *Dateline NBC* soon after Haley returned home. Steve and Kelly thought long and hard about having Haley involved in such broad ranging national exposure, and in the end felt that the *Dateline* program would be a good platform to tell the whole story. The producer who would be in charge was Carol Gable, a veteran of many *Dateline* productions in different parts of the world. Carol would discover that doing a story in Newton County, Arkansas, in July would be akin to some of her third-world exploits!

Carol contacted me early on to see if I would be available to show them around the search area. I enthusiastically agreed. Getting Lytle and William Jeff to agree to do an interview was another story. Lytle did not need a hard sell, but his partner in the rescue, William Jeff, was not too happy with the media and had dealt with them enough. It would take a great deal of politicizing to convince William Jeff to be a part of the production. I think we all were a little surprised when William Jeff finally agreed to not only do an interview but actually take his mules in to the rescue site with the crew—that would be the ultimate!

As it turned out, the only time that the crew and all parties that Carol wanted involved in the story could be available would be the last week of July. Haley's story was not time sensitive, so there was no big rush, although they did have to do it before the leaves changed colors and dropped off in the fall. Late July in Arkansas is the worst time to be here, and especially out in the wilds of the Ozarks, but that is just how it worked out.

I knew right away that Carol was going to do a great job when she showed up in Arkansas in June for a scouting trip. Without this preliminary trip, the production would have been a nightmare. She wanted me to show her some of the route that Haley had taken and talk about possible shooting sites. She also met with the Zegas in Fayetteville, and with Lytle. In fact, Lytle came out to Cloudland with Carol, and the three of us went out for a little jaunt, down over the cliff and into Dug Hollow. Carol was a bit surprised—no stunned—to discover how rugged the terrain actually was. And how beautiful.

I was quite impressed when she stated that she wanted me to take her and the production crew to the exact spot where Haley had been found to film it for the show. At this early stage in the plans, neither Lytle nor William Jeff would agree to return to that spot (in the summertime anyway). I told her, "no problem!" Lytle and I both knew that it would take a super-human effort to get the crew down to the river. "Couldn't we just float in?" Carol kept asking. While the stretch of the Buffalo River where Haley was found is floatable, it can only be done at flood stage levels, for a few hours, and then only with kayaks or covered canoes and experienced floaters.

As the time for *Dateline*'s visit drew closer, somehow Carol convinced William Jeff to do the interview. I had hiked in and located the exact spot of her rescue. I also found a relatively easy way to get into the spot, along an old pioneer road. Lytle and William Jeff had figured out the very same route and agreed to bring their mules in that way. They would even bring along an extra mule or two to help pack in all of the camera gear. Things were all coming together.

The week before *Dateline* arrived, the temperatures in the Ozarks soared into the high 90's, with humidity levels to match. In a word—miserable. The jungle-like brush, fed with unusually frequent rains this summer, was thick and impenetrable in places. Lots of ticks and chiggers too. And man it had been the worst year for poisonous snakes that I could ever recall—ticks and chiggers and snakes, oh my! Lytle and I tried to prepare Carol for all of this so that she could prepare her crew. All city slickers we thought—boy, are they going to have a big time in Arkansas!

So the schedule was set—they would film an interview with Steve and Kelly in Fayetteville the first day, then come out to the cabin the next day for interviews with Haley, Jay, Joyce, and me, plus get some footage of the trail near where Haley was lost. The third day we would venture deep into the wilderness with mules, and the last day they would meet with the helicopter pilot along with search and rescue folks, plus finish up any last minute scenes.

One problem that was creeping in was the fact that they needed a lot of power to run their big video cameras, lights, and sound equipment. The location for the Haley rescue spot was several miles from any trailhead, so going back to recharge batteries was not an option. Carol asked about packing in a generator to recharge the batteries, but since it is a wilderness area, no motors of any kind are allowed. The only solution was to borrow as many batteries as they could, which they had to get from other NBC offices. This almost turned out to be a big mistake.

I had to chuckle a little bit when the associate producer from New York City called to ask if I could recommend a nice restaurant close by the cabin where she could reserve a table for the crew to have lunch while they were shooting at the cabin. For those of you who don't know this area, I will tell you that there are no restaurants any where near here, much less a nice one. The closest one would require at least a three or four hour delay in the shooting schedule, which simply would not work. They would be staying at the Buffalo Outdoor Center cabins in Ponca—no food service near there either.

We received several nice soaking rains just a few days before the crew arrived, which brought the temps down into the 80's out in the wilderness. The humidity dropped a bit too. Still lots of critters though.

The crew arrived on a Tuesday afternoon, July 24th, 2001, and went to the Zegas residence in Fayetteville for extensive interviews with Steve and Kelly. Since they had planned to do an interview with Haley at our cabin the next morning, Kelly and Haley were going to spend the night with us (Steve had to drive to Little Rock on business right after his interview). Pam and I and Jay and Joyce hung around the cabin all evening waiting for Kelly and Haley to show up.

We got a call from Kelly at 10 p.m.—"They are still here," she whispered over the phone. "Our house is a mess and there are at least 50 camera cases spread out all over the yard!" One thing all of us would learn quickly was that this crew did a very thorough job and did not quit until they had everything covered—another sign of a great production.

It was 11 p.m. before the crew finally left the Zega's house and headed for a nearby Wal-Mart Supercenter to stock up on groceries. I heard it was sort of like those game shows where everyone gets a grocery cart and has two minutes to fill it with as much stuff as they can—they were heading into the wilderness for several days and wanted to make sure they had plenty to eat!

It was 1 a.m. before Kelly and Haley arrived at our cabin. The *Dateline* crew wouldn't reach their cabins in Ponca until much later and had to spend a bit of time repacking all of their gear for the next morning's shoot.

Jay and Joyce arrived just after daylight on Wednesday and began preparing this wonderful breakfast feast that included homemade sourdough pancakes, bacon, fresh fruit, juice, and many other goodies. Then the trucks began to appear—*five* loads of camera gear, along with a crew of seven.

The producer was Carol Gable from Anderson, South Carolina. Carol had been here back in June and knew a little of what to expect from the Ozarks in the summertime. Rob Stafford from Chicago was the correspondent (he is the one who would be doing most of the interviewing on camera and the only one of the crew to appear in the show). The associate producer was Deanna Dimuro from New York City (although a recent transplant from

California). Deanna said that she normally didn't come on the location shoots, but was asked to go on this one to help out with all of the extra "details."

Carol's hand-picked video and sound crew was a group of four guys from Houston, Texas, who all worked together on many other projects. The photographers were Bob Abrahamson (Video Bob) and Jack Razor. The sound/lighting guys were Bob Lapp (Audio Bob) and Anthony Rowland. Professionals to the bone, every one of them. It would be a treat for me to get to see them work.

We spent 30 minutes out on the back deck eating and getting to know one another a bit—the food was super, and the view was pretty darn nice.

Then I piled into one of the vehicles with Carol, Deanna, and video Bob for a quick scouting trip down to Hawksbill Crag. While we were there we radioed back to the cabin for them to begin the setup for Jay and Joyce's interview, which they would do on the back deck.

When we arrived back at the cabin, there were dozens of hard-shell cases laid out on the west deck—cameras, lights, stands, batteries, wires, more wires, more wires, and many other things which I had never seen or heard of before. It took them a couple of hours just to get everything set up. We had to remodel a bit of the back deck—including removing one of the swings and a section of handrail. But the shot they set up was really nice—Jay and Joyce would be sitting right in front of an incredible view of the wilderness.

The rest of us were busy inside, going over plans for the next couple of days for shooting sites and how we were going to be able to fit everything in. It was sort of odd reliving all of the details of the search and rescue saga while Haley was standing right there with us. At one point, she caught a walking stick, named it "Twiggy" and placed it in a cookie jar.

All quiet on the set. I hooked up a hard-wired telephone out on the deck, and they sent the audio portion of the recording session over the phone to the studio in New York—so they could begin typing for the closed captioning.

Once the actual taping began, everyone had to be absolutely still and quiet. I wanted to hear every word, so Pam and I got comfortable in chairs nearby and watched. It was quite an interview, as Rob took them through a series of questions from the very beginning of their hike with Haley to the glorious end. It was pretty emotional at times; and while the two of them held up great, I was near tears more than once.

Just as Rob was getting to the end of his questions—and I mean he only had one, perhaps two left—the sky opened up and it began to rain. They had tens of thousands of dollars worth of camera, sound, and lighting equipment sitting out there on the open deck. They were quite calm and collected and covered up some of it, hauled in other parts, and left the rest to get wet. Just about that time, both phone lines went dead.

It rained for a while—seemed like ages—but eventually let up enough for them to continue the taping and finish up the session on the deck. Then Jay and Joyce prepared lunch—which included several loaves of homemade bread and other wonderful goodies that Joyce had cooked up. The crew set up a couple of lights and filmed Jay and Joyce putting it all together in the kitchen. Good grief, we didn't know that the Cloudland kitchen might be seen by millions on national television!

After lunch, they shot a few scenes of me typing away at the computer, working on the journal (I bet I typed 10,000 words while they were shooting). Then two camera crews shot images from inside and outside the cabin.

The big moment that all of us had waited for finally arrived next—Haley's interview. They didn't want to scare her by putting her in a studio environment with all the lights and equipment, so they picked a simple location down on the lower deck, up against one of the stone walls, and shot it with a single light and two cameras. The entire crew was gathered around and hung on every word. None of us were sure if she was going to say anything at all.

Video Bob, Rob, and Haley doing the interview

211

She did talk and actually did a pretty good job of fielding Rob's questions. I picked up a bit of information from her about the route that she likely took as well as some of the things that she experienced during her time out in the wilderness. When it was all over, she passed out Reese's Peanut Butter cups to everyone (Rob had given her a bag of goodies, which included them).

The next shoot was down at Hawksbill Crag, so we packed up and drove to the trailhead, then loaded up equipment and started down the trail.

They shot a neat scene with Rob out on the Crag—the lighting was very nice—then a few shots with me walking down below the Crag. But the real scene was when Haley and Jay walked out onto the Crag—Haley got out to the very edge with him. I can only relate this story second hand because I was down below, at the bottom of the bluff, waiting for my cue. There were a number of two-way radios on site, and I could hear what was going on through them. It was one of those unexpected and un-scripted scenes that was priceless.

We hiked out as darkness approached—back to the cabin for more shooting. It was after 10 p.m. before the crew was finished and had packed up and gone. They wanted to get exterior shots of the cabin all lit up at night, just like it had been during the ordeal. *Dateline* does not try to re-create anything—nor pretends to do so—but they do want to show as many details as possible and be as accurate as possible.

Deanna had gone back to their cabins early to get started on dinner (remember, no restaurants!). It was very late when her crew finally arrived. They ended up grilling steaks outside, using car headlights for light!

Thursday morning arrived, we were to meet up with the two heroes of this story (no, I take that back—there were many hundreds of heroes!), and go with them deep into the wilderness to where they found Haley. I met first with Willard Villines down in Boxley Valley (he wrote a neat poem about the rescue). Then we were joined by Lytle James and William Jeff Villines—the two who found Haley. They had five mules between them—two mules would help pack in the camera gear.

Willard, Lytle, and William Jeff saddled up and took off from the trailhead in Boxley Valley while I took the caravan of *Dateline* four-wheel-drive vehicles up to a more remote trailhead. The mules met us there, and after a frantic thirty minutes of trying to figure out what equipment could be left behind, we headed out. There was a *ton* of gear, and I know those mules were wondering what the heck was going on!

Each of the crew members from Houston carried a big load themselves (I had loaned them a couple of backpacks for some of the gear), including two big digital video cameras and most of the sound equipment.

All of the crew had on long pants and shirts to help protect from the thick brush, and keep away bugs and spider webs. They were also wearing dog collars (one on each ankle). I have heard some reference to this being used to ward off ticks before, but had never actually seen anyone use them—at least not in public. (I had thought that perhaps Lytle and William Jeff had told them about this—just to add a bit of humor—but later found out that the idea came from Carol's husband, who is a pharmacist).

One thing that Carol had joked about to Lytle and William Jeff was that she wanted them to find a snake to take pictures of. Five minutes into the ride, a *huge* timber rattler nearly got William Jeff's mule. This five-foot monster with a dozen rattles moved off the trail into thick brush and gave us quite a show. I did not get any pictures of him because I had become the official snake wrangler and was busy pulling back brush for the cameras and poking at the snake with my hiking stick to get him to pose properly. Anthony was standing right next to me the entire time, with his microphone at the end of a long boom poised directly over the snake to get every rattle. He later remarked that he never even saw the snake. This was a great beginning to the ride/hike, and just what the producer ordered!

The next several hours were spent moving down the old road, stopping at various places to set up a shot. The mules not only carried their heavy loads well, they cooperated for every take.

At one point I was hanging back talking with Lytle and William Jeff, waiting for the crew to get something set up, when William Jeff pointed down to my feet. I was standing in the middle of a patch of ginseng. He could spot this low-growing plant from way up high in the saddle on top of his mule, Big Momma. The roots of this plant are going for $400 a pound or more these days, and it is so scarce that they have halted any harvesting of it on public lands in Arkansas for five years (to allow the plants to re-establish themselves). There are a lot of ginseng diggers in this part of the state.

It was interesting to tag along with the photographers to get a sense of how they were setting up shots. We were hiking/riding through some beautiful country, and often when I would have this vision in my head about one thing or another that would make a good scene, I would turn around and see the guys already setting up the shot. I guess photo minds work alike, no matter if it is still pictures or moving pictures.

One such scene involved Lytle and William Jeff riding through a field with the mountains in the background. Video Bob got up on the backside of one of the mules—this in itself looked pretty darn funny! Then Willard led Video Bob's mule through the field while Video Bob photographed Lytle and William Jeff riding behind him. I did not see the tape of this, however, I bet it was pretty good. Video Bob was afraid though that someone would take a picture of him riding backwards on the rump of a mule and post it in a bar somewhere—he had better look out the next time he comes to Newton County!

This crew had done a lot of stories for *Dateline* and other production companies, and had traveled all over the world and seen and dealt with many things. I overheard the guys talking about difficult situations, and then the talk shifted to family matters. One of them commented about having to change a baby's diaper. "That smell is as bad as *any* dead body I have ever been around!"

It took us all morning, but we finally arrived at the Buffalo River, right next to the spot where Haley was rescued. During a quick lunch break William Jeff passed out fried deer steaks for everyone. Quite frankly, I can't stand the taste of deer meat anymore, or any wild game for that matter. But I had to admit, these steaks were as good as any chicken-fried steak I had ever put in my mouth. He said his secret was to soak the deer meat in saltwater for 4-7 days before cooking, which would turn the meat nearly white and "soak out" the gamey flavor. Boy, he sure was right! Although one of the crew wondered out loud if it was actually possum meat they were eating.

They spent the next hour unpacking the mules and setting up lights, cameras, *big* tripods, shades, and hundreds of feet of cables. And then the second most anticipated moment of the entire shoot arrived—getting to hear from the two men who found Haley. It had been an uphill battle to get these two on camera—in fact, William Jeff had totally avoided media coverage since soon after the rescue. But here they were, not only in front of the cameras together, but back deep in the wilderness.

Lights, cameras, quiet on the set—A-C-T-I-O-N! And just as Rob was beginning to ask his first question, it began to rain. And I mean *rain*! There was no porch to hide under, no cabin to retreat into. All of that gear was out in the rain. The crew did their best to cover everything up with a batch of trash bags from our cabin, and then everyone just waited. And waited. And waited.

I was the only one who had a rain coat, and felt a little embarrassed to put it on, but I finally did so, and then crouched under the low branches of hazelnut trees with the sound and camera guys. The rest of our bunch was huddled under the light screens, which also happened to be pretty good at shedding water.

So here we were, after two months of negotiations with William Jeff and Lytle, and a long trek into the historical spot along the banks of the Buffalo River, and it was raining. "Can't argue with God," someone said. How true!

One image that will remain with me is that of Rob, the real TV star here, standing under the screen, holding up a plastic bag. Inside was his shirt, which he pulled off as soon as the rain began—he needed to keep it dry and spot-free for the close-ups of him during the interview.

Everyone seemed to take the rain in stride, and before long the sky got a bit lighter, and the rain began to let up. Within minutes we were back in business, Lytle and William Jeff were seated on their interview rock, and all was ready to go.

Once the lights were turned on, someone spoke up and asked if they should put a bit of makeup on the two stars. You should have seen their reaction—*makeup* on these two country boys—no way!!! There was a good bit of ribbing going on all the time between everyone, which made the day go a lot faster. I do believe that the good old boys in the saddles got the best of the big city folks though.

Rob, Lytle, William Jeff, Deanna (back to camera), & Jack

I had heard most of the details about the rescue before, but it was great to be able to sit there and watch it all happen for the TV cameras. These two mule men are very simple guys, with tons of backwoods savvy. They did a good job of fielding some tough questions in front of what would turn out to be literally millions of people.

The biggest problem of the day turned out to be batteries. The three lights they had set up on the "wilderness set" were eating batteries like crazy. They carried in 40 batteries (each weighed several pounds, and cost a *thousand dollars!*). At times the batteries, which were used in pairs, only lasted a minute or two. Turns out that many of the ones they borrowed were not fully charged and had little power. We were wondering if the stash would last until the end of the interviews, much less for the entire day. Turns out the rain delay put off shooting several other scenes, so the batteries did last, and all was OK.

Lytle and William Jeff tell their story to the world

The rain held off the rest of the day, and the shoot went well. Lytle and William Jeff saddled up and rode up and down the shallow river near where they had found Haley, with the cameras recording every move. At one point they rode upstream and were in the brush getting out of sight of the cameras. I heard a couple of the crew laughing out loud—"Did you hear what he just said!" Lytle and William Jeff were wearing little wireless microphones, and probably did not realize that everything they were saying was being overheard by the sound guys. I won't repeat what the sound guys heard from these two woodsmen, but I can tell you that some of it was pretty funny.

It gets dark early way down in the bottom of the Buffalo, and soon it was time to pack up and get the heck out of there—we still had a long trip back out to the cars.

Lytle points to the spot where they found Haley

The trip out was much quicker than the one in, mostly because we did not need to stop and shoot scenes along the way. Carol and Deanna got rides on the mules, Rob and I hiked on ahead at a quick pace. It was quite a sight to see a dainty New York City girl on the back of that old mule, with her arms wrapped around William Jeff, holding on for dear life!

The guys from Houston had it the worst—they had their *heavy* cameras and audio gear to carry, but did very well, especially considering how far it was back to the trailhead and what a long day it had been.

Everyone made it out OK; and after a few more shots in the dim evening light, they packed up and headed for their cabins in Ponca. They had to unpack, dry everything out, *charge* the batteries, clean everything up, get ready for the last day of shooting, then cook dinner. It would be another late night for them.

One thing not planned was any after-hours "refreshments." Not having a restaurant nearby was one thing, but being in a dry county with no booze around for miles and miles was really a problem! I gladly contributed a case of beer to the crew from the stash at Cloudland. Ironically, that very same case of beer had been brought to the cabin and left by a volunteer just minutes before Haley was found.

The next morning I got to sleep in until 6 a.m., then got up and made a scouting trip around the area to look for a couple of shooting locations. Rob and half of the crew arrived a short time later, and we headed down the ladder trail towards the river.

They set up a short interview with me at the base of the bluff. I had already gone through *three* t-shirts that morning—it was so humid. Just walking around got me soaked with sweat in a hurry. I was on my last "Cloudland" t-shirt when the camera began rolling, and I'm afraid the sweat stains did not look too good.

While it doesn't bother me in the least to be in front of a TV camera, I have never felt like I have ever done a very good job in that particular position. I am a photographer—used to being in *back* of the camera—something just never looks quite right about me when I am in *front* of the camera. As I went back through Haley's ordeal, I was overcome with emotion a couple of times, and we had to stop taping. It wasn't the potential tragedy parts that got me choked up, but rather the incredible high that came with the news that Haley had been found. That still brings me to tears thinking about it, nearly every time. Go figure.

Next we set up a shot with Rob in front of a cave. Then shot other scenes around the cabin. And overhead, a sheriff's helicopter made a few passes down low—the other photographer was with the pilot, getting the perspective of it all from the air.

Just as things got really hectic here—many more scenes to shoot and dark clouds and airline schedules approaching—Lytle showed up with a caravan of family members. They just wanted to stop by and take a look at the view from the back deck. He had at least five vehicles with him, and soon the decks were covered with his relatives, including a couple of brothers who looked a lot like him.

I didn't have time to stop and chat, as we quickly loaded up and sped off to another location. Just as they were about to begin the taping for this one, the sky opened up and it began to pour once again. Good grief, that was *three days in a row* for rain! It seemed more like the tropics, where it rains every day, than the Ozarks in July.

We had four trucks lined up along the narrow road in one location—with lights and a camera and cables all over the place. Just down the road a bit, there were four other vehicles with anxious crew members waiting out the rain, ready to head out on the trail for one last shot. And up the road came Lytle with his caravan. He always seems to draw a crowd! They all got out and stood in the rain to talk.

The rains continued, and so did the clock. Neither stopped. It soon became evident that there would be no more taping today, so the crews packed up their gear and headed to the airport—they had to make their flights back home.

There were still a couple of shots missing, so Carol later shipped me a video camera with plenty of tapes and a shot list. This camera was dubbed

"The Haley Cam." Most of what she wanted me to shoot was the trail and woods as seen from Haley's perspective. I held the camera down low and hiked along the trail, through the brush and out to the edge of the bluff. I spent several days going out on the trail shooting under different lighting situations. On two different occasions I got stung by a bee while filming— you should have seen the image go wild, and heard that audio!

Carol and others spent a great deal of time putting this show together back in the editing booths at NBC. As I am writing this, they are still working on it. The air time will be sometime in the fall of 2001, when they can get a good time slot. The Zegas plan a big watch party with family and close friends, with a local television camera or two to record the reactions. I think the story will be a great thing for Arkansas and will tell the story to the rest of the country of how great our people are.

It was wonderful to get to work with such talented folks and to see first hand just what it takes to produce and film a high-quality program like *Dateline* produces each week. They didn't cut any corners, and I appreciated their efforts and desire to tell an honest story and do it with an artistic flair. Each member of the crew seemed to enjoy what they were doing, making me believe that their final product would be very good. And even though they were all "city slickers," they held their own out here in the wilderness, they could not have been nicer, kinder, or more considerate of others. Of course, they still looked pretty funny wearing those dog collars!

William Jeff on Big Momma, Lytle on Copper, ride through the Buffalo River

Chapter 18
POEMS & SONGS
ABOUT HALEY

The story of Haley's saga inspired many poems and several songs. Some of these were published in newspapers, while others were simply private thoughts that were e-mailed to me to be used in this book.

A couple of the poems were written by volunteers who helped look for Haley. One was written by a SAR team leader who spent many long hours in the woods. Another volunteer's composition expressed the frustrations that some volunteers experienced during the mission. And a mom explained what it was like to stay behind and keep the home fires burning while her husband joined the search efforts.

A hymn was written by the music director of the Zega's church in Fayetteville, and was sung at services and used as background music for some of the television reports about Haley. And a tune by professional song writer and performer Emily Kaitz tells Haley's story with beautiful lyrics.

We Knew

We animals knew
She was there
The sweet little Haley child
We heard the anxious cries
And tried to yell
"She's here! She's here!"
For we too have young
And we know fear
She trusted us
And talked to us
She somehow knew
We were there for her
And we would help her
Find her way back home

Cindy Prince

Chapter 18

Footprints Tell the Story

Footprints of grandparents, traveling dazed and confused, round and round in circles where they had last seen their beloved grandchild.

Footprints of friends, seen and unseen, moving and seeking in every direction.

Footprints of volunteers, experienced and inexperienced, known and unknown, numbering in the hundreds and each giving a part of themselves to this child, once a stranger.

Footprints of family, paced into hardwood belonging to people who are now friends.

Footprints of dogs, searching for the scent left on small dress-up clothes retrieved from home.

Footprints of horses, carrying their loads and listening for a child's cry.

Footprints of a teacher, calling to the pupil she loved and knew so well.

Footprints of pilots, flying again and again, straining for tiny clues on the nearly invisible ground below.

Footprints of the forest animals, telling us all was well with the world yet sharing nothing about their new blonde-haired companion.

Footprints of the tired, the frustrated, the hopeful, each dedicated to finishing what they had started.

Footprints of trackers, trying to make sense of these many, many prints now scattered everywhere along the way.

And then, a child's footprint, found and traced by a young hiker from Missouri whose earlier treks in these hills compelled him to once again return to this place. A lone hiker who looked for and found the small clue we desperately sought. A footprint in the sand a great distance down river. A footprint we believed would lead to great rejoicing or enormous sorrow.

And almost immediately thereafter, footprints of an unidentified man telling us that Haley had been found, that she was safe and full of chocolate pudding. Found by men and mules whose presence in this rugged and remote place was evidenced only by tracks left during their long journey into and out of the wilderness.

Then the footprints of her parents, made by feet scarcely touching the ground as they ran to be reunited with their joy, their life.

And later, many more small, beautiful footprints, found so near and yet so far. Old footprints belonging to a child now safe in the arms of her parents. Footprints still capable of bringing tears to our eyes.

While these footprints in the wilderness have faded and speak to us no more, the footprint of Haley will remain on our minds and in our hearts forever.

Christy Comstock

Chapter 18

Little Haley

Little Haley Zega one fine Spring day,
Got lost near Point Whitaker in the woods far away.
They called in the park rangers and all the great planners,
But brother-in-law Danny Woods heard it on one of those scanners.
He called up his brothers saying, "Oh what can we do?"
They said let's get together and call up the local volunteer crew.
They searched one day and two nights.
That little angel was no where in sight.
Danny's wife Sharon said, "I'm no fool;
I'll call brother-in-law Willard and tell him to bring his fine mules."
Willard said, "I'll be there; I know that I can,
but first I'll call William Jeff: I know he's our man."
Willard called Jeff on his telephone,
But to his surprise he was already gone.
Willard went up on Cave Mountain and sat there from seven 'til ten.
Someone told him, "Oh those professionals; they are planning again."
Jeff saddled "Big Momma" so strong and so tall.
He said, "By golly, I'll make my own law."
Jeff called his friend Lytle who rode his mule "Copper."
Those two mountain men were sure enough Brush Poppers.
They rode through rough terrain, hollows and logs.
Those two mule men were better than bloodhound dogs.
They rode until two thirty o'clock when,
Lytle said, "I see that little girl upon that old rock."
They hugged her and fed her pudding and lifesavers.
She told Lytle and Jeff that red was her best flavor.
They fed her because she looked so scrawny,
And then Haley said, "I want to see my mommy"
Back on Cave Mountain near Hawks' Bill Bluff,
Those poor professionals were still planning their stuff.
They thanked us volunteers and said tomorrow don't you come back.
We have got to do some more planning;
You know that is a fact.
Fifty-three hours in that rough wilderness the people did pray.
God sent her a guardian angel, a spotted caterpillar they say.
Just one more verse before this poem can end.
God led the search for those two Good Samaritan men.

Willard "Sonny Boy" Villines

Every Mother

To every mother who got that phone call—Haley is missing! She felt the ground below her turn to quicksand and could actually feel the depth of her soul. She knew that her own child's name could have been said, and Haley became every mother's child.

To every mother who so wanted to drop everything and run to find her, but instead she frantically helped her husband throw a few things together to get ready to leave. She kissed him and watched him drive away. Please find her.

To every mother who heard the little footsteps and giggles coming down the hall. How does she tell them? The sweet smell of her child as they sat in her lap, and she explained that their friend was missing. We want to go find her they say, but they are told that Daddy and many, many others are there looking for her. But what can we do?

To every mother who searched for something for her and her children to wrap their hands and hearts around to pass the time till the next phone call—the next news report. What can we do? The most powerful thing of all, and they dropped to their knees to pray. They got up and picked up the phone and called everyone they knew to ask for prayers. They activated every prayer tree they could find, and slowly as more and more mothers prayed, this child became their child.

To every mother who went about the daily routines of taking care of her children those two days just as she always does—but differently. She had a sense of what a gift it was to make lunch, to get a drink of water, to brush their hair, to tuck them snuggly into bed. Every activity was done with a tear in the eye and a prayer that the next night, every mother's child would be tucked in her bed.

To every mother whose blood turned colder as every hour passed that last day. Whose heart poured out with every tear of the one mother on television begging for her child's life. The struggle to push aside the thoughts of the unthinkable—and then the phone rings and someone is screaming, *"They found her!"*

To every mother who finally took a breath and cried and jumped up and down with her children. Whose soul ached with joy as they watched a mother jump out of a car and run to her child. The one mother who endured it all and never lost hope. Deep in their hearts, every mother hopes that they would have been as strong as this one mother.

Paulla Goodwin

She's Alive

Flow gently Buffalo River among the green sprays.
Flow gently, and I'll sing thee a song in thy praise.
Little Haley is sleeping by thy murmuring stream.
I charge you big Buffalo, disturb not her dream.
Flow gently big Buffalo among the rocks and the hills.
Her safety depended on God's holy will.
The wild beasts of the wilderness did her no harm.
She must have been protected with God's loving arms.
53 hours in the wilderness without food she survived.
Her rescuers were surprised to find her alive.
William Jeff Villines and Lytle James gave her food they had brought.
To serve to the little girl they so diligently sought.
And little Haley Zega will remain in their thoughts.

Joe W. Vaughn

*Here is a hymn written by the music minister of the Sequoia Methodist
Church in Fayetteville*

Oh Lord can you help us one last time,
Help us to help to find a friend of ours,
Cold and scared and lost and all alone,
Send us an angel to help us bring an angel home.

And this will be the last prayer that I ever pray,
Just like the last prayer that I prayed for yesterday,
And I give praise and the glory to my Lord,
'Cause everytime that I have asked for one last prayer
He's always given more.

Oh Lord what a sight to see,
People gathered round the church like a family,
Some will cry and some will pray all night,
Praying to God that everything will be alright.

And this will be the last prayer that I ever pray,
Just like the last prayer that I prayed for yesterday,
And I give praise and the glory to my Lord,
'Cause everytime that I have asked for one last prayer
He's always given more.

And all the sudden Lord we hear the word,
That every prayer that we had prayed for had been heard,
So let's give praise and all the glory to our Lord,
'Cause everytime that we asked for one last prayer
He always gives us more.

Oh Lord can you help us one last time...

Don Hart

Little Girl Lost on the Buffalo
A song by Emily Kaitz

At the end of April in Arkansas
On a trail in the Ozark National Forest
Came a group of hikers with a little child
Enchanted and entranced by a place so wild.

The terrain was rugged, the slope unkind
And stubborn little Haley lagged way behind
"Let's go on ahead," her grandmother exclaimed.
"She'll catch up when she's tired of playing this game."

So the grownups rounded a bend in the trail
Where they waited for Haley to no avail
How she vanished so quickly they'll never know.
Little girl lost on the Buffalo.

Now the Buffalo River with its cliffs and caves
Is the home of cottonmouth and rattlesnakes,
And one careless step is all it takes.
For a six-year-old child it's a treacherous place.

The party of hikers scattered and called,
Combing woods so vast for a child so small
When they went seeking help in a rising panic
They stumbled on a nature photographer's cabin.

The man had a phone and a fax machine,
And out into the world the story streamed
Of a girl lost alone in a National Park.
Outside it was slowly growing dark.

Relatives and friends poured in that day
From nearby towns and far away
Tramping high and low through the lichens and moss
Their hearts united in a common cause.

Now the Buffalo River with its cliffs and caves
Is the home of cottonmouth and rattlesnakes
And one careless step is all it takes.
But Haley was traveling in a state of grace.

A voice came to her from a spirit guide
Who told her how to get down the mountainside
To the banks of the river from the bluff so high.
Meanwhile two days and two nights passed by.

The family wouldn't give up hope
As the searching parties scoured the slopes
Though the tension and suspense had everyone frightened.
But soon word from a psychic made the mood brighten.

She said she saw Haley by the waterside
With two men on horses out for a ride
And when word reached the dowsers in Eureka Springs,
They sent back predictions of similar things.

Volunteer crews kept hunting hard
Boy Scouts, helicopters, and the National Guard
Ministers and mothers from around the world
Were praying for the safety of the little lost girl.

'Cause the Buffalo River with its cliffs and caves
Is the home of cottonmouth and rattlesnakes
And one careless step is all it takes
But the fearful ordeal was about to break.

Two local men from Mt. Sherman woods
Thought they'd find the girl if anyone could
They gathered supplies and their mules they did load
Then set out along Cave Mountain Road.

William Jeff Villines and Lytle James
Had hunted coons in that very place
When they sighted human tracks down in Dug Hollow
They knew they were close and commenced to follow.

She was lying down by the riverside
Hungry and tired but very much alive
And the first words Haley spoke to them were these:
"I want my Mommy and Daddy and some ice cream please."

At the end of April in Arkansas
On a trail in the Ozark National Forest
Came a group of hikers with a little child
Enchanted and entranced by a place so wild.

Emily Kaitz

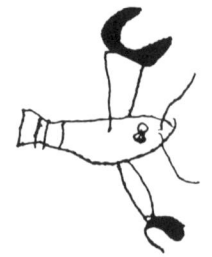

Chapter 19
LOST IN THE WOODS PROGRAM

If you are the proud owner of any make or model child and would like to protect your investment, I URGE you to read this chapter before taking your child into the woods (and have your kid read it too). I asked David Comstock from the Washington County Sheriff's Search and Rescue Team for a brief discussion of some things that every child should know before heading out on a hike. What follows is part of their "Lost In The Woods Program" that they regularly teach to youngsters. Their SAR team played a vital role in the search for Haley.

This program is one that has been adapted from several similar programs developed in North America. It is directed towards children ages 6–12 and their caregivers, although many of all ages have benefitted from it. This program is not intended as a "Long Term Survival Guide," so we are not going to discuss a crashed plane on a desert island in the Pacific (you've seen the movie, anyway). What we are going to discuss is short term survival....usually just overnight.

Most incidents involving missing persons in Arkansas are resolved in less than twelve hours. The search for Haley Zega was, of course, an exception to the norm. Nevertheless, survival for a twelve-hour period can be a challenging situation given the weather, terrain, and the age and health of the person. It probably also means that we have to survive through the night (which can be a little scary). But, if you will remember and follow a few simple steps, a Search and Rescue Team will probably find you the following day.

Surviving through the night means we may have to overcome the most common killer of the outdoors, hypothermia. The best way to prevent hypothermia is to stay warm and dry, and your best defense is the clothes you are wearing. Fabrics that dry quickly and retain heat are preferred. The old adage "cotton kills" is true because wet cotton clothing does not dry quickly and provides no insulation against the cold. This is true even in summer where a brief shower followed by a cool night can spell trouble to the unprepared. We also recommend that clothing be chosen which is brightly colored and thus highly visible. It is important for adults to make sure children in the outdoors are properly dressed.

A shelter is also important, not only to keep us warm and dry but to make us feel more comfortable. Of course, we are not going to try and build a log cabin from blown down trees What we are going to do is find a cedar tree that is big and strong. A cedar tree's long, low branches provide excellent protection from the weather. Also, fallen cedar needles under the tree provide us a soft spot on which to sit and insulation from the cold ground. To supplement our cedar tree, we need something that is small and lightweight. This something must be waterproof and windproof. Since a tent is too heavy and hard to set up, the answer is a large trash bag (we recommend the 50 gallon contractor or yard waste bags). To properly renovate the bag into a shelter, cut a "window" about 6 inches from the bottom of the bag running parallel to the bottom seam for about 6 inches. If you pull the bag over your head, the "window" should permit the child's face to peek out and breathe while covering the child's head. Once the bag is prepared (by adults at home) it should be rolled up and placed in the child's brightly colored day pack or fanny pack. A product named "Hot Hands" (available at discount or hunting supply stores) may be carried to provide a supplemental source of warmth. Just open the sealed packages, shake, and presto, a little warmth!

It would help the Search and Rescue Team to find you if you could make yourself as big and noticeable as possible. This can be done in several ways but must be done safely. So, before we retire to our trash bag under the cedar tree, we are going to make our tree different from any other tree in the forest. Children remember this as "decorating our Christmas tree," and the best way to do this is with foil. At home, take one to two feet of aluminum foil, tear it into long strips, and place it into the child's pack. Before getting under their cedar "Christmas tree," he or she takes the strips and folds them around branches all the way around the cedar tree. When the Search and Rescue Team sees a "Christmas tree" in the middle of the forest, they will know you are waiting underneath.

Another part of making yourself "big" is to listen for search planes flying overhead. If a plane flies over your cedar tree, get out from under your tree and move to a clearing where you can be seen. If you can find a clear spot near your tree, lay on the ground and wave your arms and legs.

Making yourself "big" does not mean yelling, and you should try to remember not to yell. A person can only yell for help for so long, and the human voice does not travel as far as we might like in this situation. So it is a good idea to pack a good quality plastic whistle in the child's pack. A simple blast on a whistle can carry for a mile or more and can be used from the protection of our shelter. And while you can't yell all day and night for help, you can blow your whistle.

Children generally think the most important parts of surviving are food and water. While neither are usually required for short term survival, it is important to talk to children about these two items.

Naturally, the best water a child can drink in the outdoors is water brought from home, and a small bottle should be in every child's pack. Children should know that water in the woods must be filtered and purified to be safe for human consumption. Water filters or chemical treatment are normally beyond a child's ability and are not discussed except to say that any child carrying these items should be taught how to properly use them. If a child decides he or she has no choice but to drink water found in the woods, there are a couple of things the child must know. First, the child should remember never to drink water from a body of water bigger than the child. If the child falls into a large body of water—such as a river or lake—drowning is an immediate threat which is worse than being lost. Drinking out of a mud puddle is a much better choice (even a small child can be taught to use a handkerchief to "filter" out the "big chunks"). Second, if the child does drink ground water, he or she should report that fact to the adults when found. Treatment for the bacteria and other "bugs" found in most outdoors water needs to begin.

While it is not essential, most children are much happier if they can have a snack while waiting under their cedar "Christmas tree." However, if you put a candy bar or similar favorite treat in a child's pack, it will be eaten long before you arrive at your outdoor destination! Instead, pack a high-energy protein bar which is now available at almost any grocer. These protein bars usually are not to the snacking taste of your child, which means they probably will still exist in the bottom of the pack when needed.

These few survival items can easily be carried in a child-size fanny pack that weighs very little. It is *very* important that the size and weight be kept to a minimum because the *goal* is to have the child carry the fanny pack with them everywhere they go in the outdoors. A pack left on the picnic table or beside the trail is not going to help.

Two final points are important. First, children today are taught "Stranger Danger" in elementary and preschool programs—they are taught to be wary of strangers in town and should be no less so in a State or National Park under normal conditions. However, a child needs to be reminded that, in the event he or she becomes lost, the adults will go to the authorities for help. Therefore, a person who is wearing some type of uniform and who is calling the child's name is not a "stranger" to be feared. Second, a child should know that being reunited with their parents is the most important thing to the parents. They won't be mad because you got lost, but will be proud of the way you remembered how to use the gear in your pack to survive.

Selected reading suggestions:
"Lost In The Woods" by Colleen Politano
"Safe and Sound" by Gordon Snow
Selected video suggestion:
"Lost! But Found Safe and Sound" Association of National Park Rangers

These materials can be obtained from the National Association for Search and Rescue on the web at www.NASR.org.

Here is a quick checklist of the *minimum* items that every child should have when going on a hike, even if it is a short one—remember, Haley's 30 minute jaunt turned into a three-day ordeal!

- fanny pack
- plastic whistle
- water bottle
- energy bar
- 50 gallon trash bag with window cut out
- strips of foil
- "hot hands" packet
- brightly colored, non-cotton clothing

And one final note. No matter how much gear a child does or does not have, perhaps the most important thing of all is this: *Once they realize that they are lost, they need to stay put in one place!* Find a tree to hug, make that tree their friend, and stay with it!

LOST IN THE WOODS? HUG A TREE!

If you would like to get involved with your local SAR team, contact your local Sheriff's Department for information.

Chapter 20
MORGAN NICK
FOUNDATION

The Morgan Nick Foundation (MNF) is a non-profit foundation that was formed in the aftermath of the tragic abduction of six-year-old Morgan Nick from a little league ball park in Alma, Arkansas in 1995.

MNF works closely with the Arkansas Missing Children's Clearinghouse, located in the Attorney General's Office in Little Rock, to reduce child victimization. MNF also continues to work as partners with the National Center for Missing and Exploited Children in Arlington, Virginia on behalf of missing children across our nation.

The Morgan Nick Foundation promotes a complete safety curriculum to educators, parents, and children. This curriculum, Kids and Company, has helped to raise awareness of child abduction while teaching skill tactics rather than fear tactics to children.

MNF serves the missing child in many different ways. The Morgan Nick Alert was created to broadcast information about the child and her disappearance within minutes and will broadcast across television and radio stations simultaneously across our state. This alerts thousands of people to the child's disappearance so they can be watching for that child. Through the latest technology, they are able to make colored posters of the child for immediate dissemination.

The Morgan Nick Foundation works with the families of missing children throughout their ordeal. When they learn of a disappearance of a child, either from law enforcement or by the family, they immediately offer the family support and assistance. They can, and have, sent support teams to searches where children are believed to be lost. They not only physically search for the child, but talk with the family, and at the families' wishes, can serve as a liaison between family and law enforcement officials. Their Resident Leadership Program consists of trained volunteers strategically placed across the state by region, who respond immediately when a child becomes missing.

As a part of their continued commitment to the families of missing children, the MNF offers Project Hope. Through this program, their staff and volunteers routinely check in with families to offer emotional support. In addition, each year they bring these families together to one common place where they can safely express their feelings with others in similar situations. At this conference, law enforcement officials, counselors, and media representatives meet each family personally and offer ideas on how to keep their child's story in the news, how to work with law enforcement in their case, and how to handle the emotional roller-coaster that comes with having a missing child.

MNF recognizes the dangers that teenagers face as a result of running away from home. Therefore, they broadened their perspective and created a program that focuses on this problem. L.O.S.T. (Lost on the Streets Today) brings youth, community leaders, and law enforcement together one night each year for fun, fellowship, and education about what life is like on the street. They offer alternative choices to running away, as well as provide community contacts who are willing to help should a child ever consider running away.

The Morgan Nick Foundation is supported in part by grants from VOCA (Victims of Crime Assistance), the Governor's Emergency Fund, other private foundation grants and gifts, as well as individual and corporate contributions and donations. Additionally, they hold several fund-raisers each year to offset costs not otherwise funded. MNF is a non-profit, 501(c)3, organization as recognized by the Internal Revenue Service for tax deductible contributions.

For more information about the Morgan Nick Foundation and the services they provide, contact them at:

The Morgan Nick Foundation
P.O. Box 1033
Alma, AR 72901
501–632–6382
Toll Free: 877–543–4673
E-mail: Morgannick@aol.com
Web Page: www.Morgannick.com

A portion of the proceeds from the sale of *The Search For Haley* book will be contributed to the Morgan Nick Foundation.

FINAL THOUGHTS

Haley is home and safe now. And while she did come out of the woods covered with scratches, bumps, and bruises, she has suffered no ill effects from her time alone in the woods. She is a happy, playful, smart child, and you would never know from being around her that she endured one of the most trying times that anyone could face. In the long run, I think, she is better off for having spent this time on her own in the wilderness.

Many of the volunteers and agency personnel went through great hardships as well, yet most of them will tell you that they too are better off for having participated in this event. I do believe there is something in our raw human nature, a force that comes from our inner most self, that brings out the very best in people in our greatest time of need. Perhaps it has something to do with our desire to be needed, to feel some sort of self-worth in this fast-paced, digital world that we live in today.

The potential tragic loss of one so young caused many parents to slow down and take a good look at their own kids—and what horror it would be if it was their own child out in the wilderness. There are a lot of kids today who get love and hugs much more often than before Haley's adventure, and whose parents know where they are every minute of the day.

Our terrific search and rescue community learned a great deal from this experience. Future missions will be more efficient and run smoother, and when an untrained volunteer shows up unprepared for wilderness travel, I'll bet there will be a job waiting for them.

Is hiking in the wilderness a dangerous thing to do? Absolutely. But no more so than walking down any street in this land. The wilderness swallowed up Haley whole, but it also took care of her, and taught her many valuable lessons. Kids need wilderness. So do adults. Wilderness is a place where we can meet nature, and ourselves, in the most basic form. It can teach us the value of self-reliance, and of teamwork and friendship. I say take your kids hiking as often as you can—you will both be better off for it.

Personally, I feel honored and blessed that I was able to open the doors to our Cloudland cabin and help out in some small way. I could not imagine doing otherwise. The thousands of folks who had some part in all of this can feel a great deal of pride in what they did—no matter if they were volunteers who left work and family behind and sweated in the search area, a store clerk who packed food and supplies to send out to the work site, or members of the press who felt highly enough of Steve and Kelly to respect their privacy. It was one grand and wonderful thing that all of these people did, and the world is a better place because each and every one of them is in it. Lytle and William Jeff won first place, but everyone went home a hero in my book.

Haley Zega and Tim Ernst

A FEW PEOPLE TO THANK

It took me five months to put this book together. Seems like there were as many people helping me with it as there were volunteers searching for Haley. Those who went way above and beyond to aid me in this project, and to whom I owe a great deal of thanks include: Steve & Kelly & Haley Zega, Joyce & Jay Hale, Rebecca Wood, Mark Clippinger, George Stowe-Rains, Guy Howe, Colleen Nick, Vixon James, Lytle James, William Jeff Villines, and David Comstock; in addition media folks Rhonda Justice, Dennis Graves, Chip Arledge ("The Rotund One"), Kevin Thomas, and Carol Gable; the poets and song writers Emily Kaitz, Don Hart, Joe W. Vaughn, Paulla Goodwin, Willard Villines, Christy Comstock, and Cindy Prince; text editors Nancy Williams and Judy Ferguson; the volunteers who provided stories and other information Charlie Allison, Joy Caffrey, Brad Mize, Dr. Terri Coats, Fran Alexander, Dr. Arthur Evans, Tom McKinney, Jodi Felkins, Christy Lunsford, and Billy & Mary Woods; and Newton County Sheriff's dispatcher Edd Kelton, and Newton County Judge Harold Smith. I also need to thank my own daughter, Amber, whose new dad spent way too much time working instead of playing with her. And finally, to the one who worked side-by-side with me on this project, and who not only convinced me to do this book in the first place, but also had to put up with my obsession with this project, my new bride Pam—as soon as I get this book off to the printers darling, the honeymoon will start—I promise!

AGENCIES & ORGANIZATIONS

The following list is of the agencies/organizations who were actually on-site at one time or another and helped with the search and rescue efforts—almost 80 groups! There were countless other groups away from the site who also assisted, even in other states. This was indeed a monumental effort.

Benton County Search and Rescue
Washington County Search and Rescue
Madison County Search and Rescue
Crawford County Search and Rescue
Marion County Search and Rescue
SW Missouri Search and Rescue
Explorer Scouts Search and Rescue (Jacksonville)
Newton County Sheriff's Department
Madison County Sheriff's Department
Washington County Sheriff's Department
Benton County Sheriff's Department
Franklin County Sheriff's Department
Carroll County Sheriff's Department
Baxter County Sheriff's Department
Lincoln Police Department
Fayetteville Police Department
Gravette Police Department
Bentonville Police Department
Eureka Springs Police Department
Rogers Police Department
University of Arkansas Police Department
Clarksville Police Department
Harrison Police Department
Malvern Police Department
Little Flock Police Department
Washington County Prosecutor's Office
Benton County Prosecutor's Office
Arkansas State Police
Arkansas National Guard
National Park Service, Buffalo National River
U. S. Forest Service, Ozark National Forest
Arkansas Game and Fish Commission
Arkansas Forestry Commission
Arkansas State Parks
Morgan Nick Foundation
Goss Canine Academy

Springdale K9
Malvern K9
Pope County Search and Rescue (bloodhounds)
Arkansas Department of Corrections (bloodhounds)
Newton County Judge's Office
Fayetteville Fire Department
Springdale Fire Department
Compton Volunteer Fire Department
Hasty Volunteer Fire Department
Ponca Volunteer Fire Department
Deer Volunteer Fire Department
Kingston Volunteer Fire Department
Crooked Creek Volunteer Fire Department
Pea Ridge Volunteer Fire Department
Lead Hill Volunteer Fire Department
Wedington Volunteer Fire Department
Parthenon Volunteer Fire Department
Newton County Rural Fire Association
American Red Cross (various chapters)
Arkansas Baptist State Convention
Newton County EMS
Crawford County EMS
North Arkansas Medical Center EMS
Air Evac
Carroll County Special Operations and Response Team
Benton County Central Communications
Rogers Central Dispatch
Bentonville Dispatch
Ozark Counseling Services
Cass Job Corps
Boone County Office of Emergency Services
Arkansas Department of Emergency Management
Washington County Department of Emergency Management
Newton County Department of Emergency Management
Benton County Department of Emergency Management
Arkansas Ham Radio Operators
Horseshoe Canyon Ranch
Kingston School
Sierra Club
Ozark Highlands Trail Association
Smith's Two Way Radio
Carroll Electric Coop
Tri-County Phone Company

BOOKS BY TIM ERNST

❏   THE SEARCH FOR HALEY $19.95 *
          5.5" x 8.5", 240 pages

❏   ARKANSAS HIKING TRAILS $18.95 *
          Maps and descriptions of 78 major trails in the state.
          6" x 9", 192 pages

❏   OUACHITA TRAIL GUIDE $18.95 *
          The complete guide to the longest trail in the region.
          Ten maps and elevation profiles, 5.5" x 8.5", 136 pages

❏   OZARK HIGHLANDS TRAIL GUIDE $18.95 *
          The definitive guide to this fabulous 180–mile trail.
          Thirteen maps, nine elevation profiles, 5.5" x 8.5", 136 pages

❏   BUFFALO RIVER HIKING TRAILS $18.95 *
          Maps and descriptions of over 30 trails in the river area.
          5.5" x 8.5", 136 pages

❏   ARKANSAS WATERFALL GUIDE (available mid-2002, call for price)
          Maps, photos, descriptions, & GPS info. for many great falls.

❏   ARKANSAS DAYHIKES   (available mid-2002, call for price)
          Maps and descriptions of the best dayhikes in the state.

❏   ARKANSAS PORTFOLIO picture book $ 50.00 *
          Contains 107 colorful images from all over the state.
          9" x 12", 128 pages, hardcover, gift boxed, autographed

❏   ARKANSAS SPRING picture book $ 60.00 *
          105 color images of dogwoods, waterfalls and wildflowers.
          10.5" x 11.5", 128 pages, hardcover, gift boxed, autographed

❏   BUFFALO RIVER WILDERNESS picture book $ 60.00 *
          63 photos by Ernst, 58 watercolors by William McNamara.
          10.5" x 11.5", 128 pages, hardcover, gift boxed, autographed

❏   WILDERNESS REFLECTIONS picture book $ 50.00 *
          121 color photographs from the best scenic areas in the land.
          10.5" x 11.5", 156 pages, hardcover, gift boxed, autographed

* Add $5 per order for shipping, Arkansas residents add sales tax

---

To order any of the above books, send check or money order to:

Tim Ernst
CLOUDLAND.NET
HC 33, Box 50–A
Pettigrew, AR   72752
Web page: **www.Cloudland.net**
for Visa/MasterCard/Discover: call 800–838–HIKE